Our Lady of Everyday Life

Our Lady of Everyday Life

La Virgen de Guadalupe and the Catholic Imagination of Mexican Women in America

MARÍA DEL SOCORRO
CASTAÑEDA-LILES

OXFORD
UNIVERSITY PRESS

1005107065

OXFORD
UNIVERSITY PRESS

Oxford University Press is a department of the University of Oxford. It furthers
the University's objective of excellence in research, scholarship, and education
by publishing worldwide. Oxford is a registered trade mark of Oxford University
Press in the UK and certain other countries.

Published in the United States of America by Oxford University Press
198 Madison Avenue, New York, NY 10016, United States of America.

CIP data is on file at the Library of Congress
ISBN 978–0–19–028040–6 (pbk.)
ISBN 978–0–19–028039–0 (hbk.)

1 3 5 7 9 8 6 4 2

Paperback printed by Webcom, Inc., Canada
Hardback printed by Bridgeport National Bindery, Inc., United States of America

Dedico este libro a mi hija Guadalupe Tonantzin (Lupita) Castañeda-Liles quien a tan temprana edad me ha enseñado el significado de el amor, la perseverancia, y compasión. Y a tres mujeres que han sido y siempre serán mi fuerza: Mi mamá Julia, mi suegra Gloria, y mi hermana Lorena.

I dedicate this book to my daughter Guadalupe Tonantzin (Lupita) Castañeda-Liles, who at such an early age has taught me the meaning of love, perseverance, and compassion. And to three women who have been and always will be my strength: my mother Julia, my mother-in-law Gloria, and my sister Lorena.

Contents

Acknowledgments

FIRST I WOULD like to thank the women who opened their hearts, homes, and trusted me with their life stories. Through their Catholic faith and deep devotion to *La Virgen de Guadalupe*, they have taught me the true meaning of resilience anchored on faith. *Muchísimas gracias de todo corazón*. I would also like to specially thank my editor, Cynthia Read at Oxford University Press, for her patience, guidance, and for walking with me throughout this journey.

Interdisciplinary research is challenging to say the least, because presenting a balanced analysis of multiple intellectual voices is a difficult task. I would have not been able to do this research without the mentorship of two brilliant scholars who have helped me shape this book. Denise Segura and Gastón Espinosa, your support, guidance, and thought-provoking questions have both invited and challenged me to pay close attention to how women at the grassroots live their devotion to *La Virgen de Guadalupe* in public life and in the intimacy of their homes. Thank you both for our many conversations about the need to document grassroots women's experiences, and for challenging me to understand them in the context of the multiple intersections that shape their lives. Gastón, thank you for challenging me to bring into conversation Chicana feminist views of Our Lady of Guadalupe and ordinary women's devotion to her, and for your encouragement at each step of the writing process. I am indebted to my colleagues Ana María Pineda, Thomas Tweed, Tim Matovina, and Orlando Espín— thank you for our long conversations about my work and for your encouragement and thought-provoking questions at various stages of this research. I would not have been able to navigate the interdisciplinary aspects of this book without your encouragement, expertise, and guidance. Discovering and developing one's own voice as an author is challenging, and I could not have embarked on this journey without the mentorship of Amy. Amy, thank you so much for encouraging me to trust my voice. For me, it is of utmost importance to honor the voices of the people whose lives I document. For this reason, though I provide translations I have kept the quotes in the original Spanish. However, this brings challenges—even though Spanish is my first language, I have always had trouble with the accents. Therefore, I am deeply grateful to my friend Thelma Valadez Valadez for her expertise and assistance in the Spanish language sections of this book. María Elena and Mariana Barba, thank you for helping me at the beginning stages of this work to find women willing to participate in this study. Benjamin De La Rosa, muchas gracias por la mochila de La Virgen de Guadalupe.

I am also deeply grateful to my dear friends and colleagues Lupe Martin, Joanne Rodríguez, Melissa Guzmán-Garcia, Wendy Arce, Jen Owens, Lauren Guerra Aguilar, Theresa A. Yugar, Neomi de Anda, Jaqueline M. Hidalgo, Frank Castillo, Roberto Mata, Corinna Guerrero, Lorena Garcia, Jorge Aquino, Denise Carmody, and my colleagues in the Religious Studies Department at Santa Clara University. To my colleagues in the Gender Justice and the Common Good Faculty Collaborative at Santa Clara University: Sharmila Lodhia, Mythri Jegathesan, Patrick Lopez-Aguado, Sonja Mackenzie, Stephanie Wildman, and Theresa Ladrigan-Whelpley, thank you for reading earlier drafts of the manuscript and for your valuable feedback. The writing process has multiple challenges, and one is learning the nuts and bolts of publishing, and I cannot thank enough my colleagues Gary Macy, Elizabeth Drescher, and Tricia Bruce for answering the multiple questions I had throughout this process. Gary, thank you for mentoring me at the beginning stages of the publishing process.

The early stages of this research would have not been possible without the financial support of the Ford Foundation, Hispanic Theological Initiative, UC Mexus (University of California Institute for México and the United States), and the University of California President's Office. Their support allowed me the time and financial freedom to conduct research in México. Writing is a full-time job and requires uninterrupted time set apart, and I would have not been able to complete this book without the financial support and mentorship I received from the Louisville Institute First Book Grant for Minority Scholars. The institute's consultations provided me with the opportunity to come into an interfaith dialogue with scholars and pastoral ministers. This experience allowed me the opportunity to share my work and learn from a diverse group of experts. I would also like to thank the Wabash Center for Teaching and Learning in Theology and Religion. Participating in the Center's "Teaching and Learning Workshop for Pre-tenure Latino/a Religion Faculty in Theological

Schools, Colleges, and Universities," provided me with the expert insights of religious studies scholars Ana María Pineda, Elizabeth Conde-Frazier, Eduardo C. Fernández, Miguel A. De La Torre, and Paul Myhre, Wabash Center's Associate Director. My goal with this book is to also reach out to people, especially women, outside the walls of academia. I would like to thank Modern Latina Magazine's Founder and Executive Editor, Linda Castillo, Christine Schweininger, publisher of Visión Magazine, Alex Ontiveros, Founder of Silicon Valley Latino, and Frank Carbajal, Founder of EsTiempo LLC, Founder of Silicon Valley Latino Leadership Summit, and co-author of Building the Latino Future: Success Stories for the Next Generation. Thank you for helping me reach out to a broader audience.

I would like to thank the Goddess GATE (Global Awareness Through Experience) program led by Dr. Cecilia Corcoran, FSPA, and co-facilitated by Dr. Anita de Luna, MCDP, and Dr. Jennifer Colby, Director of *Galeria Tonantzin*. My former mentors and dear friends, the late Monsignor Rev. Mateo Sheedy and Professor and Theologian Virgilio Elizondo, not only continue to be a critical influence in my scholarship and life but also continue to inspire and remind me of the importance to speak from the grassroots; to write from the lived experience of people; and to document how people in the midst of their suffering and joys find creative ways to bridge heaven and earth.

I could not have completed this book without the support of my family. *Estoy profundamente agradecida con mis padres Roberto y Julia Castañeda por su amor, apoyo y oraciones. No podría haber completado este libro sin su apoyo moral y espiritual. Muchísimas gracias por prestarme su fortaleza y fe cuando la mía desvanecía durante este transcurso. Papi gracias por las todas las veces que caminó de rodillas al altar de La Virgensita de Guadalupe para pedirle a ella y al Padre Mateo que me acompañaran y guiaran mientras escribía el libro. Papi, su amor y fe en La Virgen es realmente inquebrantable. Mami, tu vida es verdaderamente un ejemplo de amor, determinación, fortaleza y fe. Gracias por enseñarme a nunca perder la esperanza y el amor a la vida.* I thank my siblings Roberto Jr. and Lorena, and my brother-in-law Jim, for their love and unconditional support. Special thanks to my brother who, with his expertise in photography, captured the essence of the book in the cover photograph. Words cannot express how blessed I am for the unconditional spiritual and moral support of my other set of parents, Bill and Gloria Liles. Their moral and spiritual support as well as their prayers during the most difficult stages of this process have carried me throughout this journey.

Muchas gracias de todo corazón a Doña Ofe por su apoyo espiritual todos estos años cuando el terminar el libro parecía algo imposible. Jeny, tus consejos y apoyo los guardo muy dentro de mi corazón. I would like to express my deepest gratitude to my family and friends who have prayed with and for me throughout this writing journey. I could have not done it without your spiritual support. José Iván, thank you for your prayers as I worked toward meeting my last deadline. The closest translation of the term *comadre* is co-mother, which refers to a female who helps raise a child, and this is what Molly Carbajal, Elda Zuniga, and Gabi Flores are to me—*comadres*. I am eternally grateful for the many times they have cared for Lupita when I needed time to write.

I would like to thank my friend, husband, and colleague, Josef Manuel Castañeda-Liles. No words can ever describe how much his support during these years has meant to me. Josef Manuel, thank you for listening to me and providing advice when I had a new insight for the book. Thank you for sacrificing time away from your own writing to allow me uninterrupted time to complete this book. You have been a Girl Scouts, soccer, and ice-skating dad. Without the many intellectual exchanges we had and your unconditional love, support, and patience, I would have not been able to complete this book. Last, but most certainly not least, Lupita, at such a young age you have taught me the real meaning of love, kindness, and self-drive. You have been and will always be my inspiration and my guiding light—*te quiero mucho, mi amor.*

November 22, 2017
San José, California

Our Lady of Everyday Life

Introduction

LOOKING AT ME with a smile, Ester slowly reaches into her blouse. The room is full to capacity, but she does not seem to care. The space overflows with youthful smiles and laughter. Most of the women are wearing colorful outfits with earrings, necklaces, and bracelets to match their outfits, not to mention the ankle bracelets that seem to be popular among some of them. It appears to me that some have dressed to impress. Ester, on the other hand, sits shyly at her table, waiting. As she reached deeper into her blouse, I have to confess I was puzzled. What was she going to do?

She carefully places her hand in her brassiere, looks at me, smiles, and says, "*La traigo aquí todo el tiempo y hasta platico con ella*" (I keep her here all the time, and I even talk to Her), as she pulls out a small, worn, laminated prayer card of *La Virgen de Guadalupe*.[1] When the other two women sitting at the table see Ester, one pulls a rosary from her handbag as the other shows me a medallion that she is wearing of *La Virgen*. Ester and the other two women, who are in their late 70s, assure me that "*a ella nunca la abandonamos*" (we never abandon her). They never leave the house without *La Virgen* (the Virgin) because, as Ester states, "*La Virgen es nuestra madre; Eso es lo que mi mamá me enseñó cuando yo era una niña*" (La Virgen is our mother; that is what my mom taught me when I was a child).

A few months ago I saw an image of Our Lady of Guadalupe again in an unexpected place. She was surrounded by a pile of white towels, rather than roses, and a stack of paper cups, rather than candles. And she was accompanied not by statuettes of other heavenly figures like the Sacred Heart of Jesus and Saint Jude, but by what many consider an "all-American" symbol—Mickey Mouse. This is a different type of altar—a cleaning cart in a hotel hallway. I waited to see who was using that cart. I wanted to know why the person carried the image of *La Virgen* and why it was next to a sticker of Mickey Mouse. A middle-aged woman came out of one of the rooms she was cleaning and grabbed a few towels. I approached her and told her that I loved the image of Our Lady of Guadalupe on her cart. She responded, "*a ella siempre la traigo conmigo, nunca la abandono*" (I have her with me all the time, I never abandon her). She then introduced herself as Marisa.[2]

Ester is 76 years old, and Marisa appears to be in her mid-40s; both were born in México. Ester has been in the United States for many decades, whereas Marisa has only been here a few years; along with her two sons, she is undocumented. Marisa shared with me that *La Virgen* has granted her many miracles, including the implementation of DACA (Deferred Action for Childhood Arrivals) right at the time when her two sons were looking for work. She also told me that she bought the sticker of Mickey Mouse when she went to Disneyland for the first time and that she wanted to share it with *La Virgen*.

These two encounters with Our Lady of Guadalupe make me recall a memory from graduate school. At the end of the academic year, a gradu-ate school colleague (who was in her mid-20s at the time) and I decided to meet at the local coffee shop to review for an exam. Reaching into her bag for her notes, she took out a prayer card of Our Lady of Guadalupe that her mother had given her. With a smile, she put it under the notes and said, "So *La Virgen* can help us pass the exam." Unlike Ester and Marisa, my graduate colleague was born in the United States. Though she grew up Catholic, she does not consider herself religious and is very crit-ical of the Catholic Church, particularly the second-class status women have in it. These three women are from different generations and walks of life; two are practicing Catholics, and the third is not. Yet they share something in common—their devotion to Our Lady of Guadalupe, which was made visible in a holy card and exemplified in their need to carry an image of her.

People draw on a collective "chain of memory" that connects them with a particular shared belief system across space and time and pro-vides comfort in times of affliction (Danièle Hervieu-Léger 2000). In the West, newer generations tend to no longer to relate to the chain of memory into which they were socialized; instead, they seek spirit-ual alternatives that speak more directly to their present needs (ibid.). Following Hervieu-Léger's argument would lead one to suspect that my graduate colleague no longer relates to the chain of memory into which she was socialized. She has not, however, sought out religious alternatives, and as far as I know, her devotion to Our Lady of Guadalupe has not changed. In other words, there is something quite distinct about the devotion that these women have to *La Virgen*. It was to investigate precisely this phenomenon of her staying power that I began to study three groups of Mexican-origin women at three different stages of life and their devotion to Our Lady of Guadalupe.

As the participants in the study (college students, mothers, and older women) shared with me their devotion to Guadalupe, their life histories unfolded before my eyes. I soon realized that my initial race/class/gender focus was too narrow to capture the intricate ways in which devotion to Our Lady of Guadalupe and Catholic faith in general were interwoven in their lives as women, immigrants (or first-generation US-born), daughters, mothers, grandmothers, and sexual beings. Though I recognize the contributions of a race/class/gender analysis, such a framework does not entirely explain how women of Mexican origin come to understand their sexuality in the context of their religious beliefs.[3] Furthermore, the consequences of the Catholic Church's fixation on sexuality as it pertains to women are too critical to be left out of our investigations. Unfortunately, the existing literature in Latina feminist theology and religious studies does not address sexuality extensively. It seems almost as if the silence in the Catholic Church about sex and sexuality, as it relates to women, has trickled into research agendas—as it almost did to mine.[4]

The effort to gain a more multidimensional understanding of women is evidenced by social science literature, which increasingly uses a race/class/gender/sexuality analytical framework.[5] Previous studies have concluded that religion does not influence women's decisions about their lives and bodies.[6] However, like Latina feminist theology and Latinx religious studies, social science research on Latinas has considerable gaps. While religion may not influence how Latinas think about sex and sexuality, the stories of the women in my study reveal that race, class, gender, and sexuality intersect with religion to different degrees. Their life narratives allow me to see that by not including a systematic analysis of the intersection of these categories, we contribute to an academic discourse that makes it seem as if religion has little or no influence on how Latinas are socialized into their gender roles and expectations in their own families. At the same time, I do not argue that these gender roles and expectations are fixed. In the subsequent chapters, I analyze how these women's life experiences influence how they adapt and readapt their religious beliefs. In this regard, *Our Lady of Everyday Life* advances the understanding of lived religion and of Latinas more specifically by asking how women's choices about their bodies and sexuality influence their lived religion.

Certainly, not all women of Mexican origin, whether in the United States or México, identify as religious. However, it is important to recognize that the conquest of México established a sociopolitical and cultural system rooted in Catholicism.[7] This consequently created a perspective where Mexican culture is embedded in a Catholic and male understanding of being in this world, relegating women to the status of second-class citizens. Therefore, by omitting religion as a category of analysis we limit our understanding of women's lives and the consequences of México's conquest across generations.[8]

As I proceeded with my investigation, my initial findings indicated that devotion to Our Lady of Guadalupe among Catholic women of Mexican origin shapes and is shaped by the cultural, geographical, and historical context in which they live. It is fluid and malleable; it knows no boundaries between sacred and secular, and it adapts to—and at the same time shapes—life itself.[9] Their devotion does not "reflect or mirror the world" (Orsi 1996, 10); on the contrary, it is engaged in the making of their worlds as they experience life. This engagement takes place in the present while it draws from their childhood memories growing up with the image of Our Lady of Guadalupe, like those of Ester, Marisa, and my graduate colleague.[10]

As the women in my study spoke about Our Lady of Guadalupe, they intricately wove into their narratives childhood experiences of faith, devotion, family honor, respect, obedience, sex, guilt, shame, and sin. I understood then that their devotion to Guadalupe cannot be studied outside the context of their Catholic upbringing, and that their Catholic upbringing influences the ways race, class, gender, and sexuality intersect and shape their lives. It was in this way that their stories expanded the scope of my investigation from an ethnographic study on devotion to Our Lady of Guadalupe to a more encompassing sociological inquiry about what I call their Mexican Catholic imagination.[11]

In 1959, sociologist C. Wright Mills coined the term *sociological imagination* to refer to the state of mind in which individuals link their personal biography to larger social forces. And in 2000 Andrew Greeley wrote *The Catholic Imagination*, in which he contends that Catholics see the presence of God in all things.[12] In this book I use a new term, *Mexican Catholic imagination*, to help explain the experiences of the women in this study in relation to Our Lady of Guadalupe. What I call a Mexican Catholic imagination in this book refers to the intersection of the cultural and religious roots of their ways of understanding themselves and the world in the context of other social categories that shape their lives. More specifically, it signifies how Catholic women link their personal histories to their families, the larger society, God, and Our Lady of Guadalupe as Catholic Mexican women, and the awareness of self that comes as a result. This book's examination of the life narratives of women from three different life stages (college women, mothers, and older women) reveals the different ways these women inherit this imagination and how it evolves as they experience life.

We cannot fully comprehend women's devotion without first understanding the degree of significance of Our Lady of Guadalupe in the larger social and binational framework. In the context of increased migration and immigration and as a consequence of globalization, religious practices have become, in essence, transnational. To understand Mexican immigrants' cultural contributions to the United States' religious tapestry requires an examination of their sociohistorical context. Therefore, I lay the groundwork for this book by asking a number of Mexican immigrant women who Our Lady of Guadalupe is to them. Most responded that "*La Virgen de Guadalupe es madre de todos los mexicanos*" (Our Lady of Guadalupe is mother to all Mexicans) and that she never abandons her children—those that believe in her. Their understanding of Our Lady of Guadalupe as a mother who never abandons her children was interwoven with themes about family, culture, nationality, and the iconography of Our Lady of Guadalupe in very intricate ways.[13]

Mexican immigrant women bring with them a deeply nationalistic and Catholic understanding of Guadalupe. In their eyes *La Virgen* could have chosen to appear anywhere, but she chose México. Not only did she appear during the colonial era of a conquered México, she chose to appear to someone from the most ethnically, socially, and economically marginalized group—an indigenous man by the name of Juan Diego, whose story is featured in Chapter 1. This conceptualization of Our Lady of Guadalupe has been passed down from generation to generation, so much so that many link the apparition story with the genetic makeup of a people. Where and when does this relationship with Our Lady of Guadalupe begin?

When I asked if they could tell me about the first time that they heard about Our Lady of Guadalupe, one woman looked puzzled, laughed, and said, "*desde el nacimiento*" (since birth). Another said, "*desde siempre*" (since forever). As I continued asking questions, their responses were always tied in some way to memories of México. I am also of Mexican origin, and reflecting on their answers I too found myself not being able to remember when I first learned about Our Lady of Guadalupe. The women spoke of how they celebrated Our Lady of Guadalupe's feast day (December 12) in their communities by organizing big *fiestas, mañanitas, y peregrinaciones* (feasts, serenades at dawn, and pilgrimages). As they put it, it is a day when the country stops and many people do not work, and instead go to church to pay homage to *Nuestra Santa Madre, La Virgen de Guadalupe* (our holy mother, Our Lady of Guadalupe). With this perspective, I knew that to fully understand the devotion to Our Lady of Guadalupe for women of Mexican origin living in the United States, I had to go to México City where her image is housed at the Basilica of Our Lady of Guadalupe.

Research in México

This ongoing research began in 2004. The first time I went to México, I took part in the Goddess GATE (Global Awareness Through Experience) program. I had the opportunity to conduct informal interviews and participant observations in México City. In December 2006, I returned to México, this time to conduct fieldwork in the days prior to and following Our Lady of Guadalupe's feast day. Fieldwork included participating in a pilgrimage with people on December 11 and spending the night at the Basilica of Our Lady of Guadalupe, observing participants and conducting informal interviews with *peregrinos* (pilgrims) until the late afternoon of December 12. I went a third time in 2013 to make additional participant observation.

Returning to México as a field researcher was an act of (re)membering my own history. My conversations with people in México helped me to understand not only what Our Lady of Guadalupe means for them but also her significance in my own life and in the lives of Mexican-origin women in this study. I witnessed the ways *La Virgen* enters public, private, religious, and secular spaces. Altars to Guadalupe can be seen on the streets, at gas stations, in bathrooms, in businesses, meat markets, outside people's homes, and on buses (see Figure I.1). Religious medals of Guadalupe hang around the necks of men, women, and children. I saw her image on belt buckles, hats, and T-shirts, and tattooed on men's skin. I also saw a young woman with Our Lady of Guadalupe tattooed on her arm—an unusual sight, since México tends to hold women to well-defined gender roles in which tattooing on women is seen as inappropriate.

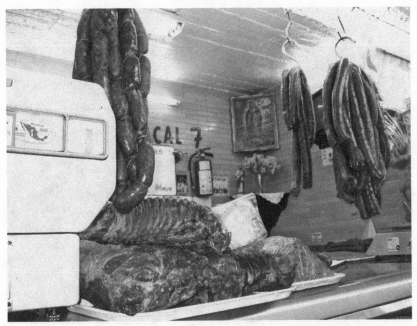

FIGURE I.I. Photograph of a meat market in México City. Courtesy: Socorro Castañeda-Liles.

One image of Our Lady of Guadalupe that caught my attention was on a wall of a building. This image was just below a candy stand (see Figure I.2). Every time I passed by there I greeted the couple that was selling the candy and always thought to myself: "The vendors are so lucky to have their candy stand right below the image of *La Virgen*." I was under the assumption that the image was there years before the couple decided to have their candy stand in that location. One day I stopped to buy candy and I soon realized that I was far from the truth about the image. The couple told me that they were devotees of Our Lady of Guadalupe and always prayed to her to help them sell their candy. The years that they had been selling their candy at this particular corner had been very good and the money from the sales had been enough to support their family. As a way of thanking Our Lady of Guadalupe they asked the owner of the building for permission to place an image of Our Lady of Guadalupe, out of tile, on the wall, to which the owner agreed. Besides allowing me to see the ways Our Lady of Guadalupe enters the lives of people in México, this experience was a reminder to not make assumptions.

My fieldwork in México revealed that the socialization processes by which devotion to Our Lady of Guadalupe takes place in *lo cotidiano*

FIGURE I.2. Photograph of a *puestesito de dulces* (candy stand) in México City. Courtesy: Socorro Castañeda-Liles.

(everyday life). It begins at a very early age, which explains why the women whom I initially asked about the meaning of Our Lady of Guadalupe in their lives could not specify when they had first learned about her. At the basilica I was able to see how, even in their mother's womb, children are introduced to devotion to Our Lady of Guadalupe. It was not surprising to see pregnant women and women with newborns or older children at the basilica. Although I also observed men with children and entire families, the majority of the pilgrims were women with children. At the basilica, one can see how even at this early stage in children's development, their mothers are spending time in a place associated with Our Lady of Guadalupe, praying in front of the *tilma* (the cloak on which her image appeared). Consequently, from a very early age, children are absorbing a culture of and devotion to *La Virgen* that will inform their lives (see Figure I.3).[14]

I saw the color and felt the texture of Mexican popular Catholicism, particularly *Guadalupanismo*, through the use of fabrics, flowers, candles, incense, and memorabilia of *La Virgen*, San Juan Diego, and Pope John Paul II, who had a deep devotion to her. Verbal exchanges between sellers and buyers bargaining for a good price, coupled with religious music and

FIGURE I.3. Family taking a photograph at the Basílica de Nuestra Señora de Guadalupe in México City. Courtesy: Socorro Castañeda-Liles.

occasional Aztec dancers making their way to the basilica, created a poetic and festive atmosphere. Popular Catholicism at the entrance of the basilica consists of the smells of fresh *tortillas, tacos, tortas, mole,* and the sweet smell of Mexican candy.[15]

The people at the basilica form a type of *communitas* that is sustained by the devotion to Our Lady of Guadalupe. I am not arguing that all merchants and visitors are driven to the basilica by their faith. Instead, what I argue is that the faith of the people who are devotees of Our Lady of Guadalupe sustains her significance even among curious onlookers who feel compelled to visit the basilica. People's actions, responses, and interactions embody a type of Guadalupan culture at the basilica that penetrates the five senses. It inhabits not only the sacred and secular but also the creative ways it infuses the sacred with the secular and the secular with the sacred. For example, at one of the stands right outside the basilica I bought a tin *nicho* (niche) of Our Lady of Guadalupe. While this type of religious art is typical, the tin used for this piece was originally a tin can of roach spray. The seller who had made it himself did not see it as an offense to Our Lady of Guadalupe. Instead he said: "*Es que 'pa nosotros La Virgen esta*

en todas partes y ademas es importante reciclar y no desperdiciar el material"
(For us *La Virgen* is everywhere, and it is also important to recycle and not
to waste material).

Research in the United States

The research in the United States was conducted in a major city in the
Bay Area of Northern California in the Greater Washington neighborhood. This neighborhood, where most of the women who participated
in the study live, is a predominantly Latinx community, but this was not
always the case. Greater Washington was originally an Italian immigrant
enclave, but by the 1960s the demographics of the community were rapidly changing. Due to increased immigration from México and other parts
of Latin America, the community transformed from an Italian immigrant
to mostly Mexican immigrant neighborhood.

Nestled in the heart of Greater Washington's central business area
stands the local church, Sacred Heart, the tallest building on the street.
Taking a walk in the neighborhood, one can see the ways some of the
homes, local businesses, and the church together express a vibrant Mexican
Catholic imagination. There are many shops on the main street, some of
which include the neighborhood's *panadería* (bakery), *mercado* (market),
pharmacy, and *la botánica*. The sweet smell of *pan dulce* (Mexican pastries,
also referred to as Mexican sweet bread) make the bakery an inviting and
familiar place to the constant stream of clients. The *mercado* not only sells
groceries and various kinds of meats but also tickets to various events,
medicinal herbs, gold jewelry, and California lottery tickets. As you enter
la farmacia (pharmacy) a large image of *Sagrado Corazón de Jesús* (Sacred
Heart of Jesus) is at the very front. Besides offering its clients over-the-
counter medications from the United States and México, *la farmacia* also
sells herbs, votive candles, and statues of various Catholic saints.

As you walk further there is a small, almost unnoticeable shop—*la
botánica*. When you enter *la botánica* you immediately notice the scent of
oils and incense that fill the air. Catholic and folk saints (saints not recognized by the Catholic Church) all share equal space at *la botánica*. Saint
Jude, the Catholic patron saint of desperate causes, does not mind sharing
space with San Simón, a folk saint known for granting luck, health, justice, and revenge. Our Lady of Guadalupe's statue is visibly noticeable as
she stands tall, ready to welcome those that enter. Like Saint Jude, she does
not seem to mind having Jesús Malverde as her neighbor at *la botánica*.

Malverde is a folk saint who, according to oral tradition, stole from the rich to give to the poor. In recent decades he has been adopted by drug cartels as their patron saint. Rosaries, Catholic prayer books, bibles, amulets, and bottles of healing water that are guaranteed to help people find luck, happiness, and love, all occupy a shared space in *la botánica*. In essence, what the official Catholic Church divides, *la botánica* unites.

Besides the established shops, there are other businesses that include taco stands, *paleteros* (loosely translated as popsicle vendors), Mexican fruit stands, and flower vendors, making the main street of the Greater Washington neighborhood a thriving business center. As alive as the business center may seem during the year, it does not compare to the festive atmosphere that the Catholic Church, along with the shops and street vendors, all create on the feast day of Our Lady of Guadalupe.

Some shops remain open all night. They sell flowers, votive candles, T-shirts with the image of Our Lady of Guadalupe, Mexican traditional *huaraches* (sandals), and indigenous outfits for boys and girls. The custom among Mexican families on Our Lady of Guadalupe's feast day is to dress children in traditional indigenous outfits. The skirt of the sidewalk along the front side of the parish is dressed in colorful lights that illuminate the merchandise of street vendors. The scent of roses, *champurrado* (a hot corn flour and chocolate-based drink), and *tamales* evoke a familial quality as they create an ambiance of unity and national pride on the feast day of Our Lady of Guadalupe. Based on my observations in México and the United States, the emphasis of *La Virgen's* Mexican origin (according to the apparition story) is much stronger in the United States than in México. One explanation is that immigrants find in Our Lady of Guadalupe a sense of national pride, acceptance, and accompaniment in a country where they are marginalized and criminalized in multiple ways.

Right at midnight the parish holds *La Misa de Gallo* (midnight mass) in honor of Our Lady of Guadalupe, and the doors of the parish remain open all night. The faithful stream in and out throughout the night. Some come and pray for a few minutes, and others stay all night. By 4:30 am, the parish is filled to capacity. Young and old, from newborn babies to the elderly, all await *Las Mañanitas* (the morning serenade). This is followed by yet another mass and the re-enactment of the apparition of Our Lady of Guadalupe to Saint Juan Diego by the parish theater group—Teatro Corazón, directed by Arturo Gómez. Though the play retells an event that took place many centuries ago, its message resonates among the faithful for it contextualizes the story in the lived reality of Latinxs today, making it a powerful experience. In fact, some of the women I interviewed for this study shared about attending the play and learning more about the story and its meaning.

Some of the homes in the neighborhood have beautiful altars to Our Lady of Guadalupe lit with Christmas lights in their front or back yards, and every home altar has a story of love and devotion to *La Virgen* that began south of the border in México. Take for example Señora Connie's home altar (see Figure I.4). The sidewalk in front of her house has a very old tree with a natural indentation. The original family that lived there placed a statue of Our Lady of Guadalupe in it. When the family moved out they left the altar, and when Señora Connie's family moved in she added flowers and solar lights. When Señora Connie lived in México she organized the pilgrimage from her home state of Michoacán to the Basilica of Our Lady of Guadalupe. She was 15 years old when she first helped organize the event, and by the age of 17 she was the head organizer of the pilgrimage, which included over five thousand participants and lasted seven days one way. She told me that in their journey from Michoacán to the basilica, the pilgrims rested in parking lots, public school grounds, and anywhere people were willing to host them. Her home altar has become a

FIGURE I.4. Señora Connie telling the story of her altar to *La Virgen de Guadalupe* in Greater Bay Area, California. Courtesy: Roberto Castañeda, Jr.

landmark in the Greater Washington neighborhood, and it is not surprising to see passers-by make the sign of the cross as they walk by the tree, pray the rosary to *La Virgen*, or place flowers at the altar. Another home has an approximately four-foot statue of Saint Jude on their front yard. Though there are people in the neighborhood who do not attend mass, and others may belong to a different religious tradition or none at all, in general, the Greater Washington neighborhood has a very Catholic ambiance, particularly on the feast day of *La Virgen de Guadalupe.*

Initial Lessons Learned from the Binational Research

The participant observation I conducted in México, coupled with my research in the United States among the women whose narratives provide the backbone of this book, allowed me to further understand women's devotion to Our Lady of Guadalupe. For the women in this study, as for the hundreds of people I have met in the course of this research, *La Virgen* is their mother and the mother of God—a relationship that I discuss later in the book. To different degrees, their Mexican Catholic imagination interweaves the sacred and secular within a *familismo* (familism) paradigm, where the mother is the central figure and relationships are not binary but fluid. *Familismo* is a theoretical concept predominantly used in cultural anthropology, psychology, and sociology to describe the degrees and types of family cohesiveness and solidarity.[16]

For Mexicans (and Latinxs in general), the concept of family extends beyond the nuclear sphere to include extended family and close friends.[17] It is expressed in the form of behavior and attitudes, and crosses national borders in the case of binational families. Familism in a Mexican Catholic imagination goes beyond these horizontal relationships. It also includes the relationships they have with the pantheon of Catholic sacred symbols.[18] In other words, a Mexican Catholic imagination from within a familism framework manifests itself in vertical (or heavenly) and horizontal (or earthly) relationships that mutually deepen one another. For example, the horizontal relationships that the women in this study build with their kinship network coexist with the vertical relationships that they initially formed via what Orsi (1996) calls the *devotional triangle* from which they first come to understand themselves as Catholic. The devotional triangle refers to the ways devotion is passed from one generation to another; in Chapter 2, I present an in-depth analysis of this aspect of devotion.

Familism within this imagination is articulated in the significance people give to medallions and images they carry of Our Lady of Guadalupe, as in the case of Ester and Marisa, and my graduate colleague. It is expressed in what they pray for and how they talk to Our Lady of Guadalupe, in the ways *La Virgen* coexists on home altars with photographs of loved ones who have died and therefore (within this imagination) have acquired a quasi-sacred quality.[19] As I demonstrate in the last part of the book, within this network of relationships Our Lady of Guadalupe arises as the most significant female sacred symbol and as a force that moves women to transgress subjugation.

Demographics and Methods

The bulk of the study was conducted over a period of two years (2004–2005) among three groups of working-class Mexican-origin women ranging in age from 18 to 82.[20] I used various ethnographic methods to collect my data: participant observation, visual documentation (both video and digital photography), and focus groups with 100 women, out of which 45 participated in in-depth interviews. The 45 women, who were all working class and were born in either México or the United States, were divided into three groups based on their stage in life. Those in the first group were single (without children) college women between the ages of 19 and 25 (16 women). Though one might argue that working-class college students, by virtue of the fact that they are pursuing higher education, are in transition from working class to middle class, I have categorized them as working class because their parents work predominantly in the service sector. In some cases, the ages of the college women and mothers overlap, but I divided them according to their stage in life because the experience of motherhood significantly influences the ways the women relate to Our Lady of Guadalupe. I also interviewed fourteen mothers between the ages of 25 and 47, and fifteen older women between the ages of 60 and 82. Some of the older women were or had been married and others never married, which I explain later in the chapter (see Appendix).[21]

I chose to study Mexican-origin college women, mothers, and older women because I wanted to analyze their experiences of growing up Catholic. I also wanted to explore how devotion to Our Lady of Guadalupe is expressed based on stage in life and generation. Later in the chapter I offer a more nuanced explanation of the demographics of each of the groups of women.

Entering the Field

Entering this field was in some ways facilitated for me because I grew up in the Greater Washington neighborhood and identify as Catholic. However, although I grew up in this community, when I went back to conduct my research after many years of being away, the community's demographics had radically changed. Many families I knew had moved to the Central Valley, and the community was now home to new residents I had never met—the neighborhood I had known, and the city in general, were no longer the same. I began my fieldwork by reconnecting with people I knew and asked them if they could introduce me to the neighborhood's new residents.

My age allowed me to blend into the young-adult groups at the local parish and colleges, and my marital status as a newlywed facilitated my interactions with mothers and older women. But building a web of relationships with community members did not come easily. Though I came from a working-class Mexican immigrant background and people welcomed me, my more advanced academic training made me an outsider to this community where less than 8% of the residents of Greater Washington hold a college degree compared to 23.3% of the overall city population.[22]

Some scholars argue that being an insider makes the researcher less objective, and as a consequence the research outcome may be subject to bias. However, what many overlook is that the insider, like the outsider researcher, is trained "in the methodological rigors of their disciplines. This is not to say that such training by itself guarantees credibility, but simply that both insiders and outsiders are subject to the standards imposed by the scientific community" (Zinn 1979, 213).

Entering the field site is only the first step in ethnographic research. Researchers quickly find that forming and negotiating relationships in a way that is not exploitative involves an ongoing "re-entering" process throughout the study.[23] In my case, as I explain below in detail, I entered the community by participating in various activities, and then re-entered this time into the different cohorts of women at the site. I translated when parents needed to meet with their child's school counselor. I also assisted parents with student transfers. I spoke to "at-risk" youth. I participated in the local church festivals selling nachos and *raspados* (snow cones). I mentored high school and college students. I served as Spanish/English translator in community and school meetings as well as festivals, and I was also on the city's park and recreation planning board for a new park in the community.

A Name of Their Own

I refer to each of the three groups as cohorts. The three groups of women were very clear about how they wanted me to define them. The young college women constantly referred to themselves as *mujeres* (women), whereas the mothers called themselves *madres* (mothers). The older cohort was the most determined, and they corrected me until I got it right. They were neither *señoras* ("Mrs."), nor *abuelitas* (grandmothers), nor *mujeres* (women). Rather, they were *damas* (ladies). Therefore, *Mujeres, Madres,* and *Damas* are the terms I use to refer to each of the three groups. With the exception of a couple of women in the older cohort and the college students, the research participants were monolingual Spanish-speaking women. All research participants were of working-class background, and the average education level of the two older cohorts was sixth grade (see Table A.1 in the Appendix). All of the women in the study identified as heterosexual. With one exception, they were all baptized Catholic. Across the three groups the women identified as practicing Catholics. However, there were a couple of women in *Las Mujeres* cohort who, while identifying as Catholic, said that they were not "practicing Catholics" because they "had not been to Mass in a while."

Social Background of Each Group of Women

Las Damas. Most of the women in *Las Damas* cohort got married and had children, except two who never married and had no children. Twelve of the fifteen women attended the local senior center, though some attended more consistently than others. Five of *Las Damas* were widows and lived alone, but had family members living close by. One of the women who was widowed lived in a granny flat in the same property where her children lived. Of the two that never married, one lived with a sister, who also never married, and the other lived alone. Only one of the fifteen women was dating. All the women had a deep devotion to Our Lady of Guadalupe and a strong sense of what, according to them, it meant to be Catholic. Some even took pride in the fact that their children married *"por todas las leyes"* (under all the laws)—that is, both civil law and Catholic canon law.

All of the participants were dependent on Social Security, which was their main source of income. Those who attended the local senior center felt that they were fortunate to have a place where they could come together and form and nurture friendships. All of the participants felt a sense of belonging in the Greater Washington neighborhood, and for most of them the center became a central meeting place. Most of the participants attended mass at Sacred Heart Parish.[24] Others were parishioners when they were younger, but at the time of the research attended mass with their grown children who belonged to other parishes in the Diocese.

Six of the women were born in México and migrated, without documents, to the United States with their families as teenagers; seven were born in México and came to the United States as adults. *Las Damas* who were born in México eventually acquired legal status. The participants came from the coastal states of Michoacán, Jalisco, and Guerrero; the northern states of Chihuahua, Monterrey, and Durango; and the central states of Zacatecas, Guanajuato, and México City. The median age of migration was 23. Two were US-born daughters of Mexican immigrant parents who came in the 1920s.

Las Madres. The women in *Las Madres* cohort were born in the northern and central states of México. In particular, they came from the coastal states of Baja California, Sinaloa, Jalisco, Colima, and Michoacán, and from the interior states of Durango, Zacatecas, Guanajuato, Hidalgo, and México City. The average number of years of formal education attainment was six. The mean age at the time of immigration was 24. Most of *Las Madres* arrived after the Immigration Reform and Control Act of 1986 (IRCA), of which the majority arrived in the 1990s. In fact, they were part of the wave of immigration that increased the US immigrant population from 19.8 million to 31.1 million— overall, a 57% increase—between 1990 and 2000. In some cases their partners were the first to migrate; once they had established themselves, they brought their wives and children (if they had any).[25] Based on the information *Las Madres* shared, most were undocumented; the few who had documents became legal residents under IRCA because their husbands, who had legalized their own status through IRCA, sponsored them. Six participants were partnered and eight were married. The average age at the time of the interviews was 36. Most of *Las Madres* did not work outside the home with the exception of a couple who worked part-time.

Las Mujeres. Las Mujeres came from two different four-year colleges from the Greater Bay Area in California: one public, one private. Seven attended the local public university and ten attended the private university. All of the participants were first-generation college students whose parents (with the exception of a couple) were born and raised in México. Overall, *Las Mujeres* who attended the public university asserted that they really enjoyed the diversity that college provided. Those who attended the private college reported a sense of uneasiness because of the small percentage of Latinxs and students of color in general. In some cases, I found that this sense of uneasiness affected the way they moved around campus.

For example, two of the participants from the private university said that they never sat on the grass because that space was for white students. When I asked why, they said that those who tend to sit on the grass are white students, especially those who like to tan. One young woman said that if she sat on the grass, she would be considered "weird." When I asked the student what she meant by "weird," she said, "Well, white students are going to think that I want to tan, and Latinos don't tan. And my Latino friends, especially my Chicano friends, are going to think that I am trying to act white." While not all the students reported such deep feelings of unease, all of the young women at the private college felt out of place in one way or another. All of *Las Mujeres* who attended the public university lived off-campus, and all except one, who lived with other college women, continued living with their parents and commuted to school every day. However, seven out of the ten students that attended the private institution lived on campus.

All of *Las Mujeres* participants came from working-class families. Some of the students were on fellowships, and others held part-time jobs on campus, local nonprofits or grocery stores to help fund their education and/or help support their families. Some came from families that lived outside the city where the research was conducted. I recruited the younger women from the public and private colleges near the Greater Washington neighborhood. I chose to do this because I wanted to see if education influenced how Mexican-origin women in college identified as Catholics or the ways they understood Our Lady of Guadalupe in their lives. Fifty percent of the cohort was born in the United States, and 50% were born in México. Those born in the United States were from California, as far south as Los Angeles and as far north as San Francisco. The *Mujeres* born in México were primarily from the coastal states of Oaxaca, Michoacán, Jalisco, and Veracruz; one was born in México City. The median age of migration of those born in México was eight years of age. The average age of *Las Mujeres* at the time of the interview was 23. Their average age is older than the typical college student. Some, especially those from the public university, were transfer students, or they worked while attending school, which led them to take longer to finish college.

Of the Mexican-born *Mujeres*, four did not have documents and funded their education through scholarships since they were not eligible to apply for student loans. Of those who responded to the question about their parents' occupation, 28% had parents working as farm laborers in California's Central Valley; 18% reported that their mothers were fulltime homemakers; and 54% had parents working in semiskilled jobs. Of those who responded to the question about their parents' educational attainment, 80% reported that their parents had a sixth-grade education or less.

Las Mujeres said that their parents encouraged them to go to college, contrary to stereotypical assumptions that parents with very little education do not emphasize the importance of higher education. To the parents of these young women, a college education was essential. One of *Las Mujeres* told me that her father said to her, "*'mija lo único que te podemos dejar de herencia es tu educación*" (*'mija,* the only thing we could leave you with is your education).

Methods for Recruiting Participants

I went to the local church, community centers, youth groups, and student clubs at the two local colleges to recruit the women for this study. I used flyers, snowball sampling, and announcements in local newsletters; the snowball sampling method was the one that proved the most effective. The interviews were conducted in Spanish, English, or Spanglish (often referred to as "code switching" between English and Spanish). The focus groups consisted of three to five women, divided by the parameters I had assigned (*Mujeres, Madres,* and *Damas*). Each focus group lasted between 1 hour and 1 hour 45 minutes; individual interviews were between 1 and 3 hours long. For the purpose of confidentiality and to protect their identity, I give all my participants pseudonyms. I include, in either the main text or the Notes, the original quotation in Spanish followed by a loose English translation of the same. The book is based on the interviews during the primary time of this research. However, aspects of this research is ongoing.

An Intersectional Analysis of Lived Religion

Within the past two decades, the field of religious studies has moved beyond a quantitative approach to the study of religion to focus more on the nuanced ways in which people experience religion in their everyday lives outside religious institutions. This move to study people's ways of understanding religion is now a growing field in religious studies known as *lived religion*. Lived religion is a way, as historians Anne S. Brown and David D. Hall so aptly put it, of "being religious [in a fashion] that is responsive to the needs that arise within social life" (Brown and Hall 1997, 57).

What is more, lived religion is the study of how people experience the sacred in their lives and how that religious experience is connected to larger social structures, both religious and secular.[26] It does not take place apart from our social reality; rather, it exists in the cultural, geographical, and historical context of society.[27] As such, it is fluid and malleable; it knows no borders, and its practices adapt to—and at the same time shape—life itself. Therefore, a critical analysis of lived religion requires that the scholar contextualize the religious practice/devotion in the larger sociopolitical and historical context.

Engaging in the study of lived religion means investigating the areas of social life that may appear chaotic, inconsistent, and at times opposite to the practices and teachings of organized religion. I would also argue that it may not necessarily nicely fit in our theories of social life; lived religion exists in the spaces in which people construct views, opinions, and meanings of their social worlds.[28] Hence, the study of lived religion is the study of those aspects of life that do not necessarily fit into mainstream academic frameworks or that seem unclassifiable. The study of lived religion is also an invitation to understand the varied ways people experience that which they consider sacred in the context of the adversity or the happiness that life brings.[29] Likewise, lived religion is the study of devotion and of religious symbols that "do not reflect or mirror the world" but are continually engaged in its making (Orsi 1996, 10). It is important to note, however, that lived religion is not necessarily completely apart from organized religion—though it can be.

I argue that how the women in this study experience devotion to Our Lady of Guadalupe in their individual lives is directly linked to the larger

Mexican Catholic imagination that they inherited from their families, mainly their mothers and grandmothers. This imagination, though it is a product of and at the same time reproduces systems that reflect an andro-centric view of the world, is also malleable and always evolving as women experience life.

My approach draws on recent scholarship that underscores the phys-ical and material aspects of what McGuire refers to "religion as lived" McGuire (2008). This approach calls for the need to look at how people materialize and *physicalize* (embody) religion, and how the material and physical get *religioned*.[30] For Sociologist Nancy Ammerman, everyday reli-gion "may happen in both private and public life" and across class lines. "It may have to do with mundane routines, but it may also have to do with the crises and special events that punctuate those routines" (Ammerman 2007, 5).[31]

The study of lived religion is relatively new in the United States, although its roots go back to Luckmann's (1967) theory of invisible reli-gion. Therefore, because it is rather a new area within the larger spectrum of religious studies approaches to research, how it gets defined—whether it is "lived religion" (Hall 1997; Orsi 1996), "religion as lived" (McGuire 2008), or "everyday religion" (Ammerman 2007)—will continue to develop as more sociologists, especially scholars of color, participate in the ongoing theoretical conversations.

The study of religion through the lens of lived religion allows the researcher to see the fluidity between institution and religion as lived with-out necessarily demarcating boundaries. Based on my findings among the women you will meet in the chapters that follow, I maintain that there are degrees of fluidity between what are considered official and unofficial reli-gious practices, making them difficult to separate. For example, using lived religion as a methodological lens, as Hall defines it, allows us to see that Mexican popular Catholic practices, while they do not necessarily mirror the traditional Catholic Church, nonetheless follow the Catholic liturgical calendar.[32]

I argue that for lived religion as a methodological lens to capture the complexity of the human experience in society, it is necessary that we approach our work from an intersectional analysis. Crenshaw (1989) introduced the concept of intersectionality, which has since been further developed by other feminist scholars.[33] This approach seeks to examine the various systems of oppression that shape women's lives—mainly

race, class, and gender. More recently, scholars have further problema-
tized what intersectionality means beyond race, class, and gender by
including sexuality.[34] In this study, I build on this scholarly shift and
use lived religion as a methodological lens to further an intersectional
analysis of religion that takes into account race, class, gender, generation, and sexuality. This intersectional analysis offers insight into issues
including the reasons why some Latinx Catholics choose to engage in
popular Catholicism, but Sunday mass is not necessarily a priority for
them.

Indeed, the study of lived religion seen from an intersectional stance
opens up many possibilities to understand the worlds we study by allowing
the researcher to see the social patterns that link individual biographies
and larger social structures.[35] This approach to methodology can help us
see how certain practices by religious communities that have historically
been marginalized in US society (i.e., minoritized and LGBTQ individuals) may be oppositional to established organized religion and other social
institutions in subtle and not-so-subtle ways.[36]

In this study, I use lived religion as a methodological lens and apply an
intersectional analytical approach to study women's experiences growing
up Catholic and their devotion to Our Lady of Guadalupe. This has permit-
ted me to see that certain practices by the women in this study were at
times oppositional to traditional Catholic teachings at various levels due to
the "compounded intermeshed systems of oppression" they experience as
working-class women of color (Mercer et al. 2015, 438).

I invite the reader to ask the following questions as you read this
book: What does an in-depth analysis of the intersection of race, class,
gender, generation, sexuality, and religion tell us about the ways women
of Mexican origin first come to understand themselves in the context of
systems of oppression? What can we learn about the extent to which newer
generations of women are influenced by their elders' understanding of
religion and sexuality? And, in what ways do women use their creative
agency to transgress limiting notions of womanhood within a Catholic
context, and what role does their devotion to Our Lady of Guadalupe play
in the process?

Argument and Structure of the Book

In this book, I argue that instead of blindly accepting androcentric Catholic
teachings or rejecting Catholicism, first-generation Mexican women of all

ages develop a protean Catholic devotion, which allows them to transgress limiting notions of what a good Catholic woman should be while retaining the aspects of Catholicism they find life-giving. They do this while continuing to identify as Catholics. The protean Catholic devotion they develop is most visible in their relationship to Our Lady of Guadalupe, which is not fixed but instead is fluid and deeply engaged in their process of self-awareness. Each chapter offers a comparative analysis of the three groups of women to provide the evidence that supports my central argument.

The book opens with Chapter 1 and offers readers a more general understanding of the significance of Our Lady of Guadalupe in México and the United States. It begins with a synthesis of the Our Lady of Guadalupe apparition story. I follow with a general overview of Our Lady of Guadalupe in history, theology, US politics and the entertainment industry, Chicana feminist thought, and her influence in Latinx communities in the United States today.

Moving from a macroanalysis to an in-depth examination of Our Lady of Guadalupe's significance, Chapter 2, "Our Lady of *Café con Leche*: The Social Construction of Catholic Devotion,"[37] argues that Mexican children in Catholic households are introduced to Catholicism via material culture and family traditions at home. That is, religious material objects and customs form part of the life of children even before they can fully comprehend their significance. I particularly focus on the embodiment of devotion to *La Virgen de Guadalupe* and the material culture associated with this religious figure. I also borrow and expand Orsi's (1996) metaphor of the "devotional triangle" to explain how Catholic devotion is passed from one generation to the next as it strengthens the ties that bind mothers and daughters. I end this chapter with a discussion of the influence of women in the transmission of Catholic faith in the family.

In Chapter 3, "Catholicizing Girlhood: Socializing Girls into Institutional Catholicism," I argue that as the mothers of the women I interviewed for this study introduced them to Mexican popular Catholic expressions of faith, they also socialized their daughters into the strict gender expectations of the institutional Church. I offer an intersectional analysis of dress codes, Mass attendance, prayer, language, and ethnicity as experienced by the women in all three age groups. Building on the previous chapter, in Chapter 4, "The Making of Girls in the Mexican Catholic Imagination: Obedience, Respect, and Responsibility," I argue that the Catholic culture in which the mothers socialized the participants also provides the parameters within which they learn how to be good girls in ways that reduce a girl's agency to rubble. In Chapter 5, "Becoming *Señoritas*: If You Can't Talk About It in Church, You Can't Talk About It Anywhere," I analyze how and what the participants in this book learned as teenagers about the female body and what information, by contrast, was kept from them. Based on a comparative analysis of the groups of women, I contend that even while the women willingly or unwillingly complied with the codes of conduct as they were growing up, they found creative ways to circumvent some of them. In essence, Chapters 4 and 5 move the conversation to voice the silences that come with a Mexican Catholic imagination.

In Chapter 6, "Our Lady of Everyday Life," I demonstrate how the Mexican Catholic imagination of these women is not fixed but always evolving as they experience life and as their Catholic faith and devotion to Our Lady of Guadalupe grows deeper. I argue that the women's Catholic devotion is fluid and moves and is shaped by their lived experience. As a result, as the women mature, the way they relate to *La Virgen de Guadalupe* becomes more holistic and complex. In Chapter 7, "Perceptions of Our Lady of Guadalupe's Relationship to Feminism: The Time Is Now," I contend that because Catholic Mexican-origin women learn to think of Our Lady of Guadalupe as an ever-present heavenly mother, they also see her as nonjudgmental. This ultimately allows the participants to continue to identify as Catholic, retain the aspects of Catholicism they find life-giving, and transgress some traditional limiting notions of what a good Catholic woman should be. The chapter also raises the question of what feminism means to *Las Damas, Las Madres,* and *Las Mujeres* and how they think of Our Lady of Guadalupe in relation to their definitions of feminism. Chapter 8, "Why Do They Paint Her This Way? She Is Our Mother," examines their responses to some Chicana feminist artistic representations of Our Lady of Guadalupe from within their Mexican Catholic imagination in order to explore how these women articulate feminism and how their own definitions relate to their understanding of this sacred figure. In the concluding chapter, I focus on a theme that crosses the chapters and offer a more extensive definition of what I call Mexican Catholic imagination. I discuss the broader implications of this study for the advancement of the study of lived religion, feminist research, and pastoral work. I also propose the concept of (*fe*)minism as a useful theoretical lens to understand what religious beliefs and social circumstances propel women to exercise their agency on behalf of themselves, their children, and communities. Finally, I suggest a series of questions to consider for further development of Our Lady of Guadalupe studies.

The field of Our Lady of Guadalupe is vast and multilayered. The purpose of this book is not to provide a comprehensive understanding of this scholarly area. Instead, through the life narratives of the women in this book, I offer an analysis of what Our Lady of Guadalupe means for Mexican-origin women in daily life. My study explores the ways in which the lives of Mexican-origin women is shaped by religion and in turn how they shape religion within the context of the social structures they negotiate. It is my hope that this book will serve as a springboard for further qualitative research on the intersection of race, class, gender, sexuality and other social categories that may apply in the study of lived religion.

"Here It Is Told"

THOUGH THIS STUDY focuses on the significance of *La Virgen de Guadalupe* in the lives of American Catholic women of Mexican origin, her sacred inspiration crosses genders. I was struck by finding her image in an unexpected place. There she was, *La Virgen*, imprinted on a man's T-shirt. Her face reflected the brown skin tone of the man wearing her image. Her hands were clasped in prayer, and her eyes radiated compassion as if affirming his dignity. No, this man was not the San Juan Diego of 1531, and he was not on the sacred hill of Tepeyac where, according to *El Nican Mopohua*, Our Lady of Guadalupe appeared several times. On the contrary, the place was far from sacred; I could sense a level of spiritual desperation in the thick, cold air. Nor was he standing before Bishop Zumarraga to convince him to build a hermitage in honor of *La Virgen de Guadalupe* on the sacred hill, home to the Aztec goddess Tonantzin. He stood before a different type of *righteous* judge at the federal courthouse in Tucson, Arizona, where a hearing was taking place as a part of Operation Streamline—an initiative of the US Departments of Homeland Security and Justice that criminally prosecutes undocumented individuals who enter the United States. His face was lifeless and empty—no fear and no anger—almost as if his humanity had been stripped away. It seemed as though God had forgotten to be present in this space.

But he was not alone: at least 60 other people like him were bound by shackles at their ankles and wrists, held together by a heavy chain belt—men and women, young and old. Among them was a group of young women in their teens who spoke neither English nor Spanish but Zapotec. Unable to communicate, their expressions embodied the terror that the Nahua women must have felt during México's conquest. Never in my life had I witnessed so many people with their hopes, dreams, and humanity stripped away—just like San Juan Diego.

Before I could articulate to myself the range of emotions I was feeling, the man wearing the image of Our Lady of Guadalupe was called to stand: "Israel Castañeda." Hearing his name made my heart palpitate: we shared the same last name. He was sentenced to 6 months in prison. His crime (and that of the rest of the people waiting to be sentenced) was crossing the US–México border without proof of citizenship. They had all risked their lives and left family behind. They were seeking a better life, just like the European immigrants who entered the United States through Ellis Island between 1892 and 1954.

This is the story of so many people who, like Mr. Castañeda and the young Zapotec women, are in search of a new kind of Tepeyac, a place that they can call home. Why did Mr. Castañeda choose to wear a T-shirt with the image of *La Virgen de Guadalupe* imprinted on its back for the treacherous journey across the desert? Was he moved by his faith and devotion to Our Lady of Guadalupe? Did he hope she would protect him? I will never have a chance to ask him, but I suspect that intellectual debates over the right to interpret Our Lady of Guadalupe do not inform his devotion to her. But what is it about Our Lady of Guadalupe's apparition story that is so deeply significant that it resonates centuries later in a court of law?

Origins of Her Story

Though some readers already may be familiar with Our Lady of Guadalupe's origin story, I recount it here in some detail for readers who have not encountered it. Furthermore, as later chapters will demonstrate, the story of her origin and her historical and political significance play a pivotal role in how some of the women interviewed for this study understand her meaning and implications for their own lives. According to Mexican tradition, an event took place on December 12, 1531, that marked the beginning of a *mestiza/o* (mixed Aztec and Spanish Catholic) religious imagination—the apparition of Our Lady of Guadalupe to a Nahua man by the name of Juan Diego (see Figure 1.1). The traditional text *El Nican Mopohua* (whose title has been translated as either "Here it is told" or "In good order and in careful arrangement") was written in 1648. In 1746, Our Lady of Guadalupe was officially declared the patron saint of New Spain, and in 1754 Pope Benedict XIV, in the decree "Non Est Equidem," approved liturgical texts for Masses in honor of Our Lady of Guadalupe and pronounced December 12 as her official feast day (Chávez 2006; Davies 2011).[1]

FIGURE I.I. Photograph of original image of Our Lady of Guadalupe, Basílica de Nuestra Señora de Guadalupe in México City. Courtesy: Socorro Castañeda-Liles.

In 1521, after the last Aztec ruler Cuauhtémoc surrendered, Tenochtitlán (now México City) fell to Hernán Cortés. Catholicism became one of the mechanisms Spanish soldiers and some missionaries used to validate the physical, emotional, and spiritual conquest of the Nahua people. The cruelties committed against the Nahua people included the rape of women and the killing of men, women, and children alike. The Aztec sociopolitical and religious systems were shattered.[2]

The spirit of the Nahua people, whose humanity was questioned by the conquerors, grew weaker with the passing of time as they witnessed the destruction of their major social institutions and the death of loved ones at the hands of the Spanish conquerors. However, Catholic Mexican popular tradition tells us that a miraculous event took place at Mount Tepeyac, which would create something new out of two opposing worlds (Spanish and Aztec).

According to Mexican Catholic popular tradition, this event took place approximately a decade after the fall of Tenochtitlán. At early dawn on Saturday, December 9, 1531, Juan Diego, a Nahua man who had recently converted to Christianity, was walking to church. To get to the church he crossed the hill of Tepeyac, the site of worship to an Aztec goddess that the Nahua people called Tonantzin. He was walking hurriedly so as to not miss catechism class, when suddenly he heard birds singing at the top of the hill. Moments later he also heard a tender female voice calling his name. What he saw at the top of the hill left him in awe:

A woman covered with a mantle as blue as the sky, with golden sunrays gently branching out behind her. Her skin was cinnamon brown like his, her hands were together in the indigenous way of offering, and she spoke the Nahuatl language. (Castañeda-Liles 2008, 155)

She introduced herself to Juan Diego as Mary, mother of God. She then proceeded to tell him to go before Bishop Zumarraga and tell him that she wanted a hermitage in her name to be built on top of Mount Tepeyac. Juan Diego went to speak with the bishop and told him what he had seen and heard, delivering the message from the heavenly lady. Not surprisingly, the bishop did not believe Juan Diego and asked him to come back another day when he could listen to the story about his vision more attentively.

Distraught, Juan Diego went back to the site where the heavenly lady had appeared before him. There she was again, saddened as he told her that he had delivered her message but that because he was a poor Nahua, Bishop Zumarraga seemed incredulous. Juan Diego proposed that the beautiful lady send someone else with a higher social status, so that her message could be taken seriously. Looking at Juan Diego with tender eyes, she told him that it was he whom she had chosen to deliver his message. The heavenly lady told him to go before the bishop once again "and tell him that the Ever-Virgin Mary, the Mother of God, wanted a hermitage to be built on the hill of Tepeyac" (Castañeda-Liles 2008, 155). He did just as she told him. Still disbelieving, the bishop questioned him at length, but in the end he told Juan Diego to ask the heavenly lady for a sign.

When Juan Diego went home, he found his uncle Juan Bernardino ill with smallpox—a disease brought by the Spaniards to which the Nahua people had no immunity. Juan Bernardino was so ill that he thought he was going to die, and he asked Juan Diego to get a priest from Tlatelolco to come and hear his last confession. The next day, Juan Diego decided to go around the hill to avoid seeing the Lady, because he needed to go and find a priest for his uncle. However, avoiding her proved unsuccessful. She appeared to him just as he was going around the hill. Juan Diego told her that his uncle was dying, that he was deeply worried and needed to look for a priest. Lovingly looking at Juan Diego, she told him that there was no reason to be sad, for his uncle was in good health. She then proceeded to tell him that he was to walk to the top of the hill of Tepeyac, pick some roses, and bring them back. Juan Diego was perplexed, for it was December, and no flowers grow in the winter.

He did as he was told, however, and to his surprise, when he went up the hill he was enveloped by the fragrance of Castilian roses. He cut them and placed them in his *tilma* (cloak), then went back to where the heavenly Lady was waiting for him. She took the flowers and placed them back in his *tilma*. She then told Juan Diego to give the flowers to the bishop, for they were the sign he had requested. Upon his arrival at the episcopal palace, Juan Diego asked for the bishop. Noticing Juan Diego's joy, the doorkeepers, friars, and servants asked to see what he had in his *tilma*. Afraid that if he did not do as they requested they would keep him from seeing the bishop, he let them see a few flowers. The friars, doorkeeper, and servants saw the flowers, but when they tried to pick up the flowers they "disappeared into thin air" (Castañeda-Liles 2008, 155). Once he came before Bishop Zumarraga, Juan Diego opened his *tilma*; to everyone's surprise, as the flowers fell the image of the heavenly Lady became imprinted on the cloth.

Meanwhile, the heavenly Lady appeared to Juan Diego's uncle, Juan Bernardino, who was gravely ill back home. She told him that she was the Ever-Virgin Holy Mary of Guadalupe, and to worry no more for he was now healed. He was to go to the bishop and tell him about his healing and all that he had seen and heard. After the miraculous events, the bishop became convinced that the heavenly Lady was the Virgin Mary in the image and likeness of a *mestiza* woman. Not long after Our Lady of Guadalupe's miraculous apparition, a hermitage was constructed on the hill of Tepeyac in her honor.

Our Lady of Guadalupe's Historical
and Political Significance

Next to the eagle perched on the cactus in the Mexican flag, Our Lady of Guadalupe is arguably the most visible spiritual symbol for people of Mexican origin. On her feast day in 2017, the Basilica of Our Lady of Guadalupe in México City, where the original image is housed, received approximately eight million visitors, making it the most visited Catholic sanctuary in Latin America. In fact, it is the second most visited Catholic pilgrimage site in the world (exceeded only by St. Peter's basilica in the Vatican). Her image has been reproduced countless times. For those who venerate Our Lady of Guadalupe, her image represents hope, struggle, and affirmation, particularly during key historical moments.

One of the first political uses of the image was during the Mexican Revolution in 1810. Guadalupe's image on a banner became México's symbol of liberation from Spanish rule as Father Miguel Hidalgo y Costilla carried her into the battlefield. México's first president, born José Miguel Ramón Adaucto Fernández y Félix, took the name Guadalupe Victoria in honor of Our Lady of Guadalupe, as he claimed she was instrumental in gaining México's independence from Spain. In the Cristero War of 1926–1929, her image replaced that of the eagle and cactus in the Mexican flag as she led troops of armed men and women against the constitution of 1917, which intended to destabilize the influence of the Catholic Church in México.

For centuries, people of Mexican descent—regardless of class, gender, sexual orientation, or geographical location—have continued to recognize *La Virgen de Guadalupe* as the most influential Catholic, cultural, and political female symbol of México. Approximately a century later, on the northern side of the Southwest US–México border, labor leader Cesar Chávez took the image of Our Lady of Guadalupe as a symbol of justice and victory as he, along with Dolores Huerta, organized thousands of farmworkers into a successful strike against grape growers who exploited their workers. Our Lady of Guadalupe crosses the border undocumented every day as immigrants swim across the treacherous Rio Grande or walk through the scorching desert carrying her image on a chain around their necks, on a prayer card in their wallets, in their prayers, or, as in Mr. Castañeda's case, imprinted on a T-shirt. More recently, her image has been used in pro–immigration-reform rallies across the country as a symbol of justice and equality for undocumented people.

Furthermore, Our Lady of Guadalupe is a prominent Catholic figure in many neighborhoods in México and the United States. Murals of *La Virgen* can be found adorning the walls of small markets and neighborhood parks in US Latinx communities.[3] Guadalupe's significance is such that many local markets (Latinx and non-Latinx) intentionally have murals of her image to dissuade people from vandalizing the premises.[4] Devotion to Our Lady of Guadalupe has not only produced a massive amount of material culture but also has helped vest popular spaces with sacred meaning through the use of public altars and murals in parks, on the streets, and in business establishments.[5]

People appropriate this sacred image for multiple reasons. Some are moved by Catholic faith. Chicanas reinterpret her as an Aztec feminist symbol, others perceive her as a Mexican national and cultural symbol, and still others interpret her as a trendy popular icon. As her appearance on the T-shirt of the gentleman facing court charges suggests, Guadalupe evokes multiple meanings and occupies countless spaces. One can think of Our Lady of Guadalupe as a type of "transgressive religious symbol" (Espinosa 2014b) that crosses multiple racial, ethnic, gender, and class borders.[6] As I demonstrate in this chapter, her image knows no borders or boundaries; she seamlessly moves between religious denominations, racial lines, political parties, and popular culture, making her way into private and public spaces and into the lives of people who entrust to her their deepest fears, struggles, desires, and hopes.

Our Lady of Guadalupe is generally perceived as a predominantly Mexican Catholic symbol, but in the United States she has become pan-ethnic and pan-religious. Such is the case in Madison, Wisconsin. In recent years, Madison has experienced an increase in its Latinx population, and a Lutheran church looking for ways to attract converts has incorporated the celebration and veneration of Our Lady of Guadalupe.[7]

In the political arena, both conservative and liberal politicians have banked on the people's devotion to *La Virgen de Guadalupe* to attract potential voters; they have been quick to use this sacred symbol as cultural capital to fuel their political campaigns. In the 2008 US presidential campaign, during his visit to México on July 3, 2008, Senator John McCain (along with his wife Cindy McCain and former Florida Governor Jeb Bush) visited the Basilica of Our Lady of Guadalupe and was photographed next to the image.[8] The visit made news headlines and captured the attention of US Latinxs as it was featured prominently on the Spanish-language television channels Telemundo and Univisión.

On March 26, 2009, during a visit to México, then–US Secretary of State Hillary Clinton also visited the basilica and her visit also made international news.[9] More recently (March 2012), former Vice President Joe Biden visited the basilica; like the other politicians, he was photographed next to Our Lady of Guadalupe.[10] Whether or not their motives were purely political, their visits to the basilica remind us that Our Lady of Guadalupe's political, cultural, and religious capital makes her one of the most widely used sacred symbols of our times, penetrating even the most secular spaces of our capitalist society.

Our Lady of Guadalupe also occupies an important place among white Hollywood celebrities and the entertainment industry. For example, Playboy model Anna Nicole Smith (1967–2007) had a tattoo of Our Lady of Guadalupe on her left ankle. What moved Smith, a white woman (and for many the antithesis of what Our Lady of Guadalupe traditionally represents), to get a tattoo of the brown virgin? Smith was born and raised in Texas; perhaps she was exposed to the image growing up. Hollywood screenwriter Joe Eszterhas—best known for the films *Flashdance* (1983), *Basic Instinct* (1992), and *Showgirls* (1995)—embarked in 2009 on the screenplay for a film about Our Lady of Guadalupe's apparition in 1531. According to CBSNews (August 5, 2009), Eszterhas said that this project was "a labor of love." On September 11, 2016, Dominican American Hollywood actress Dascha Polanco, who plays Dayanara Díaz on the American Netflix original series, *Orange Is the New Black*, attended the Blonds New York Fashion Week wearing a bodysuit and a long flower-print coat with the image of Our Lady of Guadalupe emblazoned at the center. More recently, shortly after the death of Hollywood actress Carrie Fisher in 2016, popular cartoonist Lalo Alcaraz re-imaged Our Lady of Guadalupe and titled his new version of *La Virgen*, "Princess Lupe" claiming that this was his Mexican version of Princess Leia. In this image Princess Lupe's right hand rests on her waist and she holds a ray gun hand cannon with her left hand.[11]

Whatever the motivations of various people for manipulating or using this sacred image, it is clear that Our Lady of Guadalupe has become increasingly significant in US mainstream society. Therefore, to think of Guadalupe as a sacred symbol that has no relevance outside the Mexican American and Chicanx Catholic communities is to overlook an icon that is very much part of the US sociopolitical, cultural, and religious tapestry.

Retailers have even taken advantage of her popularity by finding creative ways to stamp the image of Our Lady of Guadalupe on T-shirts, handbags, wallets, teddy bears, lamps, posters, calling cards, computer mouse pads, jewelry, baseball caps, backpacks, dolls, shoes, and vests for dogs and cats, all for the sake of profit in the United States and in México. In México, for example, the company Distroller has modified the image of Our Lady of Guadalupe to have an infantilized look, similar to the figures of the popular brand Precious Moments (see Figure 1.2). What is more, Guadalupe's hair in the *Distroller* images ranges from black to blonde to red, and her skin color from light brown to pale white—noticeably depicting a white Europeanized version of Our Lady of Guadalupe. *Distroller* began as a small Mexican company and has now grown international, with stores in the United States and Europe; companies such as Walmart, Evenflo, and Avon now have imprinted the *Distroller* representation of Our Lady of Guadalupe on their products. Among the most popular *Distroller* items with her image are handbags, picture frames, necklaces, puzzles, and backpacks that cost between $744 and $999 Mexican pesos (US $44 to $55), clearly targeting a middle- to upper-class Mexican clientele.[12]

FIGURE 1.2. Girl wearing a *Distroller* backpack with the image of *La Virgen de Guadalupe*. Courtesy: Socorro Castañeda-Liles.

Whether because she is a symbol of the Catholic faith, a representation of Mexican nationality, or simply trendy, this sacred symbol has been appropriated across geographical, racial, ethnic, gender, religious, and class lines. With such colossal traction, it is not surprising that an extensive body of scholarly material has been published on Our Lady of Guadalupe.

An all-encompassing overview of scholarly approaches to the study Our Lady of Guadalupe is beyond the scope of this book. What follows is a general introduction to the disciplines that have been most active in defining what Our Lady of Guadalupe means for the faithful. However, it is important to recognize that the apparition story has always had a counter-narrative sustained by various arguments rejecting the authenticity of the story. On one hand there are scholars like Fidel González Fernández, Eduardo Chávez Sánchez, and José Luis Guerrero Rosado, who argue that the miraculous event did take place. On the other hand, there are scholars such as Stafford Poole (1995), Louise M. Burkhart (1993), and Margarita Zires (1994), who question the veracity of the story.[13] However, the chapters that follow do not engage with anti-apparitionist scholarly claims because the women in my study did not take an interest in questioning whether she appeared or not to San Juan Diego. When I asked the women their opinions on such claims, they said either that they did not care about such arguments or that their faith and devotion lead them to conclude that she did appear to San Juan Diego. My analysis of the words of the women in this study place these intellectual debates in a new light by showing that the anti-apparitionist arguments have no bearing on these women's devotion to *La Virgen de Guadalupe*.[14]

Theological Perspectives on Our Lady of Guadalupe

Catholic theologians see Our Lady of Guadalupe as a version of the Virgin Mary in the image and likeness of a *mestiza*. Furthermore, who Mary is and what she represents depends on the culturally specific historic context in which she came to be significant for groups of people.[15] For example, Our Lady of Guadalupe is Mexican, *La Virgen de la Caridad del Cobre* is Cuban, and Our Lady of Suyapa is Honduran. Our Lady of Guadalupe came to be during the Spanish conquest of México, a time when two worlds, two ways of knowing and relating to the sacred, collided and produced something new—*mestizaje*.[16]

Mestizaje typically refers to the genetic and cultural duality (Nahua and Spanish) of Mexican-origin people.[17] Scholars argue that *mestizaje* represents the reality of conquest and colonization of a people who were stripped of their cultural and religious ways of knowing and whose humanity was questioned by Spanish colonizers.[18] This has been a central theoretical lens through which scholars have analyzed the complexity of Our Lady of Guadalupe and the meanings she brings to life for Chicanx and Mexican Americans.[19]

Leading scholars of Mexican American Catholic theology and Our Lady of Guadalupe have interpreted her from the *mestiza/o* perspective.[20] This allows for an Nahua-Catholic analysis of the *Nican Mopohua* to develop a Guadalupe theology anchored in the *mestiza/o* experience of Mexican Americans.[21] Our Lady of Guadalupe, the *mestiza* mother, affirms the indigenous roots of her *mestiza/o* children, as religious scholars have argued.[22] However, while Guadalupe affirms the indigenous roots of the *mestiza/o* people, Catholicism—not Aztec religious tradition—is the only path to religious salvation according to this interpretation.[23] From a theological perspective, Our Lady of Guadalupe advocates for her children.[24] People find her a safe and mystical space in the midst of the uncertainty, oppression, and violence in their lives.[25]

It is important to note that Catholic theologians affirm that Our Lady of Guadalupe is not God. However, some do contend that she is the feminine face of God. In other words, she represents the attributes of God that oftentimes are stripped away by androcentric orthodox interpretations of God.[26] For scholars like Orlando Espín, devotion to Our Lady of Guadalupe has a pneumatological quality. That is, the ways people describe Our Lady of Guadalupe and the characteristics they assign to her are aligned with how the Holy Spirit is articulated by Catholic theologians. This type of interpretation has implications for how we think of Our Lady of Guadalupe's relationship to God. While in this book I do not present a pneumatological analysis (the study of the Holy Spirit) of women's relationship to Our Lady of Guadalupe, from a sociological perspective I do demonstrate the ways women display a fluid understanding of Our Lady of Guadalupe's relationship to divinity.

Since the recognition of the *Nican Mopohua* in 1754, the Catholic Church has identified Our Lady of Guadalupe as Mary of Nazareth in the image and likeness of a *mestiza* woman. Catholic apparitionist theologians argue that Our Lady of Guadalupe is the Virgin Mary, mother of Jesus. However, I join with other scholars, like Espín (1997), in challenging this interpretation and inviting theologians to step out of traditional interpretations of Guadalupe and engage in conversation with the social sciences about the ways this sacred symbol might be understood by grassroots people. For example, is Our Lady of Guadalupe Mary of Nazareth in the image and likeness of a *mestiza* woman for Catholic women at the grassroots? When women pray the rosary, which image of the virgin mother do they have in mind: Our Lady of Guadalupe or Mary of Nazareth? Chapter 6 explores these questions in depth.

For the most part, the theological interpretations of her significance to people have relied on general observations of the faithful, historical documents, and archeological evidence. What has been lacking is precisely what this study aims to offer: a social scientific methodological approach that centers on in-depth interviews to further the understanding of how and why Our Lady of Guadalupe is so significant in the daily life of Mexican-origin women at the intersections of the various social categories that shape their lives.

One notable theological study that integrated social science methods to advance our understanding of the significance of Our Lady of Guadalupe was Jeanette Rodriguez's *Our Lady of Guadalupe: Faith and Empowerment Among Mexican-American Women* (1994). This was the first empirical theological study on the devotion to Our Lady of Guadalupe from the perspective of ordinary Mexican American women. Written from a psychosocial Catholic perspective, Rodriguez's study is a significant contribution not only to Guadalupe studies but also to Latinx religious studies, theology, and Chicana feminist studies in general. Her findings take us in a new direction. This has clear implications for the field of Chicana feminist social science studies in particular, which have tended to frame Our Lady of Guadalupe as a submissive role model for women. Indeed, Marian symbols like Our Lady of Guadalupe have been traditionally interpreted to represent unattainable ideals women should aspire to—a point which elicits strong critique by Chicana feminist scholars. However, through interviews with Mexican American women, Rodriguez found that what *La Virgen* means for them is more complex. Mexican American women do not necessarily take these oppressive attributes and ideals at face value. She found that Our Lady of Guadalupe is a source of both hope and empowerment for Mexican American middle-class women. My study takes Rodriguez's work further by integrating the topic of sexuality—an understudied area in research on *La Virgen de Guadalupe*.

The field of Latina theology, though gradually changing, has had a tendency to avoid the topics of sex and sexuality. The analysis done from this scholarly discipline has been more along the lines of Crenshaw's (1989)

definition of intersectionality: race, class, and gender. Rodriguez also follows this pattern, focusing predominantly on race, class, and gender analysis. This book expands this line of research by exploring the intersection
of race, class, gender, sexuality, and religion.

Let me be clear that I commend Rodriguez (1994) for breaking ground
in the theological study of Our Lady of Guadalupe. Until Rodriguez, no
one, at least as far as I know, had ever asked what Our Lady of Guadalupe
meant to ordinary women. Rodriguez not only placed women's voices at
the center of Guadalupan theological analysis, she also inspired some
aspects of my own work. Her findings prompted me to ask additional
questions about the role of Our Lady of Guadalupe in the lives of Mexican-
origin women—questions that guided me as I attempted to understand
Guadalupe's significance for working-class, ordinary women in daily life.
For example: How do women craft a devotion to Our Lady of Guadalupe in
the midst of their subjectivity as women, mothers, daughters, and sexual
beings? Given that sex and sexuality are highly contested yet central issues
in Catholic ideology, how do women negotiate their sexuality and devotion to Our Lady of Guadalupe as they go about their everyday lives? My
study departs from Rodriguez's in various ways. She interviewed accul-
turated middle-class English-speaking women, and my sample consisted
of first-generation working-class women from three different life experience cohorts (young single women with no children, mothers, and older
women), thus providing an intergenerational analysis. What is more, with
the exception of the young college women who were fully bilingual, most
of the women in my study were monolingual Spanish speakers. Her disci-
plinary lenses are psychological and theological, and mine is sociological,
which I contend holds much promise for enhancing our understanding of
the significance of Our Lady of Guadalupe.[27]

Chicana Feminist Perspectives on Our Lady of Guadalupe

Until recently, what we knew about the significance of Our Lady of
Guadalupe was produced in the disciplines of theology and history. History
has illuminated Guadalupe with analysis that either affirms or rejects the
apparition story. Theological works strive to capture the Christian (mainly
Catholic) significance of this religious symbol to her devotees. While
these disciplines have contributed to our understanding of Our Lady of
Guadalupe, for the most part, they shed little light on the implications of

Our Lady of Guadalupe in the social construction of gender roles. Chicana feminist interpretations of Guadalupe contest traditional female roles articulated through patriarchal Catholicism and family configurations. Through their writings, paintings, and theory, they recapture historical Nahua oral history and religious imagery like Tonantzin.[28]

The Chicana feminist interpretation of Our Lady of Guadalupe has come about in two different but overlapping approaches: literature and art. These two fields have denounced the virgin–whore dichotomy in which *La Virgen de Guadalupe* is generally placed. On one end there is Our Lady of Guadalupe as the docile, all-accepting mother, the female role model that women should aspire to become. On the other end, there is *La Malinche*, a Nahua woman who has been framed as the whore—the one who betrayed her own people, facilitated the conquest of México by serving as Cortés's translator, and eventually had a child with him.[29]

In Chicana feminist consciousness, Guadalupe is not Mary of Nazareth; she is the Aztec goddess Tonantzin, or in some cases only a cultural symbol.[30] Within this interpretation that removes Our Lady of Guadalupe from Catholic understandings, scholars have reclaimed Tonantzin who, based on Nahua accounts, was venerated on the hill of Tepeyac—the same hill on which, according to Catholic tradition, Our Lady of Guadalupe appeared to San Juan Diego. What is more, scholars like Irene Lara (2008b) have presented new concepts to understand the dual aspect of Our Lady of Guadalupe—the *mestiza* Guadalupe and the Aztec Tonantzin. According to Lara, *Tonanlupanisma* (*Tonan* is a derivative of Tonantzin, an Aztec goddess; *lupanisma*, a derivative of Guadalupe) captures the meanings of duality as understood in Mesoamerican definitions of Our Lady of Guadalupe.

Furthermore, Chicana feminist literary scholars bring forth Our Lady of Guadalupe's indigenous and sexual aspect as a way of reclaiming her from Catholic interpretations.[31] A common thread of Guadalupe discourse in Chicana feminist consciousness is the juxtaposition of Our Lady of Guadalupe's potential to empower, and her own sexuality. In Chapter 8, I explore how the women in this study respond to images related to these themes emphasized in Chicana art.

Perhaps one of most significant contributions to Our Lady of Guadalupe studies from a literary perspective is Ana Castillo's (1996) collection *Goddess of the Americas: Writings on the Virgin of Guadalupe*. Bringing together renowned authors such as Gloria Anzaldúa, Sandra Cisneros, and Elena Poniatowska, this collection takes an intersectional analytical approach. That is, it analyzes Our Lady of Guadalupe's significance from a race, class, gender, and sexuality cross-sectional perspective. Through testimonies, poems, and short stories, the authors address the ways andro-centric binary (virgin–whore dichotomy) interpretations of *La Virgen de Guadalupe* have been oppressive for women, and they claim Our Lady of Guadalupe as an empowering symbol.

For example, Chicana scholar Ana Castillo (1996), in her essay "Extraordinarily Woman," experiences the love of Our Lady of Guadalupe through the relationship she has with her grandmother who was a *curandera* and a devotee of Our Lady of Guadalupe.[32] Castillo's account of her own initiation as a *curandera* resonates with San Juan Diego's experience as the one chosen by Our Lady of Guadalupe. San Juan Diego, a power-less Nahua man who had been stripped of his identity, religion, culture, and humanity, becomes the messenger of Our Lady of Guadalupe. Of all those whom she could have chosen as intermediaries, she chose San Juan Diego.[33] Similarly, Castillo relates, "Abuelita—ancient crone *curandera*, disciple of Our Mother, Mexican matriarch—took her smallest, frailest off-spring into her apprenticeship and taught me what she could until she died when I was 10 years old" (Castillo 1996, 75).

In the *Nican Mopohua*, Our Lady of Guadalupe's relationship is directly with San Juan Diego. In Castillo's story, however, the relationship is trian-gular: Our Lady of Guadalupe through the intercession of the protagonist's grandmother and the protagonist herself. The emphasis on the triangular matriarchal relationship (Our Lady of Guadalupe, grandmother, and the protagonist) in Castillo's account resembles Robert Orsi's (1996) concept of "devotional triangle" as the mode of transmission of faith and devotion from mother to daughter—the topic of the next chapter. What is important to underscore is the way that Castillo describes the relationship between herself as a young girl, her grandmother, and Our Lady of Guadalupe. Her focus on the life-giving aspects of Guadalupan devotion allows the reader to see that devotion to *La Virgen de Guadalupe* as lived in everyday life has stronger ties to the matriarchs in the family than to Catholic doctrine.

Chicana literary scholars such as Gloria Anzaldúa (1996), Ana Castillo (1996), Sandra Cisneros (1996), Cherríe Moraga (1996), Carla Trujillo (1991), and Pat Mora (1994) have brought the theme of sexuality to the cen-ter of their literary works as it relates to Our Lady of Guadalupe as a locus for women's self-empowerment.[34] This aspect of the Chicana feminist re-envisioning of Guadalupe creates strong contention because female sex-uality has always been and continues be a taboo subject among Chicanxs and Latinxs.[35] Chapter 8 demonstrates that the women in this study have their own definitions of feminism that in some ways seem similar to the agency in Chicana feminism. However, their traditional upbringings lead them to criticize the overt sexuality reflected in some Chicana feminist representations of Our Lady of Guadalupe.[36]

Latina sexuality is robbed of any agency, constraining women to a "double chastity belt of ignorance and *vergüenza*, shame" (Cisneros 1996, 46). In her childhood and on through her adult life, Cisneros rejected Our Lady of Guadalupe: "I saw *La Virgen de Guadalupe*, my culture's role model for brown women like me. She was damn dangerous, an ideal so lofty and unrealistic it was laughable" (48). Cisneros saw in Our Lady of Guadalupe a constraining role model that her culture expected her to emulate. For Cisneros, nothing good could come from "*la Lupe*" (as she refers to Our Lady of Guadalupe) except a guaranteed life of unhappiness. Given her experience growing up with an image and conception of Our Lady of Guadalupe as an oppressive symbol, one might conclude that Cisneros rejected Guadalupe in her adult years; however, this was not the case. With the passage of years the Guadalupe of Cisneros's childhood transcended the Catholic submissive female role model from which she always found herself running away.

> When I look at *La Virgen de Guadalupe* now, she is not the Lupe of my childhood, no longer the one in my grandparents' house in Tepeyac, nor is she the one of the Roman Catholic Church, the one I bolted the door against in my teens and twenties. Like every woman who matters to me, I have had to search for her in the rubble of history. And I have found her. She is Guadalupe the sex goddess, a goddess who makes me feel good about my sexual power, my sexual energy. (Cisneros 1996, 49)

This quote is important not only because it provides the reader with a clear sense of how she thinks about Our Lady of Guadalupe in her adult years but also because it is a testament to the staying power of Our Lady of Guadalupe, even among women who initially found her to be an oppressive symbol.[37]

For many Chicana feminists the ultimate liberation for women comes when they can publicly affirm, celebrate, and speak freely about their sexuality. Cisneros (1996) expresses her own freedom by re-articulating Our Lady of Guadalupe as an indigenous goddess not ashamed to express her sexuality. The outcome of this process is thus the affirmation not only of

Our Lady of Guadalupe's sexuality but also that of all women. Likewise, Chicana feminist literary lesbian reconfigurations of Guadalupe have also challenged conventional social constructions of this symbol.[38] While none of the women in this study identified as lesbian, it is important to acknowledge this facet of Chicana theorizing. In her essay "La Virgen de Guadalupe and Her Reconstruction in Chicana Lesbian Desire," Chicana scholar Carla Trujillo imagines what it would be like to have Our Lady of Guadalupe as her life partner.[39] Trujillo's essay places lesbian sexuality at the center of her analysis of Our Lady of Guadalupe.

Such interpretations appear as sacrilegious to the more traditional devotees of Our Lady of Guadalupe, who perceive these interpretations as blasphemous. However, whether one agrees with these feminist interpretations or not, a careful reading and analysis of their works in the context of their histories of marginalization reveals the reasons that drive these Chicanas to reconstruct Guadalupe's sexuality and ascribe to her a sexual preference. Guadalupe in Chicana lesbian thought represents a powerful yet palpable female subjectivity—a familiar social agent that advocates and honors Chicana lesbian ways of knowing, caring, and loving.

Chicana lesbian processes of understanding the complexity of Our Lady of Guadalupe complicate the prevailing notion of Our Lady of Guadalupe as the mother who gives her unconditional love to those who believe in her. They do so by arguing that if indeed she is all-accepting, then lesbians should share an equal spiritual space with their heterosexual counterparts.[40] Spirituality, whether it refers to space or a practice, is one theme that Chicana feminist scholars have critiqued and redefined.[41] Such Chicana critiques of Our Lady of Guadalupe do not split the spiritual from the physical; both coexist in harmony in Our Lady of Guadalupe— the Aztec goddess Tonantzin.[42]

Similarly, Gloria Anzaldúa's interpretation of *La Virgen de Guadalupe* calls for a holistic interpretation. Anzaldúa's Guadalupe is not the Virgin Mary in the image and likeness of a *mestiza* Catholic virgin; her interpretation of Our Lady of Guadalupe is rooted in the multilayered and complex Aztec Cosmo vision. Her understanding of *La Virgen de Guadalupe* has various goddess-like entities: Coatlalopeuh (she who has dominion over the serpents), Coatlicue (goddess of sexual drive), Tonantzin (the loving and nurturing goddess), Tlazolteotl (goddess of fertility and sexuality), and Cihuacoatl (goddess of childbirth).[43] The amalgamation of the goddesses Tonantzin, Tlazolteotl, and Cihuacoatl create Coatlicue, who in turn is an aspect of the goddess Coatlalopeuh. Feeling threatened by two of Coatlicue's attributes—Cihuacoatl and Tlazolteotl—the male-centered Aztec-Mexican society separated Tonantzin from Tlazolteotl and Cihuacoatl, and in doing so dismembered Coatlicue and, by extension, Coatlalopeuh. That is, Coatlalopeuh now only had the Tonantzin aspect—the loving good mother.

When the Spanish colonizers along with their Catholic Church came to Mesoamerica, they brought with them rigid gender roles and expectations that defined women's sexuality and sexual pleasure as sinful. Seeing that Tonantzin had a sexual aspect because Coatlalopeuh (though incomplete for she had been dismembered by the Nahuas) remained an aspect of her, they desexed Tonantzin by separating her from Coatlalopeuh. Disassociated from Coatlalopeuh, Tonantzin became Santa María de Guadalupe the Catholic virgin mother protector of Mexicans.[44] Therefore, according to Anzaldúa, the Catholic Church completed the dismembering process begun by the Nahua people.[45]

Anzaldúa's interpretation of Our Lady of Guadalupe argues that the split of Tonantzin from her sexual aspects is the root of the *puta* (whore)/virgin dichotomy to which women are held to this day.[46] This binary conceptualization of women demonizes their sexual agency. For example, a *puta* will always be a *puta* even if she exercises some aspects of the "virgin" counterpart. However, if a woman deviates, even slightly, from the conceptions and expectations of the "virgin," she becomes a "puta." This binary construction of Coatlalopeuh and, by extension, categorization of women is the split that Anzaldúa attempts to mend together by calling women "to see Coatlalopeuh-Coatlicue (and all her aspects: Tonantzin, Tlazolteotl, and Cihuacoatl) in the Mother, Guadalupe."[47]

Like in Cisneros and Anzaldúa's interpretation of this symbol, Our Lady of Guadalupe also has the same staying power among *Las Damas*, *Las Madres*, and *Las Mujeres*. However, unlike the aforementioned Chicana feminists who disassociate Our Lady of Guadalupe from Catholicism and instead see her as a sex goddess (Cisneros) and a decolonized fierce, loving, sexual mother goddess (Anzaldúa), the women in my study see *La Virgen de Guadalupe* as the virginal Catholic heavenly mother they were introduced to by their mothers and grandmothers.

Among the many Chicana feminist interpretations of Our Lady of Guadalupe, perhaps those that have reached farthest beyond academic circles are the artistic representations; two examples are works by Yolanda López and Alma López. The traditional image of Our Lady of Guadalupe depicts a woman with her hands together right at the chest in the form of prayer. She wears a black band, which has been interpreted by some scholars as a symbol that she is pregnant. On the right side her dress folds at the knee, signifying movement, which some scholars have interpreted as honoring Aztec sacred dances.[48] The Guadalupe in Chicana artistic feminist thought walks freely, as depicted by Yolanda López (1978) (see Figure 1.3) or celebrates her body by wearing a two-piece outfit made of roses, which exposes her arms, torso, and legs (Alma López 1999) (see Figure 1.4). I argue that from a Chicana feminist perspective, the artists' representations of *La Virgen* are visual reflections of Chicana/Mexicana women's reality. This type of feminist reflection is born out the collision

FIGURE 1.3. Mixed-media collage—Yolanda López, *Walking Guadalupe*, 1978. Courtesy: Yolanda López.

FIGURE I.4. *Iris/giclée* on canvas—Alma López, *Our Lady* (Lupe and Sirena series), 1999. Courtesy: Alma López.

between heaven (unattainable ideals and expectations for women) and earth (the raw and often unpleasant daily life), as it also visually documents women's agency. Therefore, to understand why Chicana feminist artists reconstruct and continue to make visible the inner characteristics of Our Lady of Guadalupe to represent what they visually characterize as empowering, we must first consider the ways in which patriarchy penetrates even the most sacred symbols of our times, as pointed out in Chicana feminist literature on *La Virgen de Guadalupe*. Furthermore, apart from whether the artists' true intention is to make a religious or spiritual statement, one might arrive to an interpretation of the images as attempts to extract what might be perceived to be Guadalupe's inner strengths and make them visible—inner strengths that actually resonate with how the women in Rodriguez's (1994) study describe Our Lady of Guadalupe. As we will see in Chapter 8, the ways the women in this study describe Our Lady of Guadalupe are also very much on par with some of these feminist interpretations, even as their strong affinity for traditional representations of Our Lady of Guadalupe lead some of them to challenge or be repulsed by aspects of Chicana feminist representations.

Yolanda López is one of the first Chicana feminist artists to represent Our Lady of Guadalupe. One of López's first representations of Our Lady of Guadalupe is "*Walking Guadalupe*, 1978" (Figure 1.3). In this representation, Our Lady of Guadalupe resembles the original image with a couple of exceptions: Guadalupe's mantle and dress are just below the knee, exposing the lower part of her legs, and she is wearing low-heel slip-on shoes. Davalos (2008) makes an excellent analysis of how López understands the image of Our Lady of Guadalupe. According to Davalos, López saw in Our Lady of Guadalupe an image of a woman who needed to be liberated from the excessively long dress and mantle. In doing so, her intention was also to offer women—who are taught to emulate Our Lady of Guadalupe's unattainable characteristics—a more proactive image of *La Virgen*. In representing Our Lady of Guadalupe in a more contemporary way, she thought that at most people would chuckle when seeing the now liberated Guadalupe able to walk at will; however, *Walking Guadalupe* stirred deep sentiments that shook the Mexican Catholic Church and its faithful to the core.[49] In 1984 López's piece was on the front cover of Mexican *Fem* magazine's special issue on Chicana feminists. The uproar was such that the magazine's publisher received bomb threats and, on the morning of its publication, people upset with López's representation of Our Lady of Guadalupe stole the magazine from the newspaper stands.[50]

Yolanda López's various representations of Our Lady of Guadalupe depict aspects of daily life. López's Guadalupe is an unapologetic young woman who runs (Yolanda López, *Portrait of the Artist as the Virgen of Guadalupe*, 1978), works as a seamstress for a living (Yolanda López, *Margaret F. Stewart: Our Lady of Guadalupe*, 1978), and wears heels (*Walking Guadalupe*, 1978). She breastfeeds her child (*Madre Mestiza*, 2002), and unlike the original image, López's Guadalupe is much older and sits down to rest (*Guadalupe: Victoria F. Franco*, 1978). However, López's objective has never been to make a theological or religious statement about the sacred quality of *La Virgen* in everyday life. This is precisely what concerns Davalos (2008) about the misinterpretation of López's work by some scholars who claim that López's representations have a religious and/or spiritual meaning. López's real intention is to challenge Mexican/Chicano patriarchy and the Catholic Church that sustains it by portraying México's most sacred symbol in feminist ways. According to the artist, "[t]he Virgin was not a symbol that could carry us through on our road to justice and social equality."[51] What is also important to understand is that López does not identify as Catholic. For her, Our Lady of Guadalupe is not the *mestiza* heavenly mother who miraculously appeared to San Juan Diego in 1531. *La Virgen* for López is a cultural symbol and not a spiritual or religious one. This standpoint allowed López to interpret Our Lady of Guadalupe in nontraditional ways that women in my study who see Our Lady of Guadalupe as their holy Catholic mother found challenging to comprehend.

One of the more recent representations to have engendered a great degree of contention is one directly discussed in Chapter 8. It is by Alma López (1999) who, inspired by Castillo's (1996) essay "Guadalupe the Sex Goddess," represented Our Lady of Guadalupe in a computerized photo collage titled *Our Lady*. Here, *La Virgen de Guadalupe* is wearing a two-piece outfit made out of bright, colorful roses, like the miraculous roses of the apparition account. Her eyes and posture have an assertive expression. Her veil is the dismembered Aztec goddess Coyolxauhqui; the backdrop appears to be the color and design of Guadalupe's original dress.[52] The angel carrying her is a bare-breasted female angel with butterfly wings.

During Holy Week, a museum in Santa Fe, New Mexico, exhibited *Our Lady* as part of a larger exhibit titled "Cyber Arte." The exhibit caused heated debate; on one side were the local city government, the Catholic Church hierarchy, and local parishioners; on the other were the museum, the artist, and her supporters. A city was divided; the opposition filed an appeal to remove the exhibit, and the lives of the artist and model were threatened. What led López to "undress" *La Virgen?*—a question many women in this study also asked when shown this representation.

At age 18 Raquel Salinas, the model who posed as "Our Lady," was raped. Like many women who have been victims of rape, she did not find support in those closest to her. Instead, they blamed her for being raped; they humiliated her and told her that God brought this upon her as punishment.[53] The humiliation was such that she rejected her femininity by covering herself up, and she became an alcoholic. After more than 10 years of therapy, she slowly began to accept herself again; posing for López as Our Lady became the culmination of her healing process. Thus, what for many was sacrilegious and blasphemous became for Salinas the opportunity she had been waiting for to rid herself of the "shame and guilt" she had carried for so many years. Through Alma López and Raquel Salinas, we are reminded that Chicana artists' work is contextualized in real life experiences at the nexus of race, class, gender, and sexuality. As Salinas's story shows, the full meaning of these types of representations can only be understood within the context of structural violence experienced among Chicanxs. And, as we will see in Chapter 7, in domestic violence situations Our Lady of Guadalupe moves women to confront abusive situations.

Lastly, while Chicana artistic representations of *La Virgen de Guadalupe* tend to directly challenge traditional Catholic interpretations, there are exceptions. Such is the case of Caroline Martinez, who works in the style of Mexican ex-votos (pictorial depictions of miracles granted).[54] Martinez situates Our Lady of Guadalupe in the midst of the trials and tribulations of daily life, such as verbal and physical abuse from male partners. Thomas Tweed (2010) points out that while Martinez may not identify with feminism, and not only prays to God daily but her paintings are a form of gratitude to God for protecting her, she should be included in the scholarly discourse of Chicana representations of Our Lady of Guadalupe, for her art also speaks to women's affirmation and self-empowerment in ways that are fluid. However, while *La Virgen de Guadalupe* plays a significant role in Martinez's life, we cannot conclude that her spirituality is entirely Catholic, for it is also Protestant and much more; her relationship to that which she considers sacred is enveloped in what Tweed (2010, 296) calls a "both–and spirituality." Therefore, her artistic approach to representing Our Lady of Guadalupe is complex, an example of the ways she exists for people at the intersection of religious traditions—and, like Chicana representations, Martinez's work is also transgressive. In essence, Martinez's work offers an additional layer of complexity to Chicana representations of Our Lady of Guadalupe.

Religious Studies Perspectives on Our Lady of Guadalupe

Theology, history, and Chicana feminist studies have been integral in shaping Guadalupe scholarly discourse by rejecting or supporting the apparition story, documenting her historical significance among the faithful, and redefining the meaning of the sacred symbol altogether. While I recognize the importance of these perspectives in understanding the multidimensional scholarly interpretations of Our Lady of Guadalupe, I argue that the field of religious studies with its use of social science methods has made an important and much needed contribution to Guadalupe studies in recent years by providing empirical evidence for scholarly claims.

The use of social science methods such as the case study approach (the study of a particular group of people) and ethnography (the study of a particular community) in religious studies has expanded our understanding of who Our Lady of Guadalupe is for people at the grassroots. In the past two decades the scholarly approaches in the study of Our Lady of Guadalupe have moved beyond the theological, historical, and most recently Chicana literature, to social scientific. Within the social sciences, the methods include mixed method (quantitative and qualitative), the case study approach, and ethnography. Due to their qualitative approach to the study of Our Lady of Guadalupe, such works—and I also include Rodriguez's (1994) study here—provide rich empirical evidence to claims about the meaning of Our Lady of Guadalupe devotion.

While scholars in theology and Chicana literature have well documented the powerful significance of Our Lady of Guadalupe among believers, their work has focused on theological understandings of her significance, literary criticism, historical documents, the author's personal experience, or general observations at the grassroots level. To have a greater understanding of her significance and staying power, I contend that the area of Our Lady of Guadalupe studies would greatly benefit from a social science approach to the study. Indeed, there are a few religious studies scholars who have applied qualitative methods. These studies offer empirical evidence that furthers the understanding of how and why Our Lady of Guadalupe is so significant in daily life at the intersections of race, class, and gender.

These studies demonstrate how, in their devotion to Our Lady of Guadalupe, people have found the affirmation to claim space in a country and a Catholic Church that treats Latinxs as second-class citizens in nuanced and explicit ways. From California to New York, the point of departure of these studies is *lo cotidiano* (the quotidian).[55] For example, taking a case study approach, Rebecca Berrú-Davis (2009) found that St. Joseph the Worker Parish in Northern California did not consider Latinx parishioners a priority. Even after they became the majority in the parish, their devotion to Our Lady of Guadalupe was not fully accepted by the small community of white parishioners, who objected to the permanency of the image of Guadalupe inside the church. However, in interviewing the parishioners, Berrú-Davis soon discovered that the power of the Guadalupan devotion of the Latinx parishioners moved them to claim a space for the image of Our Lady of Guadalupe, and in so doing they gained a sense of place for themselves in the parish as well. The devotion to Guadalupe blurred the racial boundaries that once kept the Latinx community from being fully members of this parish community.[56]

Moving from the Southwest to the Midwest, Theresa Torres's ethnography (2013) offers a complex understanding of the faith, devotion, and political activism of a group of *Guadalupanas* (a national group of Catholic laywomen known for promoting the Guadalupan Catholic faith in their communities) in Kansas City. The faith and devotion of these women for *La Virgen de Guadalupe* moved them to exercise their agency on behalf of their parish community. As a result, they prevented the closure of their local church in spite of experiencing a degree of animosity within the Church and their community due to their gender. The piety of *Las Guadalupanas*, which is often perceived as apolitical, was the very source for a type of self-empowerment that led to community activism anchored in Catholic faith. Such findings call for the need to revisit and realign feminist theories or, better yet, draw new theories from the faith of women at the grassroots. Berrú-Davis and Torres provide context for the emphasis on agency that *Las Damas*, *Las Madres*, and *Las Mujeres* also believed in.

Like Torres's study, the following ethnographies suggest that the significance of Our Lady of Guadalupe is not limited to the Southwest. They also demonstrate that her staying power crosses boundaries of nationality. In 2004 there was an analytical shift in Guadalupe scholarship, from the study of the impact of her devotion among Catholic Mexican Americans to the potential of this sacred symbol to reinforce ties among Latinxs in the United States. Mary E. Odem's (2004) ethnographic study in a community in Georgia (a state considered part of the Bible Belt) found that Our Lady of Guadalupe has come to function as a unifying Catholic sacred symbol among Latinx migrants across ethnicities in the area of Chamblee–Doraville. Similarly, Luisa Feline Freier's (2008) qualitative study in Madison, Wisconsin found that Our Lady of Guadalupe is an important cultural symbol for some Protestant Mexicans, whether they have been Protestant all their lives or are recent converts. She also observed that with an interest in attracting the Latinx community, a Lutheran church in Madison, Wisconsin integrated celebrations in honor of Our Lady of Guadalupe as a way to keep Latinx converts. It is equally significant that, in return, the Latinx community has influenced certain Lutheran celebrations such as First Communion and incorporated sacramentals like the *quinceañera* celebration.[57]

Elaine A. Peña's (2008) binational ethnographic study in México City and Illinois (Des Plaines and Rogers Park) found that *La Virgen de Guadalupe* has become a unifying sacred symbol for women pilgrims in México, and this sense of unity was strengthened through collective special prayers, songs, and dances to *La Virgen*. She also found that for US Latinx Catholics across ethnicities she serves as their impetus to organize politically, particularly around issues of citizenship and immigration (Peña 2008).[58] In Phoenix, Arizona, the Virgin Mary's apparition to Estela Ruiz (a middle-aged, middle-class working mother) moved her to redefine her identity from a Chicana feminist to a prophetic woman of Catholic faith. This new faith moved Estela to open ministries for the underserved Latinx community on both sides of the United States–México border.[59]

Ethnographic work by religious studies scholars also allows us to see a theme that this study corroborates, that among the faithful the sacred and secular come together not in opposition but in harmony.[60] In the faith of the people one is able to see the sacralization of the secular and the secularization of the sacred. Such is the case of the "Virgin of the Underground" (Gamboni 2009), an ethnographic study of a water leak on the floor of the Hidalgo Metro Station in México City. The leak left a permanent mark in which people claimed to see the silhouette of *La Virgen de Guadalupe*. It attracted so many devotees of *La Virgen* and curious onlookers that the city cut out that section of the floor and built a niche for it.

While these studies reveal the degree of importance of Our Lady of Guadalupe among Latinxs, such findings raise a new question: Do all Latinas see her through the same devotional lens? More specifically, how exactly do Latinas across ethnicities understand Our Lady of Guadalupe in their lives? In comparing the three largest groups of Latinxs (Mexican, Puerto Rican, and Cuban) and using a mixed-method approach (qualitative and quantitative methods), Peña and Frehill (1998) found that there is something qualitatively different in the way women of Mexican origin understand Mary.[61] For example, for Cuban and Mexican women, Our Lady of Guadalupe is a mother figure. However, they differ in how they articulate her divinity. For Cuban women, Mary is to some extent a "queen," and for Mexican women, she is godlike. Mexican women do not associate

La Virgen with the characteristics typically linked to Mary (obedient and submissive servant of God/Jesus), nor does she hold a supportive role. Instead, Mary Guadalupe, among Mexican women, is described with god-like adjectives such as infinite, powerful, redeeming, and omnipotent.[62] Puerto Rican women do not see her as a mother in the way Mexicans do. Furthermore, *La Virgen de Guadalupe* for Mexican women is both a Catholic and national symbol of pride, hope, resilience, and resistance in the midst of adversity and daily life.[63] Therefore, general assumptions about what Our Lady of Guadalupe means to Latinxs are not only limiting but lend themselves to a one-dimensional Mexican-centric understanding of Our Lady of Guadalupe.[64]

These studies, from different angles and geographical locations—from the Southwest to Chicago and New York—add substantial empirical data to theological claims about the significance of Our Lady of Guadalupe. I am not saying that the theological claims discussed earlier in this chapter were written out of thin air. Rather, case studies and ethnographies offer a closer in-depth reading via analysis of the experiences of the faithful and the words people at the grassroots use to describe their Guadalupan devotion. More broadly speaking, I argue that theories about people's religious ways of knowing need to stem from the words individuals use to describe how they understand that which they consider sacred. Doing so would bring us closer to an understanding that emerges from the complex and often contradictory quality of human experience.

Moreover, the aforementioned studies offer Chicana feminist intellectuals who have written about or visually represented Our Lady of Guadalupe a lens through which to perceive the faith and devotion of women who may not identify with feminism or may object to feminist representations of Our Lady of Guadalupe. Their connection to this sacred symbol is as powerful and life-giving as the connections described in Chicana feminist work.

Looking broadly across disciplines, fields such as theology, history, Chicana feminist studies, and religious studies have produced a plethora of scholarly books and articles, making Our Lady of Guadalupe studies a rich intellectual exchange. Apparitionist and anti-apparitionist scholars have engaged in heated debates over the veracity of her apparition. Chicana feminist scholars have openly criticized the *Marianismo* framework, which exalts the unattainable quintessential Catholic reflection of womanhood and from which the Catholic Church has interpreted Our Lady of Guadalupe. They have reclaimed her as the Aztec goddess

Tonantzin Coatlicue, a central sacred figure in Aztec religion, who was demonized by Catholic missionaries. More recently, employing social science qualitative methods such as ethnography and case studies, the field of religious studies has documented what Guadalupe means for Latinx in the United States. Because other research along these lines has focused on whole communities, usually examining a single issue, this book's contribution is to furthering the understanding of devotion to Our Lady of Guadalupe in the fullness of women's everyday lives.

The Women Speak

The purpose of this opening chapter overviewing some of the literature on *La Virgen de Guadalupe* has been to provide the reader with a general introduction to the multiple ways in which scholars have interpreted this figure and to provide context for how the women featured in this study describe Our Lady of Guadalupe. The following chapters turn to a close analysis of the lived religion of the women in this study as revealed in their words. This study features women from different life experiences (young college women, mothers, and older women) connected by devotion to a female sacred symbol that is complex and yet simple. Their relationship with Our Lady of Guadalupe is not an either/or but a both/and type of experience. Scholars call this in-between space *nepantla*, a word that comes from the Nahua language of the Aztecs. It refers to the in-between space where there is no room for dichotomy—the space in which, according to Aztec thought, life really exists. There are similarities between this *nepantla* way of seeing the world and the stories and devotion of the women in this book. While I could have chosen to use *nepantla* as my analytical lens, instead I opted to use a concept I learned from one of the women in this study, Esperanza (age 68).

Esperanza is not aware of the scholarly debates on Our Lady of Guadalupe. In fact, when I mentioned them to her, such debates were the least of her worries and had no impact on her devotion. She did not have the privilege of furthering her schooling beyond the ninth grade; yet, as will be seen in Chapter 2 and subsequent chapters, she offers the general reader and scholars alike a way of understanding *La Virgen de Guadalupe's* complexity. Her epistemological contribution to the study of Our Lady of Guadalupe does not come from a need to advance scholarship or to confirm or debunk scholarly debates. Instead, her epistemological lens comes from a sacred space in her home—the kitchen. Latinx theologians would refer to her epistemology as *abuelita theology* or perhaps *locus theologicus*; Chicana scholars would most likely use the concept of "doing theory in the flesh."[65] Esperanza's concept is highly visual—simple, yet complex, like Our Lady of Guadalupe. I invite you to meet Esperanza in the next chapter and see how her concept helps us understand the complexity of devotion to Our Lady of Guadalupe.

Our Lady of Café con Leche

THE SOCIAL CONSTRUCTION OF CATHOLIC DEVOTION

Introduction

What does coffee with milk have to do with Mexican Catholicism? According to Esperanza (age 68), it has everything to do with it. I had arranged to interview Esperanza after the 12 noon Sunday Mass. On our way to her apartment for the interview, we stopped at the local *taquería* and bought tacos to go. She lives in a one-bedroom apartment in a complex for low-income senior citizens. She never married and lived alone; and unlike the other *Damas*, she was bilingual. We had our meal and chatted; then she offered me *pan dulce* (Mexican pastries also referred to as Mexican sweet bread), an *Ojo de Pancha* (Pancha's eye) to be exact, and coffee. As I poured *leche* (milk) in my *café* (coffee)[1] and mixed it, we began the interview. She began to talk about growing up Catholic and repeatedly made reference to La Virgen de Guadalupe as the "brown Mexican Virgin, mother of all Mexicans." This prompted me to ask whether, for her, Our Lady of Guadalupe is a Mexican cultural symbol or a Catholic religious symbol.

Esperanza looked at me wordlessly, then asked me to take the spoon I had used to stir my coffee. In a firm but endearing tone, she asked: "Could please do me a favor and remove the milk from the coffee you are drinking?" Her question caught me by surprise, and I have to confess, I felt puzzled—as well as stupid. I looked at her and told her that what she asked me was impossible, for the coffee and milk were mixed. She then proceeded to say: *Exactamente mija, México es como el café con leche. No se puede separar a la Virgen de Guadalupe de la religión y la cultura, todo está mezclado* (Exactly *mija*, México is like coffee with milk. You cannot separate the Virgin of Guadalupe from religion and culture, it is all mixed together).[2] Her answer left me speechless: with a very simple example, she was able to synthesize the multilayered quality of her Mexican Catholic imagination. Esperanza's reply reveals why it is so important to pay close attention to the metaphors people use to describe their ways of knowing, for these are entryways into the complex socioreligious influences that shape people's worlds.

Children born into Mexican Catholic families become familiar with Catholic customs and imagery even before they are able to fully comprehend their significance. Religious material objects in the home such as home altars, votive candles, and *santos de bulto* (loosely translated as statuettes of saints), which typically come with family stories of miracles granted, are some of the first media for the transmission of faith.[3] In this process of religious transmission, the mother (or grandmother) is typically the one who socializes the children of the family into Catholicism.

Catholic traditions are passed on through the women in the family.[4] It is within this intricate web of matrilineal relationships between religion and secular life—or "heaven and earth"—and between children, mothers, and grandmothers that many Mexican children are first socialized into Catholic culture. The mother's Catholic devotion then becomes the first religious/cultural template from within which children learn to see themselves as people of faith in a specific sociocultural context.

The socialization into Catholicism that takes place in the home is reinforced outside in the form of altars to Our Lady of Guadalupe in front of people's homes, and other public displays of Catholic rituals and practices such as Mass, processions on particular religious holidays, theatrical reenactments of Catholic stories, and pilgrimages to sites deemed holy.[5] Therefore, not only what children learn at home but also what they learn outside contributes to the meaning-making process in a child's mind of what it means to be Catholic.[6] Early sections of this chapter describe in a general way the social dynamics of the transmission of the Guadalupan devotion, and later sections bring in the voices of these generations to demonstrate how devotion is passed on.

Traditioning and Cultivating Catholic Devotion

The repetition of the apparition story and the miracles people have attributed to *La Virgen de Guadalupe* over the centuries have validated the story in the collective consciousness of Mexican Catholics, leading people to develop a devotion to her. As Our Lady of Guadalupe's story gained acceptance, and her image was used in key political moments in Mexican history as highlighted in the previous chapter, she became one of the cornerstones of Mexican Catholicism and national identity.[7]

What gives veracity to the story in the eyes of the child is the context in which it is told to her or him. The story is not merely passed down as an event that happened many years ago but is contextualized in what the mother perceives as Our Lady of Guadalupe's intercession in the trials and tribulations of the family.

In this process of transmission of the story of Our Lady of Guadalupe, vertical (earthly) and horizontal (heavenly) relationships are formed and strengthened. Such relationships typically involve three individuals: the transmitter of the devotion (usually a mother), the receiver (usually a child), and a saint (in this case, Our Lady of Guadalupe), thus creating what Orsi (1996) calls a *devotional triangle*.[8] This metaphor of a devotional triangle is useful in helping to understand how the women in this study learned to be Catholic.

The pre-established relationship between the transmitter and the receiver is fundamental to determining the extent to which the receiver will welcome and incorporate a given religious figure into his or her life. In the case of the women in my study, the transmitter (mother) uses various methods to socialize the receiver (daughter) into a particular belief system (namely, faith in Our Lady of Guadalupe).[9] These methods include home altars, structured and unstructured prayer, family rituals, stories of miracles granted, votive candles, pilgrimages, and dressing children in traditional indigenous clothing on Our Lady of Guadalupe's feast day. These methods of religious socialization are the building blocks of the child's Mexican Catholic imagination (see Figure 2.1).

As the transmitter (the mother) teaches the receiver (the daughter) about *La Virgen de Guadalupe*, the daughter learns to associate *La Virgen de Guadalupe* with her own mother. Through this, as I demonstrate later in the chapter, the daughter learns from her mother that Our Lady of Guadalupe is special and sacred, yet warm and friendly. As the daughter grows close to *La Virgen*, the mother–daughter relationship strengthens via their shared devotion to her. This sense of Guadalupe as divine and yet part of everyday life ultimately moves the daughter to incorporate Our Lady of Guadalupe into her own ways of knowing the world and understanding her own place in it.

This shared devotion to Our Lady of Guadalupe between the mother and daughter creates and reinforces in the receiver (the daughter) a deep sense of emotional attachment to both the religious figure (Our Lady of

FIGURE 2.1. Katherine Arias (age 6) re-enacting the apparition of *La Virgen de Guadalupe* to San Juan Diego on her feast day, December 12, Greater Bay Area, California. Courtesy: Carlos Barba Iñiguez.

Guadalupe) and the transmitter (the mother). In essence, the devotion to *La Virgen de Guadalupe* that the daughter develops is anchored in the sense of her rightful inheritance of that belief. However, with time the girl internalizes this belief and makes it her own, rooted in the relationship between mother and daughter and validated through popular Catholicism. In the process, the daughter develops an internal awareness that *La Virgen de Guadalupe* is real to her. Consequently, later in life (as I demonstrate in Chapter 6) the receiver associates her devotion to the particular religious figure back to the individual who originally transmitted the religious practice. The devotional triangle thus strengthens, giving the receiver a sense of "spiritual anchorage."

The ties that bind the transmitter and receiver via devotion to Our Lady of Guadalupe are not merely tucked away in memories, prayer cards, or old photo albums once the transmitter has died.[10] On the contrary, they mature as the ties continue to form part of the receiver's religious/spiritual axis, from which she will transmit the devotion to later generations. In this way, the "devotional triangle," continues to replicate with every new generation, incorporating older devotional triangles into new ones (Orsi 1996). At the same time, while the sense of intimacy that the receiver (the daughter) builds with the transmitter (the mother) and the sacred image (of Guadalupe) may remain the same, the way the receiver imagines Our Lady of Guadalupe is not impermeable or fixed. In general, people are socialized and resocialized into (or out of) devotion to certain sacred images as they experience the joys and challenges that come with life, and as their petitions to God, *La Virgen*, and saints are granted or denied.[11] For instance, what a girl believes to be Our Lady of Guadalupe's standards of good conduct for Catholic girls will adjust and readjust as she matures—which is the topic of Chapter 7.

La Llevamos en la Sangre
(She Is in Our Blood)

On average, the women assert they first learned about *La Virgen de Guadalupe* when they were between 6 and 8 years old, though in some cases the women report learning about her at a younger age. Others, like Luz Elena (age 55) from the oldest group, claim that "*Es que ella se lleva en la sangre*" (she is in our blood). In my ethnographic research in México and in the United States, I found that the devotion to Our Lady of Guadalupe begins at such an early age that many believers, like Luz Elena, link her to the genetic make-up of Mexican Catholics—as far back as they can remember, *La Virgen de Guadalupe* has been part of their lives.

Another common answer to the question of when the participants first heard of Guadalupe is the one Eva (age 44; *Madres* group) told me: "*desde que uno tiene uso de razón*" (since one has the use of reason). This response is also present among the *Mujeres*, the youngest group. Conchita (age 21) cannot identify the age at which she learned about Our Lady of Guadalupe and simply states, "*desde que una está chiquita*" (since [one is] very young). With the exception of two women in the *Madres* group who say they learned about Our Lady of Guadalupe from their fathers, on average the women in all three groups recall being taught about Guadalupe by their mothers, starting at the age of 5 or 6.

Celebrations in honor of Our Lady of Guadalupe on December 12, the day she appeared to Saint Juan Diego, form part of families' Christmas festivities. Beatriz (age 34, from the *Madres* group) recounts: "Christmas is something big [for our family] and culturally as well, and she [Guadalupe] is always a big part of that celebration."[12] Beatriz's experience is important because it brings to light the cultural significance of the 12th of December in the context of Advent (the four weeks prior to Christmas) for Mexican Catholics—reaffirming the *café con leche* theory. For Mexican Catholic families, the festivities on December 12 in honor of *La Virgen* are a clear marker that the Christmas holiday season is in full swing; four days after the celebration of the traditional *posadas*, which lead to Christmas, begin.[13]

All the women in my study grew up with the belief that Our Lady of Guadalupe was their heavenly mother, who was there to help them whenever they were in need. Although prayers like the rosary and novenas (a special set of prayers done over nine consecutive days) were part of the traditioning of Catholic devotion (as I demonstrate in the next chapter), for the most part the process of transmission experienced by the women in all age groups as they grew up was never highly structured. Rather, it always took place in conversations and in a storytelling format between the girls and their mothers (or in some cases their grandmothers) about miracles, death, life, and survival.

For example, Amelia (age 69 from *Las Damas* group) remembers that her grandmother would share with her stories of miracles granted by Our Lady of Guadalupe. Meanwhile, her mother would teach her songs about *La Virgen* such as the popular songs *La Guadalupana* and *A Ti Virgencita* (loosely translated as "To You, *Virgensita*"), which articulate the Guadalupan devotion in a Mexican nationalistic context.[14] In Amelia's words: "All of us believed and listened to everything that [my grandmother and mother] would tell us."[15] Based on their testimony, there is no doubt that the attachment to Our Lady of Guadalupe they developed as children is strong, but to what extent is this attachment based on what they know about the historical aspect of her apparition story?

Las Damas are able to recall in detail the apparition story as they learned it from their mothers/grandmothers, but this is not always the case with the younger groups. *Las Madres* say that growing up, they learned from their mothers that Guadalupe is the mother of God. Here it is important to understand that the terms Latinxs use for God and Jesus are used interchangeably, a topic I discuss in detail in Chapter 6. I follow up by asking what they know of the apparition story. With the exception of two who tell me the story in detail, the common response of the women in the group is that Guadalupe appeared to an indigenous man named Juan Diego and asked him to build a temple in her honor. Though most do not know the details or the full context of the apparition, they nevertheless feel a deep devotion to Our Lady of Guadalupe. Candelaria (age 39), from *Las Madres* group, recalls:

> For the most part it was my grandmother who would tell me the story of Our Lady of Guadalupe. I always saw *santos de bulto* (loosely translated as statuettes) and images of Our Lady of Guadalupe in the house. I would always ask about the Virgin, and my grandmother was the one who would tell me about her. That is how I learned the story.[16]

Similarly, Meche (age 42), from *Las Madres* group:

> I learned from my mom because she always talked to us about *La Virgen de Guadalupe*. She would tell us about miracles, that she knew . . . of how she appeared to Juan Diego and how he took the roses to the bishop. She told him to build a temple . . . . That was the message.[17]

The recollection of the *Mujeres*—the youngest group—is significantly different from that of the *Madres* or *Damas*. What they recall of the apparition story of Guadalupe is notably less than what the *Madres* know. The common response to questions about the *Mujeres'* knowledge of the apparition story is: Our Lady of Guadalupe asked Juan Diego to go tell the bishop to build a temple in her honor. They are not able to provide further details about the apparition, as in the case of Yolanda (age 21):

> Wasn't it to . . . hmm . . . to go to . . . what's the name? . . . I can't remember . . . oh yeah, the bishops—I'm sorry, I'm very horrible— and they did not believe him. I remember she said something like they did not believe him, but it had something to do with [telling

Juan Diego] to do something to encourage them [bishop and the clergy]. She wanted them to build a temple in her honor on the hill of Tepeyac . . . . Oh yeah, [a temple] in her honor.

Among the two younger groups of women—*Las Madres* and *Mujeres*—devotion to Our Lady of Guadalupe is not necessarily rooted in the fine details of the apparition story but more in family religious traditions and relationships that they formed around the veneration of *La Virgen*. In part this is due to generational differences. This is coupled with the migration process (as in the case of the *Madres* and some of the *Mujeres*), a certain degree of skepticism about institutional Catholicism, and the perceived role of television as a viable mode of transmission of the apparition story.

The general answer to my question on what they were taught by their mothers and/or grandmothers is, "*La Virgen de Guadalupe* is [our] mother and the mother of God." Their response is similar to what *Las Damas* were told by their mothers. In the eyes of *Las Mujeres*, Guadalupe is a divine mother who is always present in their lives. As with *Las Madres* group, in some cases *Las Mujeres'* fathers were the ones who passed on the belief in Our Lady of Guadalupe: "My dad says, 'We need to pray to her so that nothing bad will happen to us.' My dad is a really reserved man. I think that for him she also represents a lot of hope" (Pilar, age 24). In the cases when fathers would also play an active role, the women explain that the reason why their fathers are so devout is that they grew up very close to their own mothers, who were deeply devoted to Our Lady of Guadalupe. In other words, the fathers' devotion to Our Lady of Guadalupe emerged out of the devotional triangles in which these men came to learn about *La Virgen* as children.

The mothers and grandmothers of all three groups of interviewed women used critical periods in their families' lives to pass on the tradition of devotion to Guadalupe to their children. They always made reference to God as the creator and giver of life when they spoke of Our Lady of Guadalupe. Rosario (age 65), from the oldest group, recalls the following:

When [I] was ill, I remember my great-grandmother would tell me "give thanks to our Lord that we live and for what we have, and [pray to] the Virgin so she could give us strength." She would say, "The Virgin never abandons us. The Virgin, wherever we go, she is with us and she protects us, protects our families, and our little ones, our lands." So, when we had a little bit of [food] we would go and pray to her, and the next day we would have a little more.[18]

Because God is seen as the creator and giver of life, according to *Las Damas*, thanks should always be given to him first, but as for Our Lady of Guadalupe, you "talk to her all day." In essence, *La Virgen de Guadalupe* is Our Lady of Everyday Life. Guadalupe gives strength and protection in daily life. She is the one they prayed to in their childhood when there was an illness in the family or when food was scarce (as in Rosario's case). Similarly, *Las Madres* grew up seeing God as the almighty father and protector of all people, and Our Lady of Guadalupe as the one they could fully trust with their fears, joys, and inquietudes without ever fearing her rejection. Some of *Las Madres* recall their own mothers gathering the family to pray to God and Our Lady of Guadalupe for the healing of a sick relative or for the safe journey of a family member who was going to cross the US–México border without documents.

In childhood, the participants were introduced to a Guadalupe capable of providing comfort in the midst of suffering and despair. Such moments were taken as opportunities by mothers to teach their children the meaning of *La Virgen de Guadalupe*. Anita (age 21, *Mujeres* group) remembers first hearing the story of Our Lady of Guadalupe when her grandmother died. Anita's mother explained to her that her grandmother had died because that was the way Our Lady of Guadalupe wanted it to be, so the grandmother would stop suffering.

Anita's mother explained to her that her grandmother might no longer be with her physically, but spiritually she would continue to be. What is more, in dying, her grandmother was now with *La Virgen de Guadalupe* and was watching over her. In other words, the deep devotion that the grandmother had to *La Virgen de Guadalupe* assured Anita, via her mother, that her grandmother was now sharing sacred space with Our Lady of Guadalupe, and within this space she was now protecting her.

In sum, as early as they can remember, the women in my study were taught by their mothers and grandmothers to trust Our Lady of Guadalupe, with the explanation that she was their heavenly mother. This type of intimacy between Our Lady of Guadalupe and women that began in childhood is an aspect of the devotion to her that remains consistent across the three groups of women. *La Virgen* that these women grew to love was one who was willing to share her sacred space with loved ones who have died. As I demonstrate in Chapter 7, the sense of trust that *La Virgen de Guadalupe* is by their side allows the participants in this study to confront life's hardships with a type of resilience that is driven by faith.

As girls hear testimonies of miracles granted, petitions on behalf of relatives, or stories about Our Lady of Guadalupe, they are automatically integrated into the "the emotional currents" of adult lives by which devotion is expressed (Orsi 1996, 196). They first come to know *La Virgen de Guadalupe* in the context of the joys and suffering of their families.[19] As children, the women are taught that Our Lady of Guadalupe is always present and willing to hear their pleas—as simple or as difficult as the problem may seem, from a lost toy to pleas for the healing of an ill relative.

Embodying Mexican Popular Catholicism

When people repeat and diffuse a particular belief (or piece of cultural knowledge), it eventually takes the form of something they perceive as an objective reality. In the Mexican Catholic imagination, the sacred becomes real in the lives of the faithful by diffusion of a set of beliefs that are repeated and experienced through sight, hearing, taste, smell, and touch. It materializes through images of saints, crucifixes, family photographs, votive candles, food, holy water, and rosaries—all of which are typically found in the most sacred space in a Catholic home: on the home altar. In essence, in the Mexican Catholic imagination (and I would argue, Latinx Catholic imaginations in general), religious beliefs are experienced through the five senses, as the faithful call upon the sacred to address material concerns—in other words, what McGuire (1990, 2003, 2008) calls "embodied religion."

Home altars represent life, hope, and faith. They function as the spaces in the home where the sacred transcends the walls of the church and materializes in everyday life as it coexists with the faithful.[20] The home altar (*altar* in Spanish) is a type of family shrine in the home where votive candles, religious images, symbols, offerings, and photographs of loved ones are placed.[21] They exemplify the *café con leche* quality of their Mexican popular Catholicism, for they are the physical spaces where the secularization of the sacred and the sacralization of the secular take place. During my research in México City, I came across an altar that had, besides the figures of Our Lady of Guadalupe, San Juan Diego, Saint Jude, and other representations of Mary, two statuettes of baby Jesus and each image had a balloon. One had a Sponge Bob balloon and the other had one of Tweety Bird. When I asked the gentleman at the market about it, he told me that those two statuettes are representations of Jesus as a child and, because all children love balloons, his offering was balloons (see Figure 2.2). As such, home

FIGURE 2.2. Public altar at a local market in México City. Courtesy: Socorro Castañeda-Liles.

altars are neither exclusively sacred nor secular but both. Objects otherwise considered common and/or secular such as flowers, photographs of relatives who have died, and food and drink, when placed on the altar, are perceived by the faithful to take on a quasi-divine quality (see Figure 2.3).

All the women in my study were introduced to Catholicism in ways that were far more similar than different. Their similarities are mainly attributable to three central, common variables: class, national origin, and language. They are all first-generation Mexican immigrants or children of Mexican immigrants to the United States, all are of working-class background, and Spanish is their primary language.

Rosario (age 65), from the *Damas* group, was raised by her great-grandparents and grandparents on a small farm in California.[22] For as long as Rosario remembers, there was an altar in honor of *La Virgen de Guadalupe* at her childhood home. Recalling her childhood, she says:

> Our Virgin was made of rock and as offering, we would place [in front of her] beans, rice, and flowers, but only roses. She always had roses. One way or another, we always managed to offer her roses; they were never absent.[23]

FIGURE 2.3. Home altar in Greater Bay Area, California. Courtesy: Socorro
Castañeda-Liles.

Why was the type of flower placed on the home altar so important to
Rosario's family? In the apparition story, Our Lady of Guadalupe asked San
Juan Diego to pick roses from a rosebush on Tepeyac Hill, but no flowers
ever grow on Tepeyac Hill in the dead of winter. To San Juan Diego's surprise, he found roses growing right in the area where Guadalupe told him
they would be. Roses are thus associated with Our Lady of Guadalupe, and
therefore most Mexican Catholics consider roses to have a higher status
than other flowers. For this reason, Rosario's family never placed flowers
other than roses on La Virgen's home altar.[24] Coming from a working-class
farming background, Rosario's family often experienced financial hard-
ship but always found a way to buy roses for La Virgen de Guadalupe if
their rose bush did not have any. Likewise, in spite of the difficulties, food
was always present at the altar as an offering and to petition Our Lady of
Guadalupe for food abundance. The presence of food and drink is typical
of many Mexican Catholic home altars; however, there are various reasons
for offering these items, depending on the type of altar.[25]

Ester (age 76) remembers the family tradition of setting up an altar every year for the feast of Our Lady of Guadalupe on December 12. Ester recounts that "each year, just how one dresses the Christmas tree . . . [her family] dressed the altar with Christmas lights for the Virgin" (see Figure 2.4).[26] In Ester's family, the setting of the altar would always be done with great care; much thought went into the selection of items, hence the word "*dress*" to refer to the setting of the sacred space.

The image of *La Virgen de Guadalupe* selected for the altar has to be very specific, from the depiction of her face to the color of her vestment, and most importantly—the color of her skin. For example, Anita, from *Las Mujeres* cohort, recalls that her mother is very particular when purchasing an image of Our Lady of Guadalupe. Without diverging from Guadalupe's original facial expression, her mother prefers images where *La Virgen* is depicted as being happy; the vestment needs to be colorful, and her skin must be dark brown. When I ask why her skin needed to be dark brown, she says that her mother wants it to be close to the dark skin of Mexicans. This aspect of Our Lady of Guadalupe is important because, according to *Las Mujeres*, skin color is what separates Our Lady of Guadalupe from the Virgin Mary of Nazareth, and one reason why some of *Las Mujeres* are not able to relate to the light-skinned Mary, the topic of Chapter 6.[27]

In many families, the religious images on the altar are personally brought from México, as one of the women from the youngest group, *Las Mujeres*, did. Manuela (age 24) recalls going through a great deal of trouble to bring an image of Our Lady of Guadalupe on the plane, owing to the image's large size. Except for Guadalupe's face, the rest of the image her family brought from México was made of colorful silk threads and nails. According to her, this image was particularly special because someone who was in prison made it. Manuela's family has such deep devotion that there is an image of Our Lady of Guadalupe in every room. However, this image, the one brought specially from México, sits in the dining room where the family has a home altar to honor *La Virgen*. Manuela says it is in the dining room because the room is the gathering place for the family. Manuela's family is not the only one to have an image of Our Lady of Guadalupe in the dining area. There were other *Mujeres* whose families have an image and/or altar to Guadalupe in the dining area because as Manuela says, "it is where the family hosts guests, celebrates birthdays, prepares food together during the holidays, and eats dinner." Every time Manuela's family goes to Costco (a large warehouse club), they buy Guadalupe fresh flowers, and they always light a candle whenever

FIGURE 2.4. Home altar in Greater Bay Area, California. Courtesy: Monica Rodríguez.

someone is going through difficult times or as an offer of gratitude. Other women across the groups also remember their mothers or other family members lighting candles as an offering when asking or giving thanks to *La Virgen de Guadalupe* for a petition or miracle. Candelaria (age 39) from *Las Madres* cohort has an image of Our Lady of Guadalupe hanging from one of the walls in her bedroom right next to the mounted TV set. Her explanation is that the family spends a great deal of time watching TV in the master bedroom, and she wants her husband and children to see Our Lady of Guadalupe as part of their everyday life.

While women typically do the setting of the home altar, in some cases a man takes the initiative. Among *Las Madres* group is Vicky (age 31), who grew up in Hidalgo, México. She recalls that as a child her favorite time of year was the month of October, when her father would set up a home altar in honor of Our Lady of Guadalupe:

> My dad would build an altar to the Virgin and place [on it] an image of the Last Supper. [He would go to the store and buy] the best candy for the Virgin. I really liked these times because I would steal *La Virgen*'s candy from the altar. I loved to steal the candy because he always bought the good kind, the kind that he would never buy us because it was expensive.[28]

The devotion that Vicky's (*Madres* cohort) and Rosario's (oldest cohort) families have for Our Lady of Guadalupe transcended their families' economic means, as they found ways to offer *La Virgen* the very best in spite of their economic struggles. Vicky, for one, said that she does not think Our Lady of Guadalupe became upset at her act of stealing candy from the altar because, after all, *La Virgen* is her mother. In such instances, we begin to see the familiar relationship that children develop at an early age with Our Lady of Guadalupe. *La Virgen* does not mind sharing her candy. The material representation of their heavenly mother was perceived by the young girls as having a sacred, yet palpable, quality—via the material representation of Our Lady of Guadalupe they could talk to and be in communion with her.

Lived religion is about how people experience the sacred in their lives and how that religious experience is connected to larger social structures, both religious and secular.[29] The altars in the homes of my research participants of all ages are not art installations commemorating the sacred or those who have died. They are physical spaces that ordinary people sacralize as they pray, sing, and talk to *La Virgen de Guadalupe*, saints, and God. Home altars are the spaces where people bring the worries in their lives that they can no longer bear alone. They function as gateways between the divine and the mundane, between the impossible and possible.[30] Having a home altar to a saint or to *La Virgen de Guadalupe* in particular was a common family practice during the childhood of all my participants, with the exception of a couple of women in *Las Mujeres* group. However, even in the latter case, their mothers would have a central, sacred image in the house—usually of Our Lady of Guadalupe or the Sacred Heart of Jesus—to which the family would pray, talk, and make offerings such as flowers or a votive candle.

Anita (age 21), from *Las Mujeres* cohort, does not have an altar all year round, but in the weeks preceding the feast day of Our Lady of Guadalupe, her mother always sets up an altar in the latter's honor. Each year, Anita's mother dresses the altar with fresh flowers and the hand-embroidered linen of Anita's grandmother. In other cases, besides flowers, the families of *Las Mujeres* cohort (as in the case of *Las Damas* and *Las Madres*) also offer food such as maize.

It is important, however, to note that while altars are part of the home among *Las Damas* and *Las Madres*, they are present to a lesser extent among the families of *Las Mujeres*, the youngest cohort. One of the women from the oldest cohort commented about this sociocultural change in practice. Emphasizing the differences between generations and in reference to her own grandchildren, Paloma (age 80), from *Las Damas* group, recounts:

> Everything was so different in those days. Look, in my house everyone was very Catholic. My mom and my grandmother told me the story of *La Virgencita* [the Virgin], and we also had a small altar and images of *La Virgen*, the Sacred Heart [of Jesus], and the Holy Child of Atocha; there was no room that did not have a sacred image.[31]

Of the Catholic images and saints, *La Virgen de Guadalupe* is the ever-present sacred gateway, which connects families to God. She is in their living rooms, kitchens, bedrooms, and front yards—in one case, even in the bathroom. At the same time, as Paloma recounts, Guadalupe is not alone; she "shares" the home altar with other religious figures like Saint Jude who is typically a faithful companion of *La Virgen* in the home altars in Mexican Catholic households (see Figure 2.5).

FIGURE 2.5. Home altar in Greater Bay Area, California, Familia Andres Mejia. Courtesy: Roberto Castañeda, Jr.

The women also learn from their mothers (and in some cases their grandmothers) about the importance of sustaining an ongoing relationship with *La Virgen de Guadalupe* through material or symbolic offerings such as votive candles or doing good deeds. They understand that to sustain a relationship with Our Lady of Guadalupe, it is important to dedicate a space in the house to her, even if it is a small corner or an area of the wall. The repetition and diffusion of the importance of Our Lady of Guadalupe in Mexican Catholicism is a constant reminder for the women growing up that *La Virgen* is not only their mother but also an ever-present support to which they can turn whenever they find themselves in need. The place Our Lady of Guadalupe holds in these families is an example of the *familismo* quality of their Mexican Catholic imagination. That is, the relationships they develop with Our Lady of Guadalupe are rooted in the belief that she is part of their family life.

Home altars weave earth and heaven through the five senses in intricate ways, creating a type of Catholic imagination that represents what is most meaningful about being Mexican Catholic in their daily lives. Sacred figures are found not only on altars but in the most intimate spaces of people's homes, whether on walls or on the tops of dressers, making themselves familiar to children when the latter are very young. It is in this way that the homegrown trust children develop in Our Lady of Guadalupe (and other sacred figures) initially shapes their Catholic faith. As Esperanza from the oldest cohort so succinctly put it, Our Lady of Guadalupe, religion, and culture are like coffee with milk; they cannot be separated. Indeed, as Mexican Catholic children learn to see Our Lady of Guadalupe as a Catholic symbol, they also learn to associate her with México's indigenous roots.

In Mexican popular Catholicism it is a custom for parents to dress children in traditional indigenous clothing on Guadalupe's feast day (December 12). Those unfamiliar with this custom might assume that only boys are dressed in this way, as *La Virgen de Guadalupe* appeared to a man, but this is not the case. This tradition cuts across gender because in Mexican popular Catholic thought, Our Lady of Guadalupe recognizes that boys and girls alike are called to be her messengers, just like Saint Juan Diego (see Figure 2.6). It is also a form of remembering that, according to the apparition story, *La Virgen* could have chosen to appear to anybody— for example, a Spanish conqueror or a *criollo* (someone born in México of Spanish parents)—but instead chose to appear to an indigenous person. Her choice is significant because she appeared at a time in Mexican history when the Nahuatl-speaking people's very humanity was questioned by the Spanish invaders. Therefore, by dressing children in this particular clothing style, parents are socializing them into the belief that December 12 is both a celebration of Our Lady of Guadalupe's apparition and of México's indigenous heritage and national pride.[32]

For Mexicans, December 12 has become a day of national—and more specifically, indigenous—pride.[33] It is a day when popular Catholicism is visibly embodied in Mexican nationalism. December 12 is, as religious studies scholar Lara Medina (pers. comm.) once told me, "the one day

FIGURE 2.6. Girl (age 3) dressed in traditional indigenous clothing on the feast day of *La Virgen de Guadalupe*. Courtesy: Socorro Castañeda-Liles.

when Mexican Catholics are visibly and openly proud of their indigenous heritage."

Las Damas recount the joy they would feel on that day:

Luz Elena (age 55): My mom would dress us up like "indigenous girls" [ed. note: loosely translated] with our sandals, *rebozo* [shawl], our braids in ribbons, and with our little baskets [hanging from the back]. I really liked it, because almost all the little girls would be dressed in this way and we took flowers to *La Virgen*. It was such a beautiful and cheerful day. I really liked that day because my mom

and my grandma would make *champurrado* [a hot drink made with
milk, maize, and chocolate] and cornbread for everyone . . . . It was
a beautiful time, full of faith.[34]

Juanita (age 82) recounts that they would get up at dawn, something children and adults alike would look forward to. Her family and—according to
Juanita—the whole town would attend *Las Mañanitas* (morning serenade).
Similarly, Olivia (age 57) and MariChuy (age 78) remember accompanying
their families to Mass at early dawn, but their mothers did not dress them
in the special attire. Dressing a child in indigenous attire on December 12
could be expensive. Such was the case for the families of MariChuy, Olivia,
and Juanita, who say that their mothers did not dress them in the special
attire because they had many children and could not afford it.

On some occasions, the Feast of *La Virgen de Guadalupe* begins days—
even weeks—in advance of December 12, with a pilgrimage to petition or
give thanks for a miracle. The act of making a petition or giving thanks is
known in Spanish as a *manda*. A *manda* can be thought of as a form of
embodied faith that typically involves some type of sacrifice—for example,
walking to a holy site barefoot, with the last stretch of the journey made on
the knees. While living in México, when the families of the women I interviewed were able to save enough money, they would go on a pilgrimage to
the Basilica of *La Virgen de Guadalupe* in México City. If they were not able
to make the trip to the basilica, they would participate in processions in
honor of Our Lady of Guadalupe to their local church. In most cases, the
pilgrimage or procession would not be an individual act but a collective
religious practice involving the family (e.g., children), as in the following
anecdote from Josefa (age 77) from *Las Damas* cohort.[35]

I remember that when my grandma was very sick, my mom took us
all to the town's cathedral on the 12th of December. It was pretty far,
but we all walked. My mom was barefoot, and she said that it was an
offering to Our Lady of Guadalupe so my grandma could get well.
Then, when we were almost there, my mom walked on her knees
all the way to the altar. My poor mom, she almost didn't make it. But
her faith was so strong that she was able. I was, let's see, about eight
years old. That happened in México. I will never forget.[36]

Most of *Las Madres* also grew up with this tradition. In reference to the
communities in which they grew up, *Las Madres* talk about the months of

planning that would go into organizing the *fiesta* in honor of Guadalupe. Those who grew up in small communities remember that each family would be in charge of one aspect of the celebration—for example, decorating the church, making elaborate flower arrangements, reenacting the apparition, making the traditional drinks *champurrado* and *ponche caliente* (hot fruit punch) to accompany the *pan dulce* from the local bakery, making homemade *tamales*, and so forth. Generally both men and women would participate in the preparation of the feast day, but the women were most involved, particularly with the cooking. This is still the case today.

Las Madres recall their mothers dressing them in traditional indigenous attire and taking them to Mass at dawn every December 12. Julia (age 24) vividly remembers her traditional indigenous dress, hair in braids, and sandals she wore for Mass on *La Virgen's* feast day. What I found most revealing is that in the *Madres* group I was able to see the "devotional triangle" repeating itself in the next generation. For instance, many of the mothers proudly shared with me that they continue the custom by dressing their own children in traditional indigenous attire and taking them to *Las Mañanitas* at dawn on December 12.

Dressing a child in traditional indigenous attire is predominantly done for two reasons. One, as mentioned above, is to commemorate Guadalupe's apparition to Saint Juan Diego, as families publicly celebrate their indigenous heritage. The second reason (less common in the United States than in México) is to thank *La Virgen* for a miracle granted, as in the case of Raquel (age 46). When Raquel (from *Las Madres* group) was living in México, she became very ill. She went to the doctor, but none of the remedies that were prescribed seemed to work. Raquel felt that her last resort was to rely exclusively on praying to Our Lady of Guadalupe for a cure. As part of her prayer, she made a *manda* that if *La Virgen de Guadalupe* healed her, she would dress her daughter in traditional indigenous clothing on December 12. According to Raquel, Our Lady of Guadalupe restored her health that same year, and Raquel fulfilled her promise. The following December 12, she dressed her daughter in traditional indigenous clothing to thank *La Virgen de Guadalupe*.

As children, *Las Mujeres* (the youngest group) would also celebrate Our Lady of Guadalupe on her feast day. December 12 would be a big event in their families. The preparation for the celebration would begin the night before the feast. Mothers (of *Las Mujeres*) would get the children's outfits ready for the traditional *Mañanitas* the next day, and everyone would go to sleep early to get enough rest. The big day would begin around four o'clock in the morning (in some cases earlier), with people attending Mass in honor of *La Virgen* at their local church. Like *Las Damas* and *Las Madres, Las Mujeres* remember how their mothers would dress them that day. Conchita (age 21) recalls:

> My mom dressed us up as indigenous girls with our braids and she would hang a small sack, kinda like a backpack. She would dress my brother as San Juan Diego. My mom would wear a Mexican shawl and my dad, a Mexican poncho.

Similarly, Dolores (age 19) recalls:

> Ever since I remember, my mom would dress us up on the 12th of December to go to church, you know, dress my brother and me like indigenous children. Maybe when I was six or seven ... when I was more aware of what was going on ... She would put a little basket on [our] back ... She used to go all out.

Attending *Las Mañanitas* and Mass is a family celebration of life and hope. It is a day when the faithful feel Our Lady of Guadalupe's presence particularly closely.

Those who were born and lived in México until about the age of 9 make comparisons between Our Lady of Guadalupe celebrations in México and in the United States. According to Conchita, who grew up in the Mexican state of Michoacán, people celebrate the feast day to a greater extent in México than in the United States. She remembers the all-night celebrations in México beginning on December 11 as people would wait for the big day. Right at midnight, townspeople would walk together in song and prayer to the church to serenade *La Virgen de Guadalupe*. People would bring *ponche caliente* to share with everyone, and also blankets, for it is particularly cold in Michoacán at that time of year. *Las Mañanitas* would be led by a local band, followed by Aztec dancers who would dance out in the fields. The music and dance would be preceded by Mass. Conchita says that on that day she would feel joy. The feast day had a sense of *communitas* making this celebration so meaningful for the believers as it strengthened their devotion and attachment to *La Virgen de Guadalupe*.

Although Guadalupan celebrations tend to be smaller in scale in the United States than in México, Mexican popular Catholicism and Guadalupan celebrations in particular are changing the face of American

Catholicism as Mexican immigration increases, as we learned in Chapter 1. Throughout the United States, Mexican Catholics claim not only the physical space of the church but also streets across the nation.[37]

Unlike other Marian apparition holidays, Our Lady of Guadalupe's feast day has a unique sociopolitical, religious quality. In recent years in the United States and México, December 12 has also been a day of prayer for immigration reform. For example, the annual binational *Carrera Antorcha Guadalupana* (Guadalupe Torch Run) celebrates Guadalupe's apparition to Saint Juan Diego as it advocates for the reunification of families that have been torn apart due to current immigration laws. The run begins in México City at the Basilica of Our Lady of Guadalupe on September 18 and ends at Saint Patrick's Cathedral in New York City on December 12. The more than 2,500 mile run is an 86-day (one-way) pilgrimage-like journey in which approximately 8,000 runners pass the torch as it makes its way through various states of the Mexican Republic, crosses the US–México international border, and continues through 13 states in the United States. The run is a way of reflecting on and representing the journey that migrants take as they risk their lives and cross the border to escape poverty, corruption, and the ongoing drug cartel wars.[38]

Religious Popular Theater and Film as Theological Texts

Home altars are spaces where the women come to pray and venerate *La Virgen de Guadalupe*; they also bring their pleas, worries, and gratitude. They function as the spaces where "communicative exchange" with the divine takes place (Turner 2008, 192). It is in these encounters, which they perceive as real, that they feel they find themselves in communion with *La Virgen*. But this encounter does not end at the altar; films and popular religious theater function as extensions of those sacred spaces, and I would argue that they function as theological texts for the people. What follows is a brief explanation of the roots of popular religious theater (*teatro popular religioso*) to provide a context to this faith-based creative expression and understand its role and significance in contemporary times.

Popular religious theater as it exists today has pre-Columbian and Spanish roots. These two ways of embodying the sacred had distinct purposes. In pre-Columbian theater, the performances were not shows for mere entertainment; they were highly complex performance practices. First, regardless of type, they always had a religious aspect. [39] They were embodied practices of paying tribute to gods and goddesses and in doing so, reaffirming religious beliefs and practices.[40] Through theater, people (spectators and performers) were in communion with their gods and goddesses in a type of poetic prayer, in other words, in *flor y canto*. Second, they were also, to some extent, opportunities to transmit political messages.[41] Thus, the religious and political aspects of these theological performance practices reinforced for the people their faith in the context of secular life.[42]

Spanish popular theater can be traced back to Tridentine times in Spain and was later transplanted to the Americas with the conquest. In the Americas, this type of performance practice was not a ritual, as in the case of pre-Columbian theater; instead, it was a type of religious reprogramming mechanism. In other words, it was an evangelizing tool. The missionaries used theatrical reenactments of biblical stories as vehicles to convert the Nahuatl-speaking people to Christianity.[43]

Today, popular religious theater is not necessarily the evangelizing mechanism that it once was during the conquest of the Americas, but it is an embodied form of grassroots theological text used to reaffirm Catholic devotion and transmit it to younger generations.[44] Like pre-Columbian performance practices, these contemporary reenactments are accessible political and theological resources for people. Reenactments of Jesus' journey to his crucifixion (*Via Crucis*) and of Our Lady of Guadalupe's apparition to Saint Juan Diego not only recreate the stories in the tradition of popular Catholicism but also have a political message. For example, in reenactments of the apparition story across the United States, Our Lady of Guadalupe not only defends Saint Juan Diego and the many Nahua people who suffered at the hands of Spanish conquerors centuries ago. She also continues to advocate for the disenfranchised. In particular, she advocates on behalf of the undocumented. In the United States, these types of religio-political performance practices are more likely to be found in communities with a large population of Latinxs.[45]

Based on the women in this study, I argue that popular religious theater is not only a central transmitter of the *La Virgen de Guadalupe* story but also a living grassroots theology. Manuela (age 24) says that in addition to what her mother told her and what she heard in catechism class, she learned about Our Lady of Guadalupe through the performance of the apparition story at her local church. For Manuela, the reenactment is something she wholeheartedly looks forward to every year. Similarly, Rosita (age 20) remembers that as a child she "used to like going to the [Our Lady of Guadalupe] play because it made [her] think of how everything was back then." In particular, the youngest group (*Las Mujeres*) speaks about the reenactments of the apparition story as an opportunity to learn about racism and discrimination against the indigenous population during colonial times.[46] The play reaffirmed to *Las Mujeres* that by choosing an indigenous man to deliver her request, Our Lady of Guadalupe recognized the dignity of a people whom the colonizers deemed insignificant—and in so doing, *La Virgen* reaffirms their ethnic identity in the United States.

Las Madres and *Damas* are more specific in how the apparition story, as told via popular theater, relates to their lives. It is an opportunity to see themselves and their trials and tribulations reflected in the suffering, denial, and disbelief Saint Juan Diego experienced as he tried to deliver Our Lady of Guadalupe's message to Bishop Zumarraga. I attribute this to the fact that for adults more than younger people, religious popular theater is an important way of reflecting on these religious narratives in a sociocultural and political context that speaks to their contemporary realities.[47] For *Las Madres* and *Damas*, who have experienced life's hardships longer that the youngest group of women, the Our Lady of Guadalupe play is a type of religious "cultural template" (Zavella 2003) on which they are able to "place" their reality and struggles in Saint Juan Diego's experience.[48]

The apparition story as recounted on television also plays a significant role in strengthening devotion to *La Virgen de Guadalupe*.[49] Since the 1940s, the film industry has been instrumental in bringing to life the apparition story. In 1942, Mexican director Julio Bracho produced *La Virgen que Forjó una Patria* (The Virgin Who Forged a Nation), the first film based on the apparition story and one that is still a favorite among many believers. This film in particular braids Catholicism and national identity in intricate ways as it covers the period between 1531 (the year of the apparition) and 1810 (the year of México's independence from Spain). It tells the story of the birth of México and its national identity as it depicts the significance of Our Lady of Guadalupe for the Mexican people.

La Sonrisa de La Virgen (The Virgin's Smile), produced by Roberto Rodriguez in 1958, is now considered a classic. What is unique about the film is that it is not a retelling of the apparition story per se. Instead, it is about Guadalupan faith and devotion through the eyes of a young girl of 5 or 6 years of age who prays to Our Lady of Guadalupe to grant her the miracle of not going to school. Others have followed since then, such as *La Virgen de Guadalupe*, produced in 1976 by director Alfredo Salazar—another popular Mexican film about the apparition story.

These films have gained popularity and are now considered masterpieces of México's film industry. What impact did films on *La Virgen de Guadalupe* have on the women's childhoods? For the families of *Las Damas*, who grew up in lower working-class families, owning a television set or going to the movies was a luxury that they could not afford. Therefore, although they knew about some of the movies made about Our Lady of Guadalupe, they did not see them until much later in life. However, by the time the subsequent generations (*Madres* and *Mujeres*) were growing up, owning a television set was significantly more affordable. María (age 36), from *Las Madres* group, recalls, "We learned about *La Virgen* from my mom and my grandmother, but [also from] the movies that they show on TV. It was from there that I learned more about her."[50]

Las Mujeres, like *Las Madres*, also learned about *La Virgen* by watching the story of her apparition to Saint Juan Diego on Spanish-language television channels during the month of December. In fact, the role that television plays in the transmission of the apparition story is not only gaining more currency in the United States, it is an important venue in which younger generations learn about the significance of Our Lady of Guadalupe. Today, one can see movies about the Guadalupan story or the Guadalupan message year round. In particular, there is a television series that runs throughout the year and now is also offered on Netflix. Since the summer of 2008, Univisión (the largest Spanish-language television network in the United States) has broadcast a Mexican TV series entitled *La Rosa de Guadalupe* (Guadalupe's Rose). The program is a series of one-hour *mini-novelas* (short soap operas) that dramatize everyday miracles of faith granted by *La Virgen de Guadalupe*. What is most notable about the television series is that it has a very specific audience in mind: middle- and upper-class Mexican teenagers. Most of the episodes in the series center on the lives of wealthy, light-skinned Mexican teenagers and their families. Although the series is filled with messages of love, hope, forgiveness, and faith, it is important to note that it provides an upper-class perspective of life and faith among Mexicans in México.

Conclusion

At a very young age, these women were socialized into certain sets of religious beliefs and parameters. As I demonstrate in later chapters, some have continued to use such parameters as they have grown older, but they have also challenged and reconfigured them while incorporating new parameters as they experience life (the topic of Chapter 7). In first-generation working-class, Mexican-origin Catholic families, children are introduced to religion by seeing their parents (mainly their mothers) and other relatives embody what it means to be a Mexican Catholic. One central religious figure in the socialization process is *La Virgen de Guadalupe*, who early in a child's life becomes a sacred symbol capable of synthesizing the Catholic culture into which he or she is being socialized.

Some scholars have questioned the authenticity of the apparition story of Our Lady of Guadalupe.[51] However, in spite of the ongoing debates, over the centuries people have attributed miraculous qualities to *La Virgen*, creating a cultural knowledge about her that transcends any academic theory about her veracity. Furthermore, the three groups of women were first introduced to Catholicism through popular Catholic rituals and practices and the presence of material objects in the home, such as home altars and statuettes of saints, which speaks to the important role of popular Catholicism among the faithful. Such home practices were part of the lived religion of these families and functioned as the first spiritual building blocks of the child's Mexican Catholic imagination in the early years. Our Lady of Guadalupe's presence was further reinforced through the embodiment of religious nationalism and religious popular theater and film.[52]

The women I interviewed learned from their mothers in early childhood to perceive *La Virgen de Guadalupe* as their heavenly mother. This belief was reinforced via religious material objects around the house and certain family traditions. It was also experienced through the five senses.[53] I argue that through the mothers and grandmothers as transmitters and fomenters of Catholic faith and devotion, "*la familia* [the family] is the *locus theologicus*" (Valeria Torres 2010, 1). In the eyes of Mexican Catholic women, *La Virgen de Guadalupe* is real, and her capacity to comfort is endless; she is always there, ready to hear the pleas of the faithful. At the same time, far more happens in the socialization process than simply learning to perceive Our Lady of Guadalupe as a mother figure. A closer look at the socialization process among the *Mujeres*, *Madres*, and *Damas* reveals that within its meaning-making social web, parallel and vertical relationships— those of child, mother, and Our Lady of Guadalupe—develop into a "devotional triangle."[54]

The initial connection that the women felt to Our Lady of Guadalupe in their childhoods was not necessarily tied to the details of the apparition story. *La Virgen de Guadalupe* became real to them through family stories about miracles that their mothers passed on to them. She came to life in films and theatrical plays about the apparition story. The women learned to embody a sense of pride in their indigenous heritage through their mothers' practice of dressing them in traditional indigenous clothing— a practice that some have passed on to their children. In essence, Our Lady of Guadalupe became a palpable, sacred figure in the celebrations on her feast day through the reenactment of the story, songs, flowers, food, and family traditions like dressing girls and boys in traditional indigenous clothing. In the childhoods of the women across the three groups, all these family traditions together reinforced their belief that *La Virgen de Guadalupe* is the ever-present mother and protector.

In sum, Mexican Catholicism (in México and the United States alike) exists not only in the psyche of the individual but is also embodied and experienced physically. Catholic religious beliefs in the childhood years of the women in all three groups were reflected in both physical body and cultural imagery. Indeed, I found that it was through popular Catholic practices that *Las Damas*, *Madres*, and *Mujeres* first came to understand the horizontal and vertical relationships between themselves and family, community, and the sacred. Most significantly, whether they spent their childhood years in México or the United States, they learned what it means to be not just Catholic but Mexican Catholic in particular.

3

Catholicizing Girlhood

SOCIALIZING GIRLS INTO
INSTITUTIONAL CATHOLICISM

IT WAS A fall Friday afternoon on the day of the interview, and although the sun was out, the passing clouds created a cool breeze. When I arrived at her house, a small-framed woman greeted me. Angelita (age 70) was wearing a sheer light blue scarf that covered her graying hair. The scarf was tied back behind her ears so as to reveal her silver earrings. She was wearing a pink dress with a peach and blue apron that covered her from the chest to the knees, and a pair of dark blue suede slippers wrapped her feet. She greeted me with a smile, and when she shook my hand she said to me, "*Mija entra 'pa que te tomes un café calientito, o un jugo, tambien tengo frijoles recien hechos o te puedo hacer una quesadilla*" (My dear one, come in, you can drink coffee or juice, I also have beans that I just baked or I could make you a quesadilla).[1]

As I entered her home, the smell of coffee, freshly made corn tortillas, and beans enveloped me and brought memories of my *abuelita* (grandmother). As I made my way down the hallway, I saw the numerous framed photographs of relatives and images of saints that covered the walls. When I entered she directed me to the kitchen, saying, "*Aquí podemos platicar mas a gusto*" (Here we can talk more comfortably). We ate quesadillas and drank Jumex juice at the kitchen table as she began to share with me her childhood memories.

Angelita's family lived in one of the few towns in México that had a permanent priest. As the oldest of ten children, she was the one who accompanied her mother to Mass every morning. Recalling her childhood in México, she told me about the time when she almost missed Mass. When

Angelita was eight, she woke up late one morning. Carefully getting out of bed so as not to disturb the four siblings who slept with her, she noticed that her mother was already outside waiting for her. She then heard the church bells ring, indicating that Mass was about to start, and her mantilla was nowhere to be found. "I could not find my mantilla. I looked for it and looked for it, but nothing. I didn't want to wake up my siblings and guess what, *mija* . . ." Giggling, she continues, "I went where my mom had the soiled cloth diapers to be washed and I got one that was all urinated on . . . . I put it over my head and left for church. At church people would stare and stare at me, [though it was dried] I think that they could smell the urine [on the] diaper. But I had my mantilla," she says and bursts out laughing, and then in a serious tone continues, "*mija*, it was the devotion and faith that one had . . . . In those times . . . people had so much devotion."[2] Abiding by the strict dress code expectations imposed by the institutional church for girls and women were read by *Las Damas* as demonstrations of the degree of their faith, devotion, and respect. When I asked Angelita why she had to wear a mantilla, she responded that her mother and grandmother told her that doing otherwise showed a lack of respect for the house of God.[3]

Angelita's story is emblematic of the kind of institutionalized Catholic practices this chapter describes— practices that were passed on to the women by their mothers and, in some cases, grandmothers. Therefore, rather than offering an exhaustive overview of all Catholic customs, this chapter provides in-depth descriptions of the religious practices that the women remembered most. I investigate how the women were initiated into Catholic practices to better understand their relationship to Our Lady of Guadalupe in the chapters that follow.

The stories told by each cohort tended to emphasize different issues in the varying contexts that informed their religious education, development of their Catholic faith, and devotion to *La Virgen de Guadalupe* in particular. The oldest cohort (*Las Damas*) described their Catholic faith within a framework of institutional teachings and expectations. The middle cohort (*Las Madres*) described their experience growing up Catholic in a pre- and post-migration context, in which some of their pre-migration Catholic experience resembled that of the older cohort. The youngest cohort (*Las Mujeres*) spoke of the importance of language and Mass attendance, among other topics. And like *Las Madres*, the *Mujeres* who were born in México also shared about their experiences growing up Catholic in a pre- and post-migration context. In this chapter, I argue that the differences in the women's religious education and practices relate to whether they grew up in a pre– or post–Vatican II Catholic Church, their generation, geo-graphical location, and migration. The extent to which these women were expected by their mothers and the Church to abide by a strict Catholic code of conduct also influenced the development of their religious practices. The institutional Catholic practices of the three cohorts took shape within three sociopolitical periods in history that built upon one another. For this reason, Chapter 3 is organized in chronological order, beginning with *Las Damas* and followed by *Las Madres* and *Las Mujeres*. Each section discusses the sociopolitical context in which each of the cohorts grew up to situate their lived experience in a broader context.

Shifting Plates: Las Damas

On average, *Las Damas* grew up in the late 1930s to 1950s, a time when US–México binational political tensions were heightened. This was partly as a result of the Bracero Program (1942–1964), which allowed temporary contract laborers from México legal entry to the United States.[4] During this time, the Catholic Church in México was still recovering from the repression imposed by the government during the presidencies of Álvaro Obregón Salido (1920–1924) and Plutarco Elías Calles (1924–1928). These events impacted the cultural landscape somewhat like shifting tectonic plates shape the geology of a region. The shifting political plates occurred in a pre–Vatican II culture that held women and girls to higher standards of conduct and demureness than males, while relegating them to second-class citizen status.

With no source of income to support their families, many Mexican nationals took advantage of the Bracero Program. The fathers of six of the 15 *Damas* were among those who migrated during the Bracero Program in the hope of better opportunities, and they eventually brought their families. Other *Damas* migrated without documents as adults at a time when there were far less restrictions, and later in life gained citizenship. However, the program was not the economic panacea that many Mexicans on both sides of the border thought it would be. The families of the 15 *Damas*, whether in México or the United States, were farm laborers who lived a life immersed in socioeconomic disadvantages.

The experiences of growing up, as they were told to me, did not differ much between *Las Damas* who grew up in the United States and those who grew up in México. Access to education was very limited for all 15 women, and there were no stark differences in language. Spanish was the predominant language spoken at home. When I interviewed them, all spoke to me in Spanish, with the exception of one who code-switched during the interview. With a couple of exceptions, most of *Las Damas* did not attend school beyond the fourth grade. The lack of educational opportunities, coupled with the interdependence of the United States' and Mexican economic and political systems, locked working-class families into a life of continual struggle on both sides of the border.

Early in the century, the Mexican government had adopted an anticlerical ideology in the Constitution of 1917 after the Mexican Revolution because it was both tired of the influence that the Catholic Church had at all sociopolitical levels and eager to jump on the modernization bandwagon with its neighbor to the north. The tension between the Mexican government and the Church hierarchy escalated as the Elías Calles administration sanctioned and penalized the public practice of Catholic rituals and beliefs. The situation quickly turned violent and ultimately led to the Cristero Movement or Cristero War (1926–1929), which spilled over into the early 1930s.[5]

The Cristero Movement, or *La Cristiada* in Spanish, was an armed civilian movement against the Constitution of 1917, which included several articles that attempted to suppress the social and political influence of the Catholic Church. Several articles of the Constitution banned the Catholic Church from owning real estate or operating schools and prohibited Catholics from participating in religious rituals and sacraments.[6] What few people know is that women played a central role in the Cristero Movement by transporting weapons, fighting in the trenches, and hosting clandestine Masses at their homes.[7] It is estimated that more than 250,000 people died in what ultimately became a war. The constant threat of the Mexican government to persecute and kill clergy and lay people who failed to leave the Catholic faith led many families across social classes to place a stronger emphasis on the importance of a sacred space at home. By the mid-1930s and 1940s, Catholic fervor among the faithful began to see daylight once again. Though *Las Damas* were just babies or toddlers and therefore too young to recall the Cristero Movement, they grew up in a Catholic culture that had experienced repression and survived.

What *Las Damas* remember is that home altars, devotion to saints, and prayer were central to daily domestic life. Mass was celebrated in Latin, and the priest, like the rest of the congregation, always faced the altar. In México, the pews were gendered. Men sat on one side and women and children on the other. Women and girls were expected to wear skirts or dresses and a mantilla (headdress) to Mass, as Angelita's story demonstrates. Wearing a mantilla during Mass was a sign of respect for God and the Church.

These guidelines instilled in *Las Damas* a sense of obligation to abide by the expectations of Catholic culture, which stressed the importance of daily Mass attendance. According to Paloma (age 80), attending Mass *"era una obligación, si uno llegaba a faltar un domingo tenía que ir a confersarse"* ([Attending Mass] was an obligation. If one did not attend Mass on Sunday, one had to go to confession). However, according to *Las Damas*, the obligation did not apply equally across gender lines. MariChuy (age 78) observed that boys and men were not held accountable for not attending Mass. The reasoning was that they had to work along with their fathers to support the family.

Mass attendance was also a type of "public performance" (Goffman 1959) that demonstrated to the extended family, community, and the parish priest that people were "good abiding Catholics." Being a "good Catholic woman"—and by extension, a "good Catholic girl"—also meant wearing the proper attire. According to *Las Damas*, regardless of the weather, attending Mass and dressing properly were expected of women and girls alike. This expectation was instilled in girls from a very early age, to the extent that they felt they had to do whatever it took to comply with the dress code—even if that meant using a soiled cloth diaper as a mantilla.

Amelia (age 69), who was very active at the local senior center—she enjoyed calling out the cards during *Lotería* (Bingo) after lunch—shared with me what it was like for her growing up Catholic. As the oldest of eight siblings, it was her duty to accompany her mother and grandmother every day to Mass. One morning, when she was seven years old, she was running late for Mass.

> Guess what, *'mija* "the blankets got stuck to me" and I woke up late for Mass. Boy, I got up and got dressed very quickly, I braided my hair, and then one of my shoes was nowhere to be found. And I looked and looked for it but nothing. My mom and grandmother were waiting for me outside, and the church was across town. When . . . guess what? I went to Mass wearing only one shoe. That is the way it was before, one could not miss Mass because it was a sin and you had to go to confession and the priest would scold you.[8]

Sunday services, in México more than the United States, were a gendered space. The majority of parishioners who attended Sunday Mass were women, children, and the elderly. As mentioned earlier, the Church required men and women to be seated separately to avoid distractions. However, according to *Las Damas*, women and not men were considered the cause of distraction—which they read as one of the reasons why wearing the mantilla was an obligation.

Among the more traditional families, interaction between young men and women was highly restricted, especially if they did not know each other. However, young men always found ways to look at the young women, at least from afar. According to Roberta (age 79), "*eran los muchachos que les gustaba pararse en la entrada 'pa ver a las muchachas*" (It was the young men who preferred to stand at the entrance so that they could see the young women). Young women were highly supervised, mainly by elderly women, and contact with the opposite sex was virtually nonexistent. Thus, Sunday Mass was one of the few opportunities when young men and women came together, at least through eye contact. This was followed by surreptitious courtships, primarily consisting of an exchange of love letters delivered by kids in the neighborhood. As one of *Las Damas* explained, one had to be a good girl "*porque Dios no es ciego*" (because God is not blind).

On the north side of the US–Mexican border, for Esperanza (age 68), attending Mass was part of her family life. She was born into a family of 12 children, but three died. When she was six, her family moved back to México. But for reasons that she cannot recall, her younger sister fell sick and her parents were afraid that she might die, so they came back to the United States and settled in Texas. Sunday mornings always began with Mass and, according to Esperanza, her mother and siblings would fill an entire pew. As *Las Damas* recalled their childhood experiences attending Mass, some also shared that when they migrated to the United States, got married, and had children they attended Mass on Sundays with their own families. However, as they got older some listened to Mass on television because they did not have transportation to and from church.

Besides attending daily Mass, the sacrament of Penance—or confession—was an obligation for those that had received the sacrament of the Eucharist, and was never questioned. As Amelia points out, missing Mass meant going to confession and asking forgiveness for not complying with Church expectations. What is more, weekly confessions were not out of the ordinary. Josefa (age 77) recounts that after children received the sacrament of the Eucharist,

We always had to confess on Sundays, and I was afraid. I would
spend all week writing down the bad things I did, like talking back
to my eldest brother or complaining because I didn't want to do the
house chores. I wrote everything so I would not forget when I con-
fessed on Sunday. I was afraid that one of the times the priest would
not forgive me. I was about eight years old.[9]

During the interviews, *Las Damas* did not share much about catechism
instruction. There are two possible explanations. First, when I asked, some
had trouble recalling details of their experience in catechism. Second, the
towns where some of *Las Damas* lived had no permanent priest and thus
no formal catechism instruction. However, some did say that either their
mothers or grandmothers taught them *los rezos* (the prayers) as part of
their preparation to receive the sacrament of the Eucharist. *Las Damas*
also did not remember details about their First Communion, but they did
say that it was a very important day for they felt special and closer to God.
Others focused on how the whole family attended their First Communion
Mass, and this made them feel very special. Some wore new white dresses
to their First Communion Mass, but others wore a dress that they already
owned because it was too expensive to buy a new dress or to purchase fabric for their mothers to make it.

As children, the women across the three cohorts were introduced to the
Lord's Prayer, the Hail Mary, and the Rosary. Of the three prayers, the one
that *Las Damas* vividly remember (and not necessarily as something they
looked forward to) was the Rosary.[10] Though they did not fully appreciate
the Rosary as children, a daily routine for this cohort, it was one way that
Catholic ritual mediated their relationship with Our Lady of Guadalupe.
Saying the Rosary or a novena (a prayer done over a period of nine days),
as far as *Las Damas* can remember, was the only time when devotion to
La Virgen was structured around a traditional Catholic prayer. In the afternoon or early evening the women of the family, children, and the elderly
gathered around their home altars to pray using the rosary. In some cases
the father joined them in prayer, but generally it was a gendered practice.
The women, in the company of their children and the elderly (in some
cases elderly men), were in charge of expressing the family's or community's needs, gratitude, or pleas to *La Virgen*. They not only prayed for the
well-being of their families, they also prayed for the health of a loved one,
for the elderly, the abused, the hungry, and the sick.[11]

Not only were the children expected to pray, they also had to follow the etiquette that the Rosary required. For example, praying the Rosary involved reciting certain parts of the prayer and kneeling for the duration of the ritual. Esperanza (age 68) vividly remembers the daily afternoon Rosary to *La Virgen de Guadalupe*. She recalls praying the Rosary with her mother and grandmother ever since she was about seven years of age. In her words,

> We were really small, she [mother] would make me kneel for the entire Rosary prayer to *La Virgen*. It was hard because I did not really know how to kneel . . . . Then came the litany, and I would say, "Oh no, that is the longest litany." By the end of the Rosary prayers . . . I was tired. My knees were tired, and she [mother] would still go with this litany.[12]

Esperanza refers to the Litany of the Saints—a prayer of invocation to the saints for one's salvation. Esperanza says that as a child she would complain, but now as an adult she does not pray the Rosary without the Litany. When I asked her why, her immediate response was that this is how her mother taught her.

When they were children they understood the ritual of prayer as part of their life, but it was not something *Las Damas* necessarily looked forward to doing in their childhood—they preferred to "simply talk to *La Virgen*." They reported preferring to talk to her about their day, how sometimes they hated school or doing house chores. When they did say traditional Catholic prayers, they were accompanied by pleas that range from asking for the healing of a loved one to daily protection of their families. Praying for others was something they learned from their mothers, and is a practice they continue as adults. The issue of talking versus praying to *La Virgen de Guadalupe* became more prominent in their adult years, for reasons I discuss in Chapter 6. Looking back to their childhood, *Las Damas* giggle as they remember how all day they were fine and full of energy; it was only during the Rosary that they felt sleepy and wanted to nap because, as they put it, *"era muy largo"* (it was too long). Some recall that as they were dozing off they would suddenly be woken up by their mother (or another adult) with a quick pinch.

As adults, *Las Damas* say that even though they did not like the religious custom as children, they continue to do it—not only because they were taught that as good Catholics they had to do it, but also because they want to honor the teachings of their mothers. As in Esperanza's case, the tradition of Rosary prayer was passed down to the rest of *Las Damas* by their mothers and grandmothers. The Rosary was not an individual act but a collective religious and family practice. It was an opportunity for family members to come together and worship, a tradition that is still to some extent present among *Las Madres* but has dissipated significantly among the *Las Mujeres* generation.

In sum, *Las Damas* and their families lived at a time of collision between unique sociopolitical and Catholic shifting plates. First, their social world was enveloped in a type of Catholic fervor that came about as a result of governmental repression of the Catholic Church, mainly for the sake of modernization. Second, their daily bread was Catholic practices mediated by their mothers (or in some cases their grandmothers) at home. Third, though these practices had a "matriarchal core" (Diaz-Stevens 1993), they nonetheless were rooted in a pre–Vatican II Catholic culture that held women to higher standards than men. Fourth, all this occurred while the Mexican government was becoming increasingly dependent on foreign investments—mainly from the United States—to finance modernization, leading to a wider gap between social classes and causing migration waves that continue to be part of our reality.[13]

Seismic Shifts: Las Madres

Las Madres grew up in México between the mid-1960s and late 1980s before migrating, with the exception of the younger ones who grew up in the early 1990s. This was a period of economic struggle that was deeply felt among the working class in México, causing a wave of migration, which I discuss in a later section of this chapter. It was also a time when the Catholic Church underwent a significant transformation. By the time *Las Madres* came of age, these changes were well underway.

With the Second Vatican Council (1962–1965) came some degree of openness in the Church. For example, Mass was no longer celebrated in Latin but in the vernacular, and priests could now say Mass facing the congregation. The physical space of the church was no longer segregated based on gender: men and women could now sit together. Women were allowed to wear pants to religious services and no longer required to wear mantillas. While wearing head coverings was still considered ideal in the eyes of the Church, it was less reinforced than in *Las Damas'* generation. According to journalist Jackie Freppon (2002), this change in dress code came about not by a decree from the Vatican Council but through a misunderstanding.

The commotion and excitement that surrounded the council meetings in Rome led to a misinterpretation about the Church's stance on women's dress. After one of the sessions, the international press asked Monsignor Annibale Bugnini, then secretary of the Congregation for Divine Worship, if women had to continue wearing mantillas to religious services. Bugnini responded that the council meetings were focused on other matters of importance and that this did not include women's use of head coverings. The international press took his response to mean that women no longer had to wear mantillas and published the news. By the time Bugnini came forth to say that he never meant to say that women no longer had to wear mantillas, it was too late—the news had spread.

Although the Catholic Church seemed more open to women, the androcentric hierarchal structure remained intact. Mexican women were still indoctrinated by the Church, community, and family to see priests as the ultimate authority in ecclesiastical and moral matters. By the time Las Madres were growing up, it was more common for churches to have priests appointed to serve as pastors, and thus more opportunities for formal catechetical instruction. Catechism class then became another way in which Catholic children were socialized to be obedient, respectful, and of service to God. Las Madres remember their First Communion as a special day in their lives because, through the sacrament of the Eucharist, they became closer to God. Those whose families were financially more stable had a small fiesta after the First Communion Mass.

The qualities of obedience and respect still were emphasized more heavily for girls than boys. In essence, gendered disparity in expectations continued for this generation, even though they could leave the mantilla at home. The father was considered the ultimate authority in the home. However, the mother was the one who continued to influence what and how religious traditions were passed on, and in so doing initially shaped their daughters' Mexican Catholic imagination. For Las Madres, who grew up in the late 1960s through the 1980s, the Church continued to influence many aspects of their lives.

For Las Madres, like Las Damas, religion was still very important in family life. Sunday Mass was a big event. It was the day when children got to wear their best clothes. But Las Madres, unlike Las Damas, were open to sharing with me that they did not like that their brothers were excused from attending Mass. For example, Gabriela (age 37) felt it was not fair that her brothers never got reprimanded for not going to Mass. Some of the fathers attended Mass with their families, but Sunday Mass continued to be generally understood as women's obligation.

Besides obedience at home and later in catechism class, young girls were taught about the importance of the sacrament of Penance. Furthermore, Mass attendance was still to some extent a public performance, but not to the degree that *Las Damas* had experienced. Many of *Las Madres* grew up in larger towns, but they were still small enough that parishioners and the priest took notice of who attended Mass. However, *Las Madres* did not feel as guilty for missing Mass once in a while, unlike *Las Damas*. Nevertheless, attending Sunday Mass was a weekly ritual that was very much a part of how they, as children, lived their Catholicism.

Most of the women in the *Las Madres* generation also grew up praying the Rosary. Though their mothers were part of the Rosary prayer circle, in most cases, the grandmothers more than the mothers kept the tradition alive among *Las Madres*. Many of the women recall their grandmothers leading the Rosary prayer and learning about *La Virgen de Guadalupe* from them. As in the case of *Las Damas*, it was customary for the children, young women, and their mothers to gather to pray the Rosary; in some families the fathers would occasionally join them.

Other *Madres* recounted how in December the women and children would gather to make a novena prayer to Our Lady of Guadalupe. Inez (age 36) recalls her mother teaching her the story of *La Virgen de Guadalupe*. And, from about age eight, she remembers that praying a novena to *La Virgen* on the nine days before December 12 was a family tradition. Among *Las Damas* it was common for their families to use the rosary in prayer. Among *Las Madres* I found that, with the exception of two, they prayed the Rosary with their families every day as well. Rosary prayer among *Las Madres*, just as among *Las Damas*, functioned as a unifying religious act that brought mainly women and children together. Faviola's (age 46) experience exemplifies what I found among *Las Madres*.

> Since we were little my grandmother and my mom gathered us all to pray the Rosary in the afternoon. We had to stop what we were doing. I would get very sleepy when we prayed the Rosary, but as soon as the Rosary ended I wasn't sleepy anymore.[14]

Like most of the participants, Faviola found that the Rosary, with its recitation of the Lord's Prayer and the Hail Mary for each of the long string of rosary beads, made her sleepy. Kneeling for the entire series of prayers was something that in their childhood Las Madres sometimes found tedious; yet looking back, like Las Damas, those experiences of boredom are now fond memories. As Mereides (age 47) explains with a giggle, "teníamos que incarnos 'pa todo el rosario, olvídate nos cansabamos . . . pero eran tiempos bonitos, no ahora son otros tiempos" (We had to kneel for the entire Rosary, forget it, we would get really tired . . . But they were beautiful times, now times have changed).

For Faviola and Mereides, as for the other participants, prayer time with the family also represented a tradition of respect toward the elderly, particularly grandparents. In the families of some of Las Madres, it was customary to kiss the hand of the elderly (particularly grandparents) at the end of the Rosary as an act of love and respect. Another common childhood experience that Las Damas and Las Madres generations shared was a preference for talking with La Virgen de Guadalupe over praying the Rosary, because they felt much closer to her when simply talking with her. And, like Las Damas, talking with La Virgen became a significant way of becoming one with Our Lady of Guadalupe in their adult years (which is further discussed in Chapter 6).

This was the Catholic culture in which Las Madres grew up in México. But once they migrated to the United States, some things changed. Before I continue to discuss some of these changes, I want to revisit the political climate that propelled migration in the first place. The Bracero Program was only part of what destabilized México's working class, driving an increased wave of migration to the United States from México ever since. In 1965, México's Border Industrialization Program (BIP) allowed the United States to establish manufacturing companies known as maquiladoras along the border. This program became part of the political framework for the North American Free Trade Agreement (NAFTA) of the early 1990s.[15] In the early 1960s, at the end of the US Bracero Program, thousands of Mexican workers were deported back to México. Without enough money to return to their hometowns, many Mexican citizens had no option but to reside in border towns. As a result, the unemployment rate in border cities—Tijuana in the West; Mexicali, Ciudad Juárez, Nuevo Laredo, and Matamoros to the East—rose rapidly.[16]

The consequences of NAFTA were only the beginning of a decade of political and economic upheaval that often led to violence.[17] In December 1994 the Mexican foreign exchange market crashed, and in 1995 the value of the Mexican peso was $7.55 pesos per US dollar. Thousands were left unemployed throughout the country, and those who were able to retain their jobs could no longer afford the cost of living. These are the sociopolitical seismic changes—or in Mills's (1959) term, "earthquakes of change"—that caused the wave of migration in the 1990s of which *Las Madres* formed a part.

Their families experienced the strains of an economy that was rapidly declining, coupled with a government that increasingly failed to provide safety to its citizens, particularly women. For example, according to Amnesty International (2005), between 1993 and 2005 more than 370 women were murdered in the border city of Ciudad Juárez, Chihuahua. However, if the other hundreds of young women who went missing and were never found are taken into account, the number is staggering.[18]

No longer able to support their families and hoping for a better life and educational opportunities for their children, *Las Madres* migrated to the United States to reunite with their husbands or migrated with their husbands and families.[19] At the time I conducted the interviews *Las Madres* who were undocumented were concerned about their legal status, and prayed to *La Virgen de Guadalupe* and God for protection, but they did not experience the level of stress and fear that undocumented people feel under the Trump administration today as I finish preparing this book for publication.

In the United States, the women found a post–Vatican II Catholic culture quite different from the one in which they had lived in México. In México, it is customary for priests to hear confessions on Sundays, so that people can take communion at Sunday Mass. The participants in *Las Madres* group, like *Las Damas*, grew up in a Catholic culture where confession was a weekly practice and not optional.

Gabriela (age 37) was born in Guadalajara, Jalisco, and migrated to the United States at the age of 19. She is now married and has three young children. She grew up in a very traditional Catholic family, in which weekly confession was part of Sunday Mass. In her family, the adults (particularly women) and children who had made their First Communion were expected to go to confession on Sunday before attending Mass. Gabriela was surprised that in her new parish in the United States, the sacrament of confession did not take place every Sunday. Puzzled, she asked the priest why the sacrament of confession did not take place on Sundays. To her disbelief and disappointment, the priest responded,

"No. What for? Have you killed someone? Have you abused somebody? Have you cheated on your husband?" And I told him "No." He then said, "Just talk to God and confess to Him."[20]

She could not understand why a sacrament that was so central to her Catholic upbringing since childhood in México had so little importance in the US Catholic Church. She was more confused than before, but also frustrated.

> I think that this is how the beliefs that we bring with us [from México] begin to break apart [when you come to the United States]. In México you confess every Sunday and then take communion. Today, I sit and talk to my God and then I take communion, but you still need the contact with the priest.[21]

For Gabriela, contact with the priest—the person who, since childhood, she was taught to see as the authority in matters of faith in the Catholic Church—was essential. It was difficult for Gabriela to understand the priest's logic for not hearing her confession.

Migration brings about many changes, such as family reconfiguration and gender role adaptation, topics that have been extensively researched.[22] But less is known about the way migration moves people to readjust their religious imaginations, and what they teach their children about what it means to be a person of faith in a new country. Gabriela continues,

> I always try teach my daughter [about the importance of going] to confession, and . . . I always have trouble [convincing her]. And I said [to the priest] I want my daughter to go to confession as much as possible, and he said, "I bet you have more sins than she does." And I said wow, let me think . . . . I collapsed. Little things like that . . . bring you down.[23]

Gabriela not only had to readjust to a new secular cultural system but also to a Catholicism that did not always reflect the teachings she grew up with in México.

Attending Sunday Mass was a weekly practice that was very much a part of how *Las Madres* lived their Catholicism in México; it was also another way of expressing the sense of family. Once they migrated to the United States, things changed for some of them. Being apart from their families due to forced migration discouraged some of *Las Madres* from attending Mass. They went to Mass only occasionally or on special holidays, such as December 12, Ash Wednesday, and Easter Sunday. Though the local church was only a few blocks from where they lived, with the exception of two, *Las Madres* were not active in the church other than attending Mass occasionally.

In México, attending Mass was a family tradition sustained by the encouragement of the matriarch of the family—usually the mother or grandmother. Now in the United States, apart from the rest of the family, the motivation to attend Mass decreased. Besides, it was up to *Las Madres* to take the initiative, and some (particularly the youngest mothers of the cohort) found it challenging to transition into the matriarchal role of their mothers and grandmothers. As Vicky (age 31) put it: "*En México mi mamá nos juntaba a todos 'pa ir a misa, aquí en Estados Unidos es diferente. Ella no esta aquí y yo no tengo la motivación, pero voy a tratar*" (In México my mom used to gather us all to go to Mass, here in the United States it's different. She is not here and I don't have the motivation, but I am going to try).

Whether by force, as in the case of the Cristero Movement, or by happenstance, due to family separation caused by migration, the likelihood of the faithful attending Mass either decreased or stopped all together. However, this did not mean that their Catholic faith ceased. When I visited the homes of some of *Las Madres*, I encountered images of Our Lady of Guadalupe and crucifixes hanging from walls, or home altars with statues of *La Virgen de Guadalupe* and other saints. Their homes had become a type of domestic chapel. Such domestic sacred spaces helped sustain and nurture their Catholic devotion in a country where their Catholic imagination was experiencing seismic shifts.

Aftershocks: Las Mujeres

Las Mujeres grew up in California in the 1990s at a time when California experienced multiple political aftershocks that placed many undocumented citizens at a social, political, and educational disadvantage. These aftershocks came in the form of Propositions 187 (1994), 209 (1995), and 227 (1998). The referendums were instrumental in fueling the anti-immigrant climate that dominates the national debate about immigration reform to this day.

Proposition 187, which was introduced in 1994 as the "Save Our State" initiative, restricted access to certain social services (e.g., education, employment, and health services) for those without legal documents. In addition, the initiative made racial and ethnic profiling legal.[24] The purpose of this proposition, in essence, was to economically and educationally debilitate undocumented people so that they would have no choice but to return to their countries of origin.

The anti-immigrant aftershocks were rapidly felt throughout California, triggering pro-immigration reform rallies across the state in which the image of Our Lady of Guadalupe was used on a banner representing a call for justice. The US Conference of Catholic Bishops protested against Proposition 187, denouncing it as an inhumane act toward the most vulnerable.[25] At the local level, Catholic priests across the country allocated time during their sermons or held town hall meetings to speak out against the proposition.[26]

Some of Las Mujeres witnessed the Catholic Church's commitment to the "preferential option for the poor"—that is, to the most vulnerable and underserved in society.[27] Five participants from Las Mujeres cohort described going to Mass and hearing the priest inform the congregation about Proposition 187. Some recall rallies against it, in which the image of La Virgen de Guadalupe was used as the movement's coat of arms. In fact, Catholic parishes organized such rallies across the nation. In two instances, participants reported that on Christmas Day in 1994, the reenactment of the Pastorela—the journey of a group of shepherds to visit the newborn Jesus, performed by Teatro Corazón—was about a contemporary family facing possible deportation, in which the devil (a central character in the original Pastorela reenactment) was Proposition 187.[28]

In 1995, by the time Las Mujeres were in their teenage years, University of California Regent Ward Connerly introduced the "California Civil Rights Initiative," commonly known as Proposition 209. The proposition was approved in November of that year by a 54% margin.[29] This law prohibited state employers from hiring employees and state universities from admitting students on the basis of gender, race, and ethnicity.

By the time Las Mujeres were entering high school, the anti-immigration aftershocks were reconfiguring the national sociopolitical landscape by pushing undocumented people back to México. Republican Ron Unz, who had previously opposed Proposition 187, introduced Proposition 227 to end bilingual education in California; it was passed by a margin of 61% to 39% on June 2, 1998. Schools no longer provided bilingual education to migrant children, under the premise that bilingual instruction was detrimental to the integration of non–English speaking children into the US education system.[30] Las Mujeres grew up in a political reality that left migrant families and children at a great disadvantage and prohibited the use of Spanish in public schools. In spite of political attempts to repress the Spanish language, as I demonstrate below, Spanish was and continues to be central in shaping their Mexican Catholic imagination.

Las Mujeres did not endure the same restrictions, unreasonable expectations, or gender bias to the degree that *Las Damas* and *Las Madres* experienced. In fact, they were not even aware that before the Second Vatican Council, the Catholic Church had a specific dress code for women, including the use of mantillas, for attending Mass. Religion for this cohort continued to be central in their families, but there was variation. More specifically, the families of the young women who were born in México and migrated as children placed a greater emphasis on the importance of Catholicism and its teachings than the families of the young women who were born in the United States. This may be explained in part by the strength of the ties immigrant families maintain with Mexican Catholic customs. That is, more recently arrived immigrants may tend to adhere closer to the Catholic customs and traditions they brought from México compared to those who have been longer in the United States.

While attendance at Sunday Mass was also expected in the families of *Las Mujeres*, it was not strictly enforced. What is worth noting is that *Las Mujeres* preferred to attend Mass in Spanish because, according to them, in the English-language Mass they found no connection to their Catholic faith. There was one more similarity between *Las Mujeres* and *Las Madres*. *Las Mujeres* who lived on campus during college did not attend Mass regularly because, according to them, going alone did not feel right; they were used to going with their families. However, most of *Las Mujeres* who lived at home and commuted to college continued to attend Sunday Mass with their families.

Like *Las Damas* and *Las Madres*, they preferred talking with Our Lady of Guadalupe. Structured prayer was still significant among the families of *Las Mujeres*, but to a lesser degree compared to *Las Damas* and *Las Madres*. For five of the 15 participants in *Las Mujeres*, Rosary prayer (at least once a week) was a common practice growing up. This was especially the case for those who lived the first part of their childhood in México. Of those who participated in Rosary prayer, some recall that their grandmothers usually led the prayer, with their mothers, siblings, and (in a few cases) their fathers and grandfathers. In Mexican popular Catholicism, older women play a central role in passing on religious customs. This explains why the practice of Rosary prayer was common among *Las Mujeres* who grew up close to their grandmothers.

Rosary prayer was part of the daily life of *Las Damas* and a significant part in the lives of *Las Madres*; among *Las Mujeres*, however, only one-third reported praying the Rosary as children. One explanation for this is the interruption and readjustment of daily life as an outcome of the migration process. For many families, migration brings changes such as separation from family members; some, usually the elderly, stay behind. Families also readjust or discontinue family traditions like Rosary prayer as they reconfigure their Catholic imagination. *Las Mujeres* who migrated with their families said that in México they were much more involved in Catholic religious traditions, which they described as festive, compared to their degree of involvement in the United States.

Though structured prayer was not as common among *Las Mujeres* when compared to the other two cohorts, what was most revealing was that the language—the systematic means of communication—in which they prayed remained Spanish. In addition to the material means used in the socialization process (such as images of saints), language plays a significant role not only in how the process begins but in how it continues to shape the Catholic imagination of the youngest cohort. The in-depth interviews and focus groups among *Las Mujeres* on their Catholic upbringing brought to light the influence of language in their religious faith.

The Catholic socialization in which *Las Mujeres* came to understand their religious belief system had a very particular relationship with language. When I asked *Las Mujeres* in what language they prayed, 15 of 16 said that although they are fluent in English and mostly use English, they have prayed in Spanish ever since they were very young because that is the language used by their mothers and grandmothers. As Leonor (age 22) explains, "I feel more comfortable doing it in Spanish, because ever since I was little I've always attended church with my parents, and it was always in Spanish." Chavelita (age 23), shared a similar experience: "When I was little I remember that we would pray the Rosary with my mom and my grandmother and it was always in Spanish—the Mass, the prayers, the stories that they told us were all in Spanish."

Another place where language played a significant part was in Catholic formal instruction via catechism. While some of *Las Mujeres* attended catechism instruction in México, most attended catechism instruction in the United States. The mothers of *Las Mujeres* who grew up in the United States registered their daughters in Spanish-language catechism class;

since they had taught their daughters the prayers in Spanish, it was easier for the girls to continue with their religious education in Spanish. In
México and in Spanish-language catechetical instruction in the United
States, the transmission of Our Lady of Guadalupe's apparition story continues almost organically from the privacy of the home to the classroom.
Those like Neida (age 19) that attended catechism in México said that
they learned about *La Virgen de Guadalupe* at home from their mothers
or grandmothers and later in catechism. Similarly, Manuela (age 24), who
attended catechism in the United States, said that she first learned about
Our Lady of Guadalupe from her mother but learned more about her
significance in catechism class. However, this is not the case in English-
language religious instruction in the United States, which tends to emphasize a white Euro-ethnic interpretation of Mary. What is more, feast days
like December 12 tend not to play a central part in English-language religious instruction. Anita's (age 21) case is one example of the significance
of language and ethnicity in religious education.

Learning that there was no space in the Spanish-language classes,
Anita's mother registered her in the English-language catechism class
until space became available in the Spanish-language one. Little did Anita
and her mother know that this experience would allow Anita to see the
difference in what is and is not taught to children about Our Lady of
Guadalupe, depending on the language of religious instruction—even in
the same parish. In Anita's words,

> The demographics where I lived were very clear-cut. Like in the
> English catechism you'll see all the Caucasians . . . . If you go to
> the Spanish one you'll see all the Latino kids. I remember in the
> English one we never really talked about *La Virgen*. It wasn't until
> I took the Spanish class that we did. They were like talking about
> *La Virgen*, and stuff like that you know, and I was like, Wow!!! They
> didn't tell me this the first time I took this class. I saw . . . the differ-
> ence, you know, where religion meets culture. Yeah.

For Anita, this experience was very revealing. It allowed her see how religion is shaped by ethnic and cultural social structures, and by extension,
language. In the first English catechism class, the story of *La Virgen de
Guadalupe* was absent from the syllabus, whereas in the Spanish catechism class, Guadalupe was an essential part of Catholic instruction. In
essence, *Las Mujeres* learned the basic message about *La Virgen* in their

homes from their mothers, grandmothers, and (in some cases) their fathers, and it was further reinforced through formal religious instruction in Spanish.

Conclusion

The contexts shaping the religious socialization of the three cohorts differ in various ways. Those who migrated differ in length of residence in the United States. *Las Damas* grew up in a time when the Mexican Catholic Church was coming out of a period of persecution and repression. The United States and México rested on shifting binational political plates that pushed working-class Mexicans on both sides of the border further to the margins. *Las Damas* who were born in México came to the United States without documents at a time when there were far less restrictions, and later in life gained citizenship.

By the 1980s, the binational agreements between the United States and México led to political seismic shifts that created a tsunami of migration from México to the United States, of which *Las Madres* formed part. Most of *Las Madres* fled México due to the economic crisis that was largely due to NAFTA. Most of those that came from México are undocumented. Some of *Las Madres* have moved out of the neighborhood since I first conducted the interviews and focus groups. Those that have kept in contact with me and are undocumented experience real fear of being separated from their US-born children, as a result of Trump administration's focus on the detainment and deportation of undocumented immigrants. For this reason they have told me that they prefer to live in anonymity.

By the 1990s, the political topography where *Las Mujeres* grew up was unstable ground that gave way to multiple aftershocks, placing many undocumented people in the State of California at a great disadvantage. At the time of the interviews, *Las Mujeres* seemed more secure than *Las Madres*. This is partly due to the fact that they are fully bilingual and have access to a college education, which in turn provides them with far more opportunities and a path to achieving a middle-class status. Unfortunately, I have not had communication with *Las Mujeres* cohort recently. So, unlike some of *Las Madres* who have kept in contact with me and shared what they feel about the current political climate, I do not know what *Las Mujeres*, most of which were born in the United States, think about the new executive order on immigration. However, just because most of these women were born in the United States does not imply that they are not worried. While they did not share their parents' legal status at the time of the interviews, I suspect that if some have undocumented parents, they are as worried as *Las Madres*, about family separation due to deportation.

Of greater relevance to their Mexican Catholic imagination, there was a significant difference across cohorts in the content and depth of their memories of growing up Catholic. A key reason is that *Las Damas* and *Las Madres* have richer faith experiences informed by the various life stages they have lived through. *Las Mujeres* are considerably younger, and therefore their faith experiences are limited to their childhood and teenage years. Differences in experience included dress code, Rosary prayer, and Mass attendance; but there were also similarities, including the preference to talk to *La Virgen* as opposed to recite a Catholic prayer. All three cohorts, with the exception of a couple of women, prefer to pray in Spanish and attend the Spanish-language Mass. Although the youngest generation was fluently bilingual, they felt a stronger connection to their Catholic faith and their devotion to *La Virgen de Guadalupe* when using the Spanish language.

In the pre–Vatican II Catholic culture in which *Las Damas* grew up, the dress code was very specific: either a dress or a skirt and blouse, and the mantilla, were required for church attendance. *Las Damas* who grew up in towns that had a permanent priest attended Mass everyday. However, there were some that grew up in smaller towns where there was no permanent priest. This may account for the fact that the older women did not mention attending formal catechetical classes. When they migrated to the United States they attended Mass on Sundays. However, this changed as they grew older. Some with whom I am still in contact tell me that they attend Mass weekly, while others listen to Mass on television because they have no access to transportation to go to church on Sundays.

By the time *Las Madres* came of age in the 1980s, the changes that resulted from the Second Vatican Council were well underway; women's dress code became flexible, and the use of the mantilla was not enforced. *Las Madres* describe attending Mass in México as a family event; but once they migrated to the United States, the younger *Madres* stopped going to Mass on Sunday because it felt strange for them to attend Mass without their mothers or grandmothers. Others said that they found it difficult to attend Mass with their small children.

By the 1990s, *Las Mujeres* were not familiar with Vatican II and were not aware that the Catholic Church had a dress code for women or that the pews were segregated based on gender. *Las Mujeres* who grew up in México compared their experience as Catholic kids to their different experience in the United States. They described their experiences attending Mass or the feast day of *La Virgen de Guadalupe* in México as more festive. Furthermore, the US American Church that the younger women grew up in is less strict compared to the Catholic Church of México, and because religious education programs such as CCD (Confraternity of Christian Doctrine) were well established by the time *Las Mujeres* were growing up, it had more influence in shaping their Mexican Catholic imagination compared to *Las Damas*. Like *Las Madres*, *Las Mujeres* who lived on campus only attended Mass when they went back home, because they said their college life kept them busy. However, *Las Mujeres* who lived off campus did attend Mass on Sundays with their families. What is most illuminating about the experience of *Las Madres* and *Las Mujeres* is that their Mass attendance reveals the importance of family in their Catholic imagination.

Additionally, while the Rosary was a daily practice among *Las Damas* and common among *Las Madres* in México, this practice stopped when they migrated, in part because they were used to their mothers or grandmothers taking the lead. Praying the Rosary for the youngest generation (*Mujeres*) was not as common. However, there were some exceptions among *Las Mujeres* whose families adhered closer to traditional Catholic customs.

Up to this point, the book has analyzed the life-giving aspects of Catholicism as experienced by the women across cohorts. Using the devotional triangle as a theoretical framework, Chapter 2 analyzed the ways the women across cohorts were socialized by their mothers and grandmothers into Mexican popular Catholicism, in particular devotion to Our Lady of Guadalupe. This chapter highlighted some of the Catholic institutional expectations their mothers and the Church had of them and how these changed over time. This chapter also situated their religious socialization in broader historical and political contexts to show how each of the cohorts' imagination was shaped in times of tumult. Ultimately, devotion to *La Virgen de Guadalupe* in the Mexican Catholic imagination of all three cohorts was not shaped in a vacuum. Despite differences related to generation, migration, and sociopolitical events, this chapter demonstrated that some common experiences related to growing up

Catholic, such as praying the Rosary and the use of the Spanish language to pray and talk to Our Lady of Guadalupe, solidified the importance of *La Virgen de Guadalupe* in their lives. The Spanish-speaking Guadalupe presents herself in familiar ways, reaffirming not only her ever-presence—she will never abandon them—but also their Spanish language and ethnicity and, with this, their sense of belonging. The next chapter looks more closely at what is not done or said in adolescence about puberty, a critical period of female development, and the consequences of those silences for shaping the Mexican Catholic imagination.

4

The Making of Girls in the Mexican Catholic Imagination

OBEDIENCE, RESPECT, AND RESPONSIBILITY

A FRESH FRAGRANCE of flowers envelops me as Artemia opens the door of her home. She is wearing a lovely, colorful flowered blouse with white capri pants, black strappy low-heeled shoes, and jewelry. As I compliment her on her beautiful outfit, she says, "*¿Esta ropa vieja? Esto fue lo primero que encontre en mi closet esta mañana*" (These old clothes? This was the first thing I found in my closet this morning). Artemia is the most fashionable of *Las Damas*. She loves dressing up, and she stands out at the senior center that she attends every day. From where I sit in her living room, I can see the beautiful backyard. She has flowers of every kind and a cute shed in one corner. As I begin sipping the glass of apple juice she gave me, she transports me to her childhood.

> My parents were great parents but very disciplinary. My dad once told us: "Look, my dear ones, I want to tell you . . . just two things that you must always remember, and one is respect. If you do not respect yourself, nobody will respect you. That is one thing, and the other is obedience." This is how they raised us. And my dad would say, "He who does not comply will be tested. Always remember this: to be respectful and obedient. How are you going to tell someone to do something you do not do? You have to respect everything within the boundaries of obedience" [meaning that everything that is worthy of obedience must also be respected]. (Artemia, age 67)[1]

Respect and obedience go hand in hand. According to Artemia's father, those who do not obey will be tested throughout their lives; most importantly, how will they pass on the importance of obedience and respect if they do not practice it? For Artemia's father, passing on—in other words, teaching about respect and obedience—had to be done by way of example.

However, when obedience is expected without questioning, a child is led to believe she has to be obedient under any circumstances. Obedience without boundaries then functions as a set of rules and regulations made manifest through certain actions and beliefs that consciously and unconsciously help sustain what feminist theologian Elisabeth Schüssler Fiorenza (2001) calls a *kyriarchal* system. According to Schüssler Fiorenza, this term describes religious institutions (as well as other institutions, for that matter) formed under a system where "the lord, slave master, husband, the elite freeborn educated, and propertied man have domination over all wo/men and subaltern men" (2001, 95). This kyriarchal system is fertile ground for a type of systemic praxis where the degree of obedience and respect not only determine a girl's self-worth, it sets the tone for a culture of silence about the stages of puberty—the topic of the next chapter. But first we need to understand how the women learned early on in childhood to perceive themselves and their position in their families, community, and society at large.

Las Damas

For *Las Damas*, respect for the elderly, parents, men, and the Church was a decree with a sanctified quality. They were taught that in the Catholic Church, the priest was a representative of God and therefore an important public authority figure. At home, the ultimately authority was the father. If the father was absent, then the oldest brother took on the role of man of the family. In some cases, even if the brother was much younger than his sisters, he was still considered the man of the family in the absence of the father. Generally, women and girls alike were expected to perform respect by obeying male authority in and outside the home and fulfilling the Church's expectations for a good Catholic girl. The performance of respect was done in what Goffman (1959) famously described as the backstage of society—the place most people consider informal, where one could normally be at ease—one's home. However, for *Las Damas* the home was a backstage that, far from being an informal space, had its own front stage (the public sphere) that required a certain etiquette, particularly in the presence of their fathers. In this complex backstage—through silence, the kiss of the father's hand, and absolute obedience veiled in respect—girls were initiated into their marginal place in society and the Church.

This gendered culture of respect for authority gave the impression of reciprocal cohesiveness and harmony that flowed from within the walls of the Church to the privacy of the home and vice versa. In the formal and informal classes that they took to prepare them for First Communion, *Las Damas* learned that being obedient and respectful was behaving in accordance to the teachings of the Church.[2] The more Catholic a girl was perceived to be, the more she was considered by her family and community to be pious, honorable, and eventually good marriage material—characteristics that are associated with *marianismo*.[3]

Rosario, a 65-year-old widowed woman, mother of 12, grew up on a small farm in California. She considers herself very religious. She spoke about the sense of respect toward the men in the family and all the protocol that came with it. Though Rosario grew up in the United States, her experience growing up Catholic resembled that of *Las Damas* that grew up in México. She recalls that every morning always began with the following greeting to her great-grandfather:

> "May God give you a good morning." I would hold his hand and kiss it as I knelt [before him], then [I] could go wherever [I] needed to go, to the market or some other place. "I'm leaving, Daddy." He would then bless [me] and then [I] would go. It was such a [mark of] respect because as the head of the household he had the authority.[4]

Teaching children to treat others with dignity is a great value indeed. Rosario and other *Damas* remember these teachings fondly, without resentment. They compare their experiences to the ways that young people behave today. *Las Damas* emphasize that *"ahora no es como antes,"* meaning that today cannot be compared to how they were raised at home. Nora (age 65) also remembers:

> *Mija*, back then we had such great respect for our parents, grandparents, and the Lord our God. There was no way we would raise our voice to them; we didn't do that. A great respect, a great respect, not like today.[5]

Artemia (age 67) recalls that in the time she was growing up, you would never hear a child speak to an adult with the informal *tú* (singular second-person pronoun), but instead with *usted*. Esperanza, Nora, and Artemia, as well as the other *Damas*, grew up in a Catholic culture where discipline was a way of life and not an option. A child never addressed an adult in an informal way; to do so was perceived as great disrespect that carried deep consequences, such as physical punishment.

Performing respect for the elderly and men—particularly their fathers and grandfathers—was a way of life for *Las Damas* cohort. But not everyone remembers the protocol that came with respect in positive terms. Esperanza (age 68), born in Arizona and raised in California, recalls her childhood in the following way:

> My father, he would say, "Go get me water," and I would bring it, and I had to cross my arms at the chest with my head down waiting for him to finish the water, you know. And we had to say "*Sí señor*" or "*No, señor*" [yes sir, no sir], we couldn't just say *no y sí* [yes or no]. Very, very respectful; very strict, very strict.[6]

Unlike Rosario, the respect that Esperanza felt for her father was closer to fear than esteem. Regardless of whether the girls perceived the practice of respect toward male figures as a positive or negative experience, at an early age girls from this generation learned to see men as loci of authority. This attitude made some girls vulnerable and even open to blame for acts they did not instigate, leading to grave outcomes. This was the case for Artemia, whose story opened this chapter.

Artemia, her mother, and her siblings had spent the Christmas of 1951 at her older sister's house (her father had died a few years before). On the way home, two men approached the family and grabbed Artemia by the hand. Her mother tried to fight the aggressors by not letting go of Artemia's other hand, and before they knew it they were in the crossfire of a gunfight. Her brother-in-law was shooting at the aggressors to save Artemia, but he was not successful. Later Artemia found out that the abductor and his accomplice were also at the Christmas party, where they first saw her. Artemia said that she was scared because she did not know what was going to happen, and that she did not see her mother for quite some time after the abduction. "*Yo estaba muy chiquilla, ni siquiera había tenido mi primer período, y todavía me gustaba jugar con muñecas*" (I was very young, I had not even had my first period, and I still liked playing with dolls). After the men kidnapped her, one took her out to eat and threatened to start shooting his gun in the restaurant if she talked to anyone.

Artemia did not share with me whether she was sexually assaulted, but she did say that three months later she married the abductor who snatched her from her mother's hands. Since she was still underage, the kidnapper had his father pay someone to generate a birth certificate that falsified Artemia's age. He told the judge that she was 20 years old, and he had money in a car parked outside the courthouse to bribe the judge in case the latter refused to perform the ceremony. Though Artemia had multiple opportunities to escape her aggressor, she did not do it, because

> there was no way I was going to disobey my mother or the man that had taken me away . . . . Back then one's honor was worth more than life itself. If I had been a little older or if I had been brave enough, I would have pushed him away, because I did have the opportunity [to do so] . . . . One day [I visited Rita—my sister-in-law] who lived about a day's worth of walking from where I lived . . . . I could have escaped but I did not, because I had to obey.[7]

Rita encouraged Artemia to escape, even though her husband would most likely hit her for letting Artemia run away, but she did not care because, according to Rita, *"aunque me pegue que tanto me puede hacer"* (even if he hits me, how much damage can he do to me?).

The Christmas of 1951 changed Artemia's life forever—she was only 14 years old. Her experience illustrates the consequences of socializing girls into a type of culture of obedience that is capable of reducing a girl's agency to rubble by making her think that obedience is far more important than her own safety, her dignity, and above all, her life. Artemia's decision to not run away from her aggressor is not surprising, given the type of socialization many girls and women at that time received not only at home but also in the Church. Obedience was more important for Artemia than her safety and life. She also believed that if she went back to her mother, people might perceive her as a dishonorable girl because she had been living with her abductor. Furthermore, the dialogue between Artemia and Rita, her sister-in-law, demonstrates the culture of violence some women experience and the extent to which women are willing to go to support one another, even if it means putting their own lives at risk. Given what Artemia learned at home from her father about respect and obedience, it is not surprising, then, that when she was abducted, she did not attempt to escape. Artemia's account is heartbreaking and unfortunately not the only one. Of the 45 women I interviewed, a total of three (including Artemia) had somewhat similar experiences.

During the period in which *Las Damas* were growing up, abduction was romanticized and in many ways systematized, particularly in small towns and villages throughout México.[8] Girls as young as 13 were kidnapped by much older men who claimed that they had fallen in love with the girls, even when there had not been any type of communication between the two; often, this abduction led to rape. Such acts of abduction are commonly referred to colloquially as *robar* (literally, "to steal"). According to the women, some girls were abducted on their way to the nearby river to get water or at large events such as family or community *fiestas*. The girls were usually taken away for one or two days and then returned to their families.[9]

Once the girls were abducted, in the eyes of a highly conservative male-centric Catholic culture they were no longer "pure," since they had spent a night with a man. It did not matter whether in fact the young girl had been sexually abused or not; the fact that she had been taken away by a man was enough evidence to taint her reputation. The village often got word of the kidnapping; usually the father, in order to save his daughter's honor and the reputation of his family, forced the girl to marry the abuser. In other cases, the kidnapper married the girl without anyone's consent.[10]

Artemia's decision not to run away from her aggressor is not surprising given the way many Mexican-origin women of her generation were socialized.[11] Artemia, now in her late 60s, is a confident woman, and one of the most progressive of *Las Damas* (as explored in Chapter 7). At the end of the interview, we went to her backyard and she opened a big shed that caught my attention when I first walked into her home. To my surprise, the shed was full of dolls of all kinds and sizes, including Barbie dolls, ceramic dolls, and rag dolls. Every corner and space in the shed was full of them—there was only space for one small stool where she sat. She had combs, brushes, hairpins of all colors, and even hair spray. She must have had at least 100 dolls. She said that dressing them and combing their hair brings her a sense of peacefulness. Is this space a reflection of the emotional and psychological scarring that the abduction experience has left in her life? Is this her way of compensating for a childhood that was violated and stolen from her more than 50 years ago?

Las Madres

Like *Las Damas*, *Las Madres* came from very traditional Catholic families where their fathers were the authority. Though the traditioning of obedience and respect were present in all my individual interviews and focus groups, the formative years of *Las Madres* centered on the need to respect their own bodies as the primary form of socialization they received at home. In part this had to do with the time in which they were coming of age, in the late 1960s to 1980s. It was a time when there was more openness about sex and sexuality, at least in the media and public arena, which went against the beliefs and customs of the more traditional Catholic families.

It was common for *Las Madres* to be told by their mothers and fathers the following: *tienes que darte a respetar* or *tienes que darte tú lugar* (you need to behave in a way that others will respect you). These messages were gendered and coded in two significant ways. First, they were mainly directed to young women and not men; second, by "others," parents really meant men and not necessarily women. Self-respect meant valuing one's dignity and self-worth, and these attributes had more to do with their female sexuality than their persona as a whole—body and mind. This was done in various ways, including dressing properly (meaning clothes that were not too revealing), behaving properly (which usually meant a young woman was not allowed to have a boyfriend until she was at least 18), and monitoring what one shared about one's body. In my focus groups and in-depth interviews, *Las Madres* shared some of the ways their mothers and grandmothers inculcated and reinforced a type of respect that was always anchored in fear and strongly bound to their Catholic imagination.

When Laura (age 37) was seven years old, her cousin who was visiting from the United States brought her a Barbie doll as a gift. Laura loved Barbie dolls but did not have one. She was very excited because she finally had that special toy she had always wanted. Laura played with her Barbie the rest of the day. The next morning she woke up and hurriedly went to where she had left her Barbie, only to find that it was missing. Someone had taken it, but who? She looked all over for it but could not find it. She asked her siblings and cousins, but no one knew where it was. She wondered why the person who took the toy did not ask for permission to borrow it instead of just taking it away.

That afternoon she found her doll out in the backyard by a trash can—it had not only been thrown away but mutilated. She recalls, "*Yo me asusté 'pos que había pasado, quién cortó mi muñeca y por qué?*" (I got scared, what happened? Who could have cut my doll, and why?). The doll had two big holes on the chest—her breasts had been cut off. Who could have done such an atrocious act? And more importantly, why? What was so wrong with the Barbie's breasts? After all, it was only a plastic doll. Seeing her doll torn apart, she was not only sad and puzzled but also began to ask herself what was wrong with women's breasts. "*Yo me preguntaba, qué tenían de malo los pechos de mi muñeca?*" (I asked myself, what was so wrong with my doll's breasts?) Later that day she found out that it was her mother who had cut out the doll's breasts.

In Laura's story, respect took the form of silence about women's bodies—even to the extent of her own mother cutting the shape of the breasts from a Barbie doll. In other words, one demonstrated respect by not exposing children to what were considered inappropriate toys. According to Laura, her mother felt that the doll's anatomy was too close to the actual female body; it was not only wrong but also inappropriate for a seven-year-old girl to see—not to mention play with—what in her mother's eyes was an obscene toy. However, her mother's attempt to protect her daughter from seeing *inappropriate* characteristics of the female anatomy at what she considered a very young age was counterproductive. Her mother's action prompted Laura to question aspects of the female body she had previously not considered. She recalls, "*Yo estaba toda confundida. ¿Qué tenían de malo los pechos de mi muñeca? ¿Los pechos de Las Mujeres son algo malo?*" (I was all confused. What was it about the Barbie's breasts that was so wrong? Are women's breasts bad?). She even asked, "*¿Qué me va a pasar a mi cuando los pechos me crezcan?*" (What will happen to me when I begin to develop breasts?). Laura's experience exemplifies the ways in which a Mexican Catholic imagination materialized for *Las Madres* that were detrimental to a girl's mental and physical health.

Lupe (age 36) also recalls her teenage years as a period where family values were based on fear.

> Look, Mexican culture [taught] you to, first, not have a boyfriend until one had . . . not until after we finished with our schooling after the age of 18. Then we were taught to take good care of ourselves. And having a boyfriend specially implied not having [sexual] relations, do you know what I mean? This was a fear that they instilled in you . . . . Because you have to respect your house, you have to study first, and one was practically prohibited from having a boyfriend before the age of 18.[12]

In Mexican popular culture, the hidden meaning behind the use of the phrase *te tienes que cuidar* (you have to take care of yourself) is that you are not allowed to have sex before you get married; the phrase *respetar tu casa* (respect your home), according to *Las Madres*, really means that you had better not get pregnant out of wedlock and dishonor the family. Inez (age 36) summarized what respect meant to the women of her generation in the following way: "*Para mí la religión significa, respeto para sí misma, y mucha fe*" (For me religion means, respect for oneself and great faith). Self-respect and faith take on a *café con leche* quality, meaning they cannot be separated—a young woman who respects herself is a person of faith. And Gabriela (age 37) expressed the frustration she felt because her mother would not allow her and her sisters to go to parties because, according to her mother, "*pueden correr peligro*" (they might run into danger).

> My mom has always been strict. In fact, my mom was the one with the strong personality, even to this day. She would not let me go out to parties and I felt very frustrated . . . she would say that something bad could happen to us.[13]

Unfortunately, the degree to which some of the mothers restricted the activities of their daughters (*Las Madres*) gave their daughters the notion that their mothers disliked them. As Candelaria (age 39) recalls: "*Mi mamá era más estricta, por eso yo pensé que ella no me quería*" (My mom was more strict, and that is why I thought she didn't love me). Like Candelaria, the other *Madres* complained about their own mothers criticizing the length of their dresses or skirts and how much makeup they put on, and they recall being sent back to change or wash their face before going outside. At the time, *Las Madres* felt very upset and considered their mothers too *anticuadas* (old school, traditional). What they did not ask, at least at that time, was how their own mothers learned to be women. In other words, it is important to recognize that *Las Madres'* own mothers were raised in a very specific sociocultural and religious framework.

According to María (36), women's social formation was significantly more rigorous than that of men, and this in part had to do with culture: "In my view it should be the same [for men and women] but unfortunately this is how it is. In Latino culture the man is always different [from women]. Yes, that is what they make us think." When I asked Lupe if this only had to do with Latinx culture, she replied, "I think that religion and culture are very closely related. As you know, in México we are typically very religious, but also our culture is deeply rooted. The Latino Mexican culture is deeply rooted."[14]

Catholicism and secular Mexican cultural values, as María points out, are very much intertwined. As Esperanza in *Las Damas* cohort succinctly summarized the relationship between Catholicism and Mexican culture, it is a *café con leche* (coffee with milk) way of life. It is a social system in which secular sexist ideology is Catholicized and Catholic sexist ideology is secularized, producing and reinforcing limiting definitions about demureness and womanhood that are then reinforced across social institutions such as the family and the Church, and reinforced by women themselves. Consequently, Mexican culture is embedded in a Catholic and male understanding of being in this world.

Las Mujeres

Respect, for *Las Mujeres*, was somewhat different from what *Las Damas* and *Las Madres* experienced growing up. Respect for their parents and fathers in particular was present but not to the extreme in which *Las Damas* experienced it. Silence about the body was seemingly instilled in *Las Mujeres*, but the messages were somewhat more direct and not as abstract as for *Las Madres*. The messages about performing proper respect revolved around the way *Las Mujeres* perceived and carried their bodies. As with the previous groups, *Las Mujeres* grew up in families with well-defined notions of women's place in society and the home. Rosita (age 20), a junior in college, lives at home and commutes to school every day; her parents' strict rules have defined the extent of her involvement in college. She finds this situation conflicting; she considers herself an educated, self-identified Chicana who enjoys getting involved in college functions, but her parents' curfew has always limited the extent of her participation.

Every time she goes out, her parents remind her that she needs to be home early. This makes Rosita feel frustrated because she is involved in various social justice organizations, including MEChA (Movimiento Estudiantil Chicano de Aztlán) at school; the meetings tend to be in the evening, since most students live on campus.[15] She explains, "I know they are protecting [me] *pero a veces* [but sometimes] it's kind of like I'm grown up, you know." This restriction on movement was an attempt on her parents' part to keep their daughter safe, not realizing that in doing so their daughter was missing out on extracurricular college opportunities that could have furthered her intellectual maturity.

Though she understands her parents' preoccupation, Rosita feels that such concern for her safety means that they do not fully realize that their daughter is a grown woman. Nevertheless, she says, "*Pero los entiendo* [but I understand them] . . . *allá en* [over in] México, you know, you live with your parents until you get married." Indeed, women's agency in México—particularly two to three generations ago—was stunted or limited at best, as we learned from Las Damas and Las Madres. Women passed from the control of their fathers to the control of their husbands. Most of Las Mujeres continue to be haunted by the belief that "good girls" do not move out of the house until marriage. Part of the explanation for why the parents of Las Mujeres were so strict is that, with the exception of a couple of cases, the parents were born in México. Furthermore, the parents of Las Mujeres all grew up in homes with very traditional values similar to those of Las Madres cohort.[16]

Rosita shared that she is considering moving to Los Angeles upon graduation because she has not been able to find employment in Northern California. Her parents' belief that "young women do not leave the house until they marry" bothers her; she wants to be independent of her parents, yet she feels restricted by their controlling attitude. Performing respect in Rosita's case means "respecting her house" by not coming home late. And what respecting the house means to her parents is preserving her bodily virtue and virginity.

Some of Las Mujeres' parents have given them the impression that they have freedom, but that freedom always came with mixed messages or restrictions. Manuela's (age 24) mother has always encouraged her to be independent, as Manuela says, "so that one day, you know, heaven forbid, that I am left alone, I don't have to depend on anybody." At the same time, Manuela recounts:

> When I was growing up . . . my parents were never like "oh, you can't have a boyfriend, or you can't go out" . . . but there was always a curfew . . . you know, you had to be home by this time. My curfew was always ten o'clock.

Not only did Manuela have a strict curfew, she also had to "report" so her parents would not worry. Manuela continues:

> I had to come from school first. You know, "I'm home, I'm still alive . . . I [am] going out." "O.K., but you need to come home by 10, and you call in." We always had to call my mom, you know . . . so she would . . . call me just so she knew where we were at.

Las Mujeres, like Las Madres, were also frustrated about the ways freedom was gendered. With the exception of two, all participants felt that the restrictions were biased along gender lines—their brothers had more freedom, even if they were younger. *Las Mujeres* not only questioned gender bias but also challenged it by planning to "untradition" limiting definitions about women's place at home and society. According to Chavelita (23), her brother could come and go as he pleased without having to "report" or come home at ten o'clock like she did. When I asked her if she agreed or disagreed with the double standard, she said that she disagreed and that when she had children she would treat them equally regardless of gender.

Chavelita is an example of the ways some young women challenge and break away from traditional gender expectations. However, others like Celene (age 20) find it more difficult. In Celene's case, respect encompassed a broader definition: to perform respect meant to attend to your responsibilities in the home. Celene, who lives on campus, considers her parents very traditional at the expense of their daughters' right to equality in the home. Her father instilled in his daughters that cooking was women's responsibility and not men's; therefore, her brothers were excused. When I asked her how she feels, she was quick to respond:

> Well, I get very angry [raising her voice, she continues] because I say, "But men also have hands to cook," but my dad says that [cooking] is for women and it is not men's work, and my brothers say: "Yes, it is true."

Celene feels frustrated because she believes that cooking should not be gendered, and she voices her concern with her father when she gets the opportunity. However, she finds it difficult to break away from this expectation, and ultimately agrees—not because she is entirely in favor of her father's view on cooking, but because, according to her, "it [the belief that it is women's responsibility to cook] is within you. And at the end not really wanting, we accept; we have to do it, it is like we have this in us." The endorsement of cooking as a woman's job is another way of instilling guidelines about what she does with her body—it is to be used to cook and clean.

The notion that "it is part of a woman's nature" and the belief that women need to comply is one example of the extent to which sexist gender roles and obedience are traditioned (i.e., passed on) in such a way that some women feel they are unavoidable. As in Celene's case, for most of *Las Mujeres* who had brothers the socialization of unequal treatment between women and men at home had a three-pronged framework: responsibility, obedience, and respect.

Not having the liberty of going out without any restrictions was another aspect of their lives that *Las Mujeres* sometimes verbally contested. On one occasion, Pilar (age 24), who lives at home and commutes to college, was not allowed to fly to Southern California from the Bay Area (a trip of approximately one hour) because, according to her father, she was female and had more to lose.

> One time when I wanted to go to LA—I'm 24—I had to tell my dad that I was going to take a plane and meet my friend, right, and he wanted to interrupt me . . . and I was kind of like "Are they going to let me say [any]thing?" So, after I said everything, he was like, "Well, no. You can't go 'cause . . . the bottom line, I don't agree with it." And I was like, "Well if you don't trust me, then that's fine, but I haven't done anything for you not to trust me."

Repeatedly, the young women in the *Las Mujeres* cohort expressed resentment because, even though (according to them) they have never done anything wrong and have always obeyed their parents out of respect, they do not receive the trust they feel they deserve. In the in-depth interview, Pilar assured me that if her brother had been traveling, her father would have reacted differently, because men tend to have more liberty.

The parents'—specifically, in most cases, the fathers'—concern was that if they gave too much liberty to their daughters, their daughters might become sexually active and consequently get pregnant. The phrase used by Pilar's father, *las mujeres tienen más que perder* (women have more to lose), is often used to refer to women's virginity and more specifically to the possibility of getting pregnant out of wedlock and being destined to live life as a single mother. Pilar, however, does not see the correlation between flying to Los Angeles to meet her friend and the possibility of getting pregnant and living life as a single mother. Despite its cultural/historical ubiquity, the type of limitation imposed on Pilar by her father is not likely to be passed on to the next generation. Pilar stated that if she ever has a child she will raise her son/daughter with beliefs and values less restraining than the ones imposed on her and her brother. Pilar, like Chavelita, does not plan to pass on such limiting notions of responsibility and respect.[17]

Under the belief that they were raising their daughters *por el buen camino* (on the right track), parents set boundaries that *Las Mujeres* experienced as suffocating and unjust.[18] Parents (particularly fathers) believed that such limitations were for their daughters' own good; according to them, women have more to lose than men if given the opportunity to exercise their free will. However, not all of *Las Mujeres* were raised with rigid rules and restrictions. For example, Neida (age 19), who lives on campus and whose mother is a single parent, says that her mother has never imposed restrictions on her. When I asked her if her mother was strict, she said with a big smile and giggle,

> Noooo, my mom is not strict at all. She never imposes rules on me. She tells me, "You make your own decisions, because if you make mistakes I want you to blame yourself; I don't want you to blame me."

Neida's mother has always been open with her. She thinks that it is because her mother is a single parent; this has made her value the need to be independent, which meant giving Neida freedom to make her own choices.

> She gives me permission for anything, and in that sense I feel that I owe respect to her 'cause she trusts me . . . . I've always felt respect for my mom. I don't want to disappoint her either, she takes pride that I am a good girl and that I didn't turn out bad.

Neida also shared that when her mother found out that she was dating in college, she took her to a health clinic to discuss the different birth control options available to her. Neida's mother (who is, according to Neida, deeply Catholic) demonstrates that the Mexican Catholic imagination is not static but always evolving in ways that heal women's sense of self. In doing so this imagination can transgress gender expectations, ultimately benefiting their daughters. Neida's friends in college cannot understand why Neida does not take full advantage of the freedom that her mother gives her. For Neida, it is because her mother has always been "very lovable" and allows her do what she wants. Thus, Neida feels a deep respect for her mother and does not want to disappoint her.

Conclusion

Obedience and respect are typically defined as a positive (both at the level of feeling and as action) toward another person or entity. However, while engaging in this type of behavior may be perceived as positive, this does not necessarily mean that it is a positive experience for women. The performance of obedience and respect can also be actions exercised by a girl who, out of free will or obligation, is moved to not disrupt the status quo imposed by a given culture, society, and religion. This was demonstrated by all three age cohorts and exemplified in Artemia's story. Indeed, the messages that Las Damas received about the importance of being obedient did not have any clear boundaries as to when and when not to be obedient. And what is most noticeably absent from the emphasis on obedience in the experience of Las Damas was respect for the integrity of a girl's subjectivity. Obedience and respect under this second definition can be a conscious or unconscious behavior that, though it is reconfigured or redefined generation after generation, nonetheless replicates patterns of oppression. This chapter demonstrates how kyriarchy (Schüssler Fiorenza 2001) plays out in the context of the women's Mexican Catholic imagination across cohorts and its consequences, even as it modifies somewhat across generations.

Not until there is a significant ideological rupture can there truly be change in the social order. The cases of Chavelita, Pilar, and Neida illustrate this point. Chavelita and Pilar are determined to break the cycle of gendered expectations when they become mothers. In Neida's case, her mother chose not to pass on the restrictions imposed by her own parents, and Neida plans to also be open to her own children someday. Neida's experience is important for two reasons: first, it demonstrates that the experiences of Las Mujeres are not monolithic; and second, it illustrates how women manage to untradition certain beliefs without compromising the cohesiveness of a solid mother–daughter relationship.

In sum, the way the women across cohorts came to understand obedience and respect took different shapes. For some, it meant not asking questions and thus being silent. For others, it meant trying to decode the messages about protecting their virginity that parents, particularly mothers, transmitted to their daughters. Yet for others, as in the youngest cohort, their movement was restricted, and the reasons behind it were framed as protecting their bodies. However, as the women grew older they transgressed this restrictive understanding of obedience and respect. Their understanding of Our Lady of Guadalupe plays a role in that transformation of their understanding. As we will see in Chapter 6, *La Virgen de Guadalupe* speaks from a Catholic perspective, but because she is materialized and philosophized by the women in real time, *La Virgen* is perceived to understand the here and now along with the pressures of the contemporary moment.

5

Becoming Señoritas

IF YOU CAN'T TALK ABOUT IT IN CHURCH,
YOU CAN'T TALK ABOUT IT ANYWHERE

ANITA (AGE 21, *MUJERES* COHORT) is a self-identified Chicana feminist. Her self-confidence and vibrant personality quickly grabbed my attention. She has the type of energy and enthusiasm that draws people to her when she enters a room. She is funny and outspoken, which made me wonder if she came from a family of women who, as we say in Spanish, *no tienen pelos en la lengua* (have overt and assertive personalities). As we begin our interview I ask her to tell me a little about her relationship with her mother and *abuelita* (grandmother). She laughs and tells me that she grew up close to her mother and her grandmother. I ask if there was any tension between them, and with a big belly laugh, Anita proceeds to share one particular incident.

> We [grandmother, mother, and Anita] were sitting at the kitchen table at home. I got up and left to [go to] the bathroom, and I found out I got my period . . . . So, *yo muy casualmente* [casually], you know, I went out of the bathroom and I told my mom "*Ya viene* [here it comes] all week *porque me bajo mi regla*" [I got my period] and my grandmother starts freaking out. *Qué porque* [Why] she told me, "*hay de esas cosas no se hablan muchachita*" [young lady, you don't talk about these things] and I'm like, I'm like "*una, estoy hablando con mi amá*" [first of all, I am speaking with my mom]. I don't mean to be disrespectful, but that was very . . . that was very awkward to me, you know . . . I was like, "Lady, I don't know why you're flipping out and this happens every month you know, and until you hit

menopause it was happening to you too, okay?" . . . Later on they both explained to me that . . . she [grandmother] was very much raised with the belief that "if you can't talk about it in church, you can't talk about it anywhere else."

In her classic book *The Second Sex*, French feminist philosopher Simone de Beauvoir (1949) wrote: "One is not born, but rather becomes, a woman." How exactly do we learn to become women? How did Anita's grandmother learn to become a woman, and how was she attempting to socialize Anita into womanhood by reprimanding her for discussing what she thought as an inappropriate topic? Anita is one example of how many young women have transgressed the Church's taboo about the menstrual cycle.

Her experience has multiple layers revealing the complexity and the extent of the taboo. Among many Mexican families, the kitchen has a quasi-religious and familial value.[1] It is not only the place where people come as a family to eat but the place where older women (usually grandmothers) share and pass on religious traditions and other stories over meals or food preparation. The practice of this type of sharing is referred to as *religión casera* (Elizondo 2003) or *abuelita theology* (Cadena 1995).

From the grandmother's perspective, Anita was not only imprudent in telling her mother that she had gotten her menstrual period, but she said it in the kitchen. Respect, for Anita's grandmother, meant not engaging in conversation about the body (menstruation, sex, sexuality) because it was wrong in the eyes of God. Anita could not understand why her grandmother was so upset about something that happens to every woman; as she said, it also happened to her grandmother when she was younger. This is one example of two women's views about the female body, from distinct generations, colliding because they learned to be women in different ways, time periods, and geographical locations (Anita grew up in the United States and her grandmother south of the US-México border). One generation is still demonstrating the obedience and respect described in the preceding chapter. For *Las Damas* as well as for Anita's grandmother, keeping silent about the menstrual cycle was central to a Mexican Catholic imagination driven by the belief that "if you cannot talk about it in church, you cannot talk about it anywhere." The other generation was driven more by a Chicana feminist worldview that did not shy away from naming and questioning the elephant of silence in the room.

I begin with the above anecdote because it brings to light generational differences. Anita's grandmother grew up at approximately the same time that *Las Damas* did, when respect meant censoring; respect meant silencing; respect meant keeping your questions or concerns about your own body and its anatomy to yourself, which meant that they were rarely, if ever, answered. Anita's grandmother was not able to understand why her granddaughter was violating the code of conduct *para las señoritas* (for young ladies) prescribed by the Catholic Church.

Furthermore, the sense of shame about women's bodies is part of a larger history. Mexican American Catholic theologian Virgilio Elizondo (2007, 164) argues that the sense of shame "for being *indio, mestizo, mulatto*" imposed on Latin America's conquered people was, and continues to be, one of the most devastating consequences of the conquest. It "brands the soul, in a way worse and more permanent than a branding of the master's mark with a hot iron on the face" (Elizondo 2007, 164). Building on Elizondo, I contend that for Latina women, this sense of shame not only has a particular race, color, and phenotype, it is also gendered, relegating women to a life of complete or selective silence about their bodies, sex, and sexuality. Consequently, this sense of shame within the context of a kyriarchal Mexican Catholic imagination has placed women in the role of involuntary perpetrators of their own mental and physical subordination. Through the use of silence and shame, the female body has traditionally been policed by society and religion (in this case, Catholicism) and highly monitored by mothers (or grandmothers, as in Anita's case). This silence is usually enveloped in messages about morality. As we have seen in Chapters 3 and 4, the morality they are socialized to abide by is ruled by male authority and leaves no room for questions or even acknowledgment of the changes in their bodies as they go through puberty.

Some scholars may contend that this taboo around puberty has to do more with Mexican culture, and allude to the role religion plays in this type of socialization. Others may recognize that religion plays a significant part, but fail to investigate to what extent. For example, Chicana/Latina social science feminist scholarship acknowledges that the Catholic Church has always been an active participant in women's subordination, particularly on issues of the body.[2] However, how exactly this takes place remains unanswered, for the most part. This chapter builds on the *café con leche* framework discussed in Chapter 1, which emphasized that culture cannot be separated from religion. Expanding on the insights of that chapter, I demonstrate that *Las Damas, Las Madres,* and *Las Mujeres* learned to become *señoritas* within a Mexican Catholic imagination in which, early on in childhood, they were socialized into a culture of respect that not only defined a girl's self-worth but also set the stage for a culture of silence about puberty, sex, and sexuality.

Another aspect of Latinx culture that is operating here is *Marianismo*.[3] *Marianismo* as originally defined by Stevens and Pescatello (1973) refers to the socialization of girls into a set of religiocultural beliefs that women should be submissive to men. The term derives from the name María— the name of the Virgin Mary of Nazareth, who in the Catholic Church has been given the following characteristics: submissive, loving, all-accepting, suffering, all-enduring, and pious. These characteristics, as we have seen, have also been assigned to Our Lady of Guadalupe.[4] These attributes have been disseminated in the front and back stage (Goffman 1959). The front stage includes the Church via sermons and catechism, and popular culture via TV commercials, soap operas, and print media; the back stage is found in girls' homes through their parents (Villegas et al. 2010).[5]

Marianismo functions at many levels. On one hand, the characteristics that have been assigned to Our Lady of Guadalupe are detrimental to women's sense of self by giving them second-class status. However on the other hand, the women in this study find some of these qualities (i.e., loving and all-accepting) to be an indication that Our Lady of Guadalupe will never reject them. Their mothers and grandmothers socialized them to believe and have faith in an all-loving and ever-present *Virgen de Guadalupe*. While it may be life-giving and affirming for these women to interpret Our Lady of Guadalupe as loving and all-accepting, these characteristics have a double edge; they are associated with "all-enduring, suffering, and pious" and are used as examples by the Church and society alike as characteristics that women should emulate (see also Hardin 2002; Villegas et al. 2010). Such portrayals reinforce traditional gender roles and place women in a binary where on one end is *La Virgen de Guadalupe* and on the other is the whore represented by Hernán Cortés's translator, the Nahua woman named Malinche.[6]

This chapter will focus on puberty as experienced in each cohort. However, the analysis of *Las Damas* will move beyond this life stage and include testimonies about their wedding night and first pregnancy. These stages are indicative of the end of puberty; yet psychologically, *Las Damas* never fully reached puberty, and consequently these stages left emotional scars. Though *Las Madres* have also gone through the above-mentioned phases, they did not share with me their experiences. I suspect that *Las Damas* were more inclined to share with me these particular aspects of their lives because the age gap between us was significantly greater. I was also a newlywed at the time of the interviews, and I believe that being married was my passport to enter and get to know more of their private lives.

Becoming Señoritas
Las Damas

By the time *Las Damas* entered their teenage years, their Mexican Catholic imagination was increasingly influenced by the teachings they learned from their parents on obedience and respect. Through this learning process *Las Damas* were socialized into a Mexican Catholic imagination that reinforced a kyriarchal system. That is, a way of life in which women's second-class status was a by-product of male socio-religious, political, and economic power over women, causing them to become victims and victimizers of each other.

Las Damas were taught about the importance of respecting God, the Church, family, adults, themselves, and those in positions of authority, which were mostly men. They were taught that "*a los adultos no se les levanta la voz*" meaning, when talking to adults you do not raise your voice, and that "*con Dios no se reniega*," that is, you don't complain to God. When inside the Church, they were expected to behave and dress properly, for it was the house of God. While this expectation may be perceived as a general rule across gender, race/ethnicity, class, geographical location, time, and religious traditions, there was more to it. Women were held more accountable than men. Besides, the priest, as representative of God, also deserved reverence, and one way of demonstrating this was by kissing his hand when greeting him.

In the family, the father, older brothers, and adults deserved utmost respect, and this also included kissing their hand when greeting them. As for respecting themselves, this meant behaving properly, being obedient, and not talking to boys, much less playing with them. Once a young woman became engaged, she was not allowed to go out to *fiestas* or social gatherings. She was not to talk to younger girls or single young women her age, because by having gotten engaged she was now considered to have entered the adult stage of her life. I argue that this was a way of preventing young or single women from asking the engaged young woman questions about "adult" topics—meaning puberty, sex, and sexuality. Within this imagination they learned to perceive themselves as subordinate to men.

From the time of puberty onward, the female body was perceived as an object of temptation capable of inciting men to commit illicit acts against them. It was a Catholic culture in which women were blamed for men's uncontrollable sexual desire. Therefore, when girls reached puberty they had to conceal their bodies as much as possible by vesting the body and the psyche with definitions of demureness that limited their sense of self in literally painful ways. Ester (age 76) recalls:

> You see, it was so different for us when we became young women [during puberty]. I think I became a young woman around 13 years of age. My mom made us our brassieres, and our breasts could not show because it was wrong to show men our breasts, it was a sin, very tight like this. I would begin to notice, you know, other girls at school [that were also developing] and my [mother] would tell us, "Oh no, not you, all of you have to be this way" . . . and I would say "Holy mother, it hurts."[7]

Ester and the other *Damas* grew up at a time when brassieres consisted of long pieces of fabric that were used to wrap young women's breasts, particularly among working-class families. Ester said that these pieces of cloth had to be tight, and it was painful, but she understood that it was not proper to show their developing breasts because *"era malo"* (it was bad), and therefore according to her *"era un pecado"* (it was also a sin). Ester also shared with me that when she became an adult and got married, she felt a little more comfortable talking to her mother about the practice of breast-binding. She would often joke by telling her, *"por eso no me crecierón porque tú me las apretates* [laughs and then in a more serious tone added] *pues sí es muy duro"* (that is why they [breasts] never grew, because you bound them tight; it was very hard). The emphasis on *recato* (modesty) made *Las Damas* believe that they had to conceal their developing breasts because it was disrespectful and bad in the eyes of God and the Church, and this made them feel uncomfortable and embarrassed about their developing bodies.

The feeling of embarrassment experienced by *Las Damas* was the result of deeper and complex social dynamics at work. Reflecting back on their mothers' attempt to conceal their bodies, *Las Damas* told me that now they understood that part of reason was that their mothers wanted to protect them from the possibility of being *robadas*. That is, it was an act of protection against the possibility of being abducted with the end of nonconsensual marriage. If we recall Artemia's story, she was *robada* and forced to marry at the age of 14. Therefore, by concealing their daughters' developing breasts the mothers hoped that men would perceive their daughters as children who had not yet reached puberty.

However, their attempt to protect their daughters instilled in the girls a sense of shame for their developing bodies that consequently reinforced the notion in them that the female body had the potential to incite men to sin. Moreover, this was not the only way women were made to feel embarrassment over their bodies. If we recall, the Catholic Church had its own ways of policing the female body by requiring the use of the *mantilla* when inside the Church. According to *Las Damas*, not wearing a mantilla gave the impression that women went to mass "*para exhibirse*," in other words, to attract attention.[8] In binding their daughters' breasts, were the mothers exercising their creative agency to protect their daughters against a socio-religious system that perceived women as sites of temptation, or were the mothers only reinforcing the notion of women as provocateurs?

For *Las Damas*, the coming of age and the type of "presentation of self" (Goffman 1959) that was involved was a physically and psychologically painful process imposed by the Church and society, and reinforced by their mothers and grandmothers. It implied the negation of one's femininity, first, for the grace of God, and second, for acceptance in a Catholic culture and society that in general had an inflexible definition and image of proper girlhood and by extension womanhood. However, even with the multiple ways the female body was policed, young girls found creative ways to exercise their agency.

One way some of *Las Damas* challenged the status quo when they were teenagers was by folding their sleeves or skirts at the waist to make them short when their mothers or family were not around. For example, Irma's (age 76) mother was very strict and did not permit her to wear sleeves above the elbow, but she nevertheless found ways to contravene her mother's orders. When she went out to play with her friends or was on her way back from school, in order to fit in with her friends who did just the same, Irma would fold her sleeves back as far as she could (which was not too far past the elbow, since the sleeves were tight). Before she got home, however, she would always undo the folds so she would not get in trouble. Whether it was folding their sleeves or rolling up their skirts, the women talked about these experiences as heroic acts of agency against the status quo, even within a social structure that had fixed definitions of modesty.

The framing of female reproductive organs as shameful has been one of the most marginalizing Church teachings for women.[9] Women's bodies have been articulated as impure and filthy due to their menstrual cycle.[10] Historically, menstruation has been considered a filthy taboo in Christianity.[11] As late as 1972, Pope Paul VI prohibited young women from serving as lectors and acolytes "out of veneration for the traditional prohibition against menstruants at the altar" (Phipps 1980, 300). It was not until 1994 that girls were allowed by the Vatican to assist as altar servers at liturgical celebrations, but it was not mandatory; therefore, priests have the power to negate this right to girls if they so choose.

The definitions and significance attached to menstruation by men are enveloped in an androcentric fear of "women's bodiliness and sexuality, and women's blood in particular has been prey to suspicion and anxiety" (Green 2009, 15). Men's suspicion and anxiety about something they cannot control has been a key underlying reason for women's second-class status within Christianity (Green 2009).

Therefore, if the menstrual cycle is dirty and filthy, and this part of women's life cycle is unavoidable, then it should be hidden and silenced. Consequently, the belief that *Las Damas* developed in the early stages of puberty about the need to asexualize their bodies, as evidenced by Ester, only grew deeper as they experienced their first menstrual cycle, leaving *Las Damas* with deeper feelings of shame and embarrassment for a natural body function that they cannot control.[12] For this reason, I contend that the sense of shame that Elizondo (2007) talks about is gendered, and thus has different implications for women. One of the most atrocious beliefs that some women of Mexican origin have inherited is shame toward the source of their own life-giving power—menstruation.

Religious-based misconceptions and misinformation about women's menstrual cycle and bodies in general have percolated into women's psyches for centuries, directly and indirectly, through Church-sanctified silence about puberty. That is, a modest and demure Catholic girl never talks about her developing body. Unaware of the biblical textual tradition that has framed the menstrual cycle as unholy, the women have inherited a Mexican Catholic imagination that denies them the right to know their own bodies. This type of Catholic imagination has taught women to feel shame in the name of God. What is more, social science research among women of Mexican origin demonstrates that for this ethnic group, instead of being a celebration of life itself, menstruation is a source of shame—a forbidden topic among mothers and daughters.[13] This privatization has psychologically affected generations of Mexican-origin women.[14]

In their teenage years, being Catholic not only meant strict dress codes and the expectation of obedience, but also the cloak of silence and shame

around issues of the body. Rosario had her first menstrual period at the age
of 12. Frightened, Rosario told her grandmother and great-grandmother.

> I was scared, I thought I was going to die. I told my grandma and
> great-grandmother and they began to cry, they took me to the river,
> bathed me, and they prayed for me. Then they took me to the Our
> Lady of Guadalupe home altar [we had] and they told me you are
> now a little woman, but that was it. They did not tell me anything
> else. I didn't know . . . I didn't know and I had to learn all by myself.[15]

While Rosario did tell her grandmother and great-grandmother what had
happened to her, she did not receive any information about what was
occurring to her body, and seeing them cry scared her even more. The
forbidden nature of any discussion of the menstrual cycle at the time led
to the privatization of this part of women's life course. Young girls themselves did not have access to information, making this healthy sign of maturation a traumatic experience that they kept to themselves and prayed to
La Virgen for it to stop.

Las Damas prayed to *La Virgen de Guadalupe* for the "illness," as they
put it, to go away. At this stage in their life cycle, this was their way to
escape the silence around the menses. The menstrual cycle was not seen
as a positive, natural part of a young woman's life. Instead, it carried a
stigma to the degree that young girls had no access to information about
this life stage, and it was perceived as an illness—thus, the term "sick" was
not unusual—that they prayed to *La Virgen* for it to soon go away.[16] One
explanation may be that since the silence that surrounded the menstrual
cycle was prevalent when *Las Damas* had their first cycle, they assumed
that they actually were ill.

The taboo and silence around the menstrual cycle that Rosario experienced was such that even at the age of 65 she did not fully understand it. One
day when I went to visit the senior center she pulled me aside and told me:

> There is something I just found out and because you are already
> married I am thinking it is important for you to know, so you won't
> be so closed off like me. Did you know that men do not get sick?
> I did not know, but my boyfriend told me yesterday.[17]

At the moment, I did not know how to respond to her question. All I could
do was to reaffirm that what she had told me was something very important

and thank her for sharing this with me. What she meant by "men do not get sick" was that men do not menstruate, as I explain below. Rosario had six grown sons, and up until her boyfriend told her, she was under the assumption—since she never asked—that they menstruated just like her daughters. That Rosario found out this late in her life that men do not menstruate is a consequence of keeping important information regarding health and the reproductive system from girls growing up at the time of *Las Damas*. Though she could have asked these questions later in her adult life, she did not, because she was socialized to think of such questions as improper. Rosario told me that she has many questions but has not had the courage to ask. Most importantly, pulling me to the side and telling me that men do not menstruate is an example of Rosario's determination to break the cycle of silence and taboo around menses.[18]

When I asked Josefa (age 77) if her mother had told her about the menstrual cycle before it happened, she was quick to respond:

> No, no, it was not the custom, it was not the custom . . . . NOOO when I got sick [menstruated], I got so scared. Even after a year since [it first happened] I did not tell my mom, anything . . . . A woman who [out of the goodness of her heart, since we were many kids, sometimes] used to help [my mom] with the laundry, she was the one who told me. She said, "you are going to get sick and give me your . . . to wash them." We did not have Kotex at the time; we used cloths . . . . You didn't talk about that with your mother . . . practically your mom never talked about that . . . . It was not like today that the little ones know everything, even more than us.[19]

Johnson & Johnson first introduced sanitary pads in 1896. However, *Las Damas* came from working class families and lived in small or rural towns. Therefore, they did not have access, and even if they did, they could not afford to buy them. Instead, they used rags or stuffed old socks with pieces of cloth. These impromptu sanitary pads were washed and reused.

While silence about menses predominated in the era of *Las Damas'* youth, there were some exceptions. Two of the women with whom I spoke did receive some information about menses: Luz Elena (age 55) from her eldest sister, and Olivia (age 57) from her mother, and in Olivia's case she referred to it by the term "menstruation" as opposed to "being sick." One explanation for their greater awareness may be that they were among the youngest in *Las Damas* cohort, meaning they lived at a time when the general culture was becoming less silent about it. Still, information about menses did not take place until the first menstrual cycle. Luz Elena stated that her sister took on the role of mother and told her about the menstrual cycle. The oldest sister was usually responsible for helping the parents— mainly the mother—with household chores and raising younger siblings. The eldest daughter in many ways played the role of surrogate mother, the mediator between her younger siblings and mother, as Luz Elena's experience demonstrates.

By contrast, Olivia was the only one whose mother told her (and her sisters) about the menstrual cycle—but again, not until the day that it first happened. Olivia's mother was open because her own mother never told her anything. When Olivia's mother menstruated for the first time, she was in bed for two days. When her mother (Olivia's grandmother) asked her "*¿Por qué estás en cama?*" (Why are you in bed?), Olivia's mother responded "*Estoy enferma mamá, estoy enferma*" (I'm sick mom, I'm sick), then she added, "*No sé mamá mire como estoy*" (I don't know mom, look at me). Olivia's mother was scared and confused because her mother had never told her anything about the different stages of puberty until she menstruated for the first time. Reflecting on her mother's experience with her own first menstrual cycle, Olivia says, "it is bad not to tell your daughters."

Because her mother shared with Olivia her own experience, Olivia recognized early on how important it is to tell daughters about menstruation. Olivia's experience is an example of the ways in which silence about the menses in this older cohort was not necessarily fixed. Some women were determined to give their daughters a greater sense of normalcy about maturation.

Las Madres

Nonetheless, *Las Madres'* socioreligious construction of the self carried on many of the beliefs and assumptions about the female body that were expressed by *Las Damas*. As with the previous group, issues about sex, sexuality, and the female anatomy were absent in discussions between *Las Madres* and their own mothers when they were growing up. Like *Las Damas*, *Las Madres* came from very traditional Catholic families where certain topics were not discussed.

A central belief that *Las Madres* learned from their parents was the importance of respecting their bodies. When they reached puberty, this translated into not asking "inappropriate" questions—not even of their own mothers—particularly if they had to do with women's maturation. With the exception of three *Madres*, menstruation was never mentioned, neither before nor after it happened. As one of *Las Madres* (Mereides, age 47) put it, "*de eso no se hablaba en ese tiempo*" (you never talked about it back then). When I asked why it was never talked about, I received a typical answer from María (age 36): "*Porque daba vergüenza hablar de esas cosas, era malo*" (because it was embarrassing to talk about those things, it was bad).

Las Madres, like the earlier generation, learned about menstruation the day of their first cycle. Some spoke of their experience with their first menstrual cycle as frightening: "*Yo pensaba que me iba a desangrar toda y morir*" (I thought I was going to bleed to death; Eva, age 44). Most of the women did not go to their mothers for an explanation of what was happening to their bodies. They were too embarrassed and scared that they might be reprimanded for having done something to cause the bleeding.

In a few cases their mothers did make some remarks about menstruation, but it was a brief and hesitant conversation that did not take place until the day the daughters' menstrual period began. Julia (age 24, one of the youngest in the cohort), who was raised by her grandmother, recounts that the day she first got her menstrual cycle she got very scared and ran to tell her mother. Her mother's response was, "That happens to women; you are not a girl anymore, and you cannot be going around jumping and running. Put something on and don't bathe until it goes away."[20]

Julia shared that she cried a lot that day because she still wanted to be a girl. She was only 12 years old, and she loved to play, run, and jump around; yet, according to her mother, she could no longer do any of those physical activities because it was inappropriate for a young woman.

Similarly, Raquel (age 46), who was significantly older than Julia, shared the same experience and did not know about the menstrual cycle until the day that it happened.

> One time in the evening I was playing and I got hurt . . . I was playing *al señor quemado* [loosely translated as "playing chase"] and I ran for the ball and I tripped with the sidewalk and hit my stomach. The next day I woke up and I was sick [menstruating] and my mom was the one who noticed, I didn't even notice myself, and then that was when she told me, but just that day. I was 11, I do remember that.[21]

Here is another instance of the use of the term "sick" to refer to the menstrual cycle, even among *Las Madres* generation.

Candelaria's (age 39) experience was different from the rest of the Madres. She told her father and not her mother the day she menstruated for the first time, because she felt closer to him. Candelaria recounts:

> It never crossed my mind to tell my mom, nor my grandmothers, because back then one did not have the freedom to ask questions, nor to express what we felt or wanted. They had power over us. When I first got my period I remember that time I told my dad what had happened to me. And he told me, "Oh, that is nothing, just put something on and that's it." But I was very scared and very worried. I bathed and bathed and bathed myself and it wouldn't go away. I would then ask myself, what is going to happen to me? Until I put something on, because back then we had nothing to put on, you didn't go to the store to buy . . . no. And then I put something on and that is how I began to learn all by myself.[22]

In some ways, perhaps the father's response could be seen as more normalizing, though still inadequate. *Las Madres* (with the exception of the younger ones), like *Las Damas*, used old rags as sanitary pads. The overt and covert messages women received about the menstrual cycle as dirty and impure led women not to be open with their own daughters about this central part of their lives. Consequently, *Las Madres* in most cases had no one to turn to for orientation and had to learn on their own by trial and error.[23] However, in the midst of the silence and shame that surrounded the menstrual cycle, women have transgressed such taboos.

Las Madres were never explicitly told about the vulnerability to pregnancy that came with the menstrual cycle. Instead, as demonstrated in the previous chapter, they received coded messages about the importance of behaving in a respectful, "ladylike" way. Beatriz's (age 34) case was also different from the rest of *Las Madres*. When she menstruated for the first time (at age 15), she got very scared because she did not know what was happening; no one had ever told her. When she told her mother, the latter broke out in mocking laughter, making Beatriz feel belittled. In her words,

> When I told my mom about three days after it had happened she just laughed, and it made me feel dumb. Do you understand what I mean? That time I remember I got frustrated because I thought

instead of encouraging me it seemed more like she just threw me on the ground. I was 15 when I first got my period and I did not know yet.[24]

Beatriz's mother opted to make fun of what was happening to her daughter so as to not make a big issue of it, not knowing that this deeply hurt her daughter.

Las Mujeres

Among *Las Mujeres*, compared to the experience of *Las Damas* and *Las Madres*, I found that their mothers were much more open (to varying degrees) about women's life cycles such as menses. However, the importance attached to the hymen was what their mothers emphasized the most. Women's virginity has been rhetorically framed as a symbol of honor, grace, modesty, and purity—qualities that have always been associated with the ideal woman. Thus, only the virginal, graceful, honorable woman who is modest in her attire, language, and character is worthy of the respect of others and of marrying "*por todas las leyes*" (by all the laws), meaning both civil law and Catholic canon law.

In traditional families, a woman's virginity functions as the family's badge of honor. Thus, the families with daughters that are *muchachas de su casa* (young women of the home)—that is, virgins who attend to household chores and are conventional in their dress, makeup, and beliefs (to the knowledge of their parents and community, at least)—are respected in their communities; their daughters are held up as role models to be emulated by other girls. This set of qualities is rooted in a type of *Marianismo* mentality that places women on a "pedestal" to the detriment of their subjectivity as sexual beings.

In the present time, however, the taboo of the menstrual cycle is not as strong as in *Las Damas*' and *Las Madres*' generations. Television ads for sanitary pads and tampons are significantly more graphic than they were two decades ago, and (unlike previous generations) young girls are taught about the menstrual cycle and sexuality in elementary school, particularly in the United States. Popular and accessible websites like http://beingirl.com, which targets 12- and 13-year-old girls, is one way Procter and Gamble advertises its sanitary products. What is more, there is an array of apps for the smartphone, only a tap away, to track the menstrual cycle. In spite of all the information now available online, what is most important is the conversation that takes place between mothers and daughters. However, most of the mothers of *Las Mujeres* were very brief, and the type of information that was passed on focused on the importance of making sure the hymen remained intact until marriage. For example, their mothers used conversations about women's menses as an opportunity to discourage their daughters from using tampons, as Rosita's case illustrates.

When Rosita (age 20) menstruated for the first time, she already knew what was happening to her because, like the rest of *Las Mujeres*, she had learned about the menstrual cycle at school. However, Rosita's experience with her first menstrual cycle was similar to that of *Las Madres*, for her mother felt uncomfortable talking to her about menstruation. According to Rosita, when it happened, her mother "mentioned it a little bit *pero casi no*" (but not really). Her mother was hesitant to talk to her about menstruation and what to expect, and thus opted to mention it only briefly. Rosita believes that it was because her mother was embarrassed to talk about it. However, she did strongly advise her against the use of tampons because they could cause Rosita to "lose" her virginity. Rosita recounts:

> I remember her talking about like . . . when you get your period, don't use Tampax [tampons], and then like she was like "oh no, no, not [until] after, you know, you get married and you lose your virginity" . . . I don't remember exactly *como lo dijo* [how she said it], *que* [that] it rips or whatever, I think that's what she said, but it was very brief.

Rosita was not the only one whose mother warned her against the use of tampons. Of the 15 women I interviewed, 12 shared similar experiences. The warning always came qualified with the phrase *"no los uses hasta que te cases"* (do not use them until you get married). However, some of the young women whose mothers opposed the use of tampons used them anyway because, as Teresa (age 20) said, "tampons are so much more comfortable and cleaner." From their mothers' perspective, if their daughters' hymen became broken then no man would want to marry them because technically they were no longer virgins. Similarly, Hurtado (2003a), in her study among young Chicanas, found that young Latinas were also discouraged from using tampons by their mothers for the same reason.

This concern about having an intact hymen relates to the Mexican Catholic imagination that holds young women accountable to the ideal image of the virgin bride. Traditionally, in Mexican families on both sides of the US–México border, mothers and not fathers are responsible for raising children, particularly girls. Therefore, if a young woman becomes pregnant out of wedlock, the mother and not the father is blamed for not raising the daughter with strong religious and moral family values. The mother is often accused of "allowing" the daughter to *manchar el nombre de la familia* (dishonor the family's name).[25]

In *Las Damas'* generation if a woman's hymen ripped before marriage (whether because she engaged in a sexual act or for non-sex-related reasons such as injury), her husband had the right to return her to her parents under the justification that she was "not pure." In the case of *Las Mujeres*, their mothers warned them that if they used tampons before marriage it could lead to a life of suffering, for the husband would always doubt whether or not his wife engaged in a sexual relationship with another man, before marriage.

Most families on both sides of the US–México border, particularly in urban areas, no longer adhere to such beliefs. Nonetheless, the sense of shame for not being pure remains present at varying degrees among women who have not only "betrayed" their most valuable attribute—virginity—but also the family, and above all God and the Church.[26] Among *Las Mujeres*, I also found that both parents attempted to monitor their daughters' bodies by instilling fear and shame in the young women. Dolores (age 19) recounts:

> My parents, they are still talking about it. "Oh, you have to main-
> tain yourself pure until you marry because if you don't this and this
> will happen . . . . If you do not want to suffer, then don't do it." Yes,
> always.

Instilling fear about the unhappy life they would lead if they were to become sexually active (not to mention pregnant) before marriage is a common way the parents of *Las Mujeres* reinforced the need to remain virginal before marriage.

Another way parents instill fear among their daughters is by telling them that people can easily tell if a woman is a virgin just by looking at her. Manuela (age 24) shared the following:

> Nobody talks about it in my family, like I said in the focus group.
> I don't remember my mom sitting me down and giving me the
> "sex talk." Never. I do know that it is very important for her. I do

remember her being like "when you have sex, I'm going to know because you are going to lose that sparkle in your eyes" or some cheesy line like that . . . . Or, "You can tell because your hips are going to get bigger" and when my time came up . . . I was like oh, my God, she knows . . . [laughs].

Being told that people can notice whether a young woman is a virgin by simply looking at her was very common among the participants; Conchita (age 21), Elena (age 21), and Teresa (age 20), for example, had very similar experiences. However, though *Las Mujeres* felt respect for their parents, particularly their mothers, they nonetheless questioned such beliefs. Manuela continues:

> You know I don't think that you being a virgin or not makes you less of a woman or of a lesser value . . . . I don't want to say that it's like [a] rite of passage . . . you know it happens, but it happens, I don't think I am less of a woman because I'm not. I don't agree with that being so important, unfortunately in our religion and our culture that's the standard of approval . . . . Everybody wants . . . you know, the whole thing that if you are not a *señorita* you cannot get married in white, I don't agree with that. But I still consider myself a religious person.

Manuela, who identifies as Catholic, disagrees with the Catholic tradition of remaining a virgin before marriage, yet at the same time she considers herself a religious person. Her multilayered relationship with the Catholic Church attests to the selective engagement with Catholicism that is evident among *Las Mujeres*. While these women disagree with many of the Church's teachings, they nonetheless consider themselves Catholic and borrow heavily on Catholic teachings to nurture their devotion to *La Virgen de Guadalupe*, as I demonstrate in the next chapter.

Becoming Women in the Time of Las Damas

Paradoxically, in Christian tradition women have been considered physically and mentally weak and yet powerful enough to seduce men to sin. This view of the female body is not surprising, given early Christianity's obsession with the flesh–spirit divide, which defined the spirit as pure and the body impure. Unfortunately, this social construction of the essence of the female person was not only a central aspect of early Christianity but also the lens through which, to this day, Christianity understands humanity, and in particular human sexuality (De La Torre 2007, 52).

As mentioned earlier in the chapter, some of *Las Damas* shared with me their experience on their wedding night and first pregnancy. At the time when the women reached adulthood, the belief that it was not proper for a Catholic woman to ask questions about sex or sexuality was common in Catholic families. One consequence of this is that older Latinas today, for the most part, know very little about the reproductive system and sexuality. Not all the women I interviewed were open about their first sexual experiences; however, based on the testimonies of those who trusted me enough to share it, I suspect that the majority of the women in *Las Damas* group did not experience pleasure on their first sexual encounter.

At the time these women entered adulthood, young women married knowing nothing about sexual intercourse. Take the example of Olivia (age 57); she was the only one of the cohort of women in my study whose mother told her about the menstrual cycle.[27] However, while Olivia's mother was open with her about the menstrual cycle, she did not talk to her about sex, which made Olivia's first sexual encounter with her husband far from pleasurable. Olivia was engaged to a man who she said was the love of her life. She was looking forward to her wedding, but little did she know that this was going to be an unforgettable experience for other reasons.

The morning after her wedding, Olivia ran to her parents' house and, terrified, told her mother that the devil had possessed her husband: "*Mami, a mi esposo se le metió el diablo.*" Fearful, crying, and hoping to get answers from her mother, Olivia was shocked when her mother replied that she should not speak that way about her husband. Olivia's husband added, "*Suegrita, mire lo que Olivia dice de mí?*" (Dear mother-in-law, do you hear what Olivia is saying about me?). Olivia reiterated that the devil had possessed her husband, but her mother's reply was the same. Thus, even though her mother was open about women's menses, she never told Olivia what to expect the day of her wedding. Neither Olivia's mother nor anyone else had told Olivia about sexual intercourse. She married knowing nothing about sex, hence her reaction to her first sexual experience with her husband. Another of *Las Damas* shared with me that on her wedding night, when her husband wanted to have sexual intercourse with her, she was so scared (because she thought he was going to hurt her) that "*cuando se me acercaba corría de un lado del cuarto' pal otro, 'pos uno no sabía nada*" (when he got close to me I ran from one side of the room to the other, for one did not know anything).

Many Catholic women, particularly those of lower economic status (as was the case for the women in my study), knew very little about sex or sexuality when they got married. If we recall, Rosario did not know that men do not menstruate until much later in life. Silence around the body and human sexuality has had consequences for women's health. Working-class older Latinas are less likely to get breast exams or Pap smears compared to older white women from the same class status. According to a recent study published in 2012, Latinas "ages 65 and older are less likely than Caucasians to participate in cancer screening services," and one of the central factors has to do with cultural and religious values (Maramaldi et al. 2012, 537). This is not surprising when the Catholic Church, obsessed with sanctifying virginity, vests women's ignorance about sexuality with a "purity" veil. Women are thus socialized to think that the degree of purity (i.e., unawareness about sexuality) they possess represents the level of commitment and love they have for God and the Church.

From the Catholic Church's point of view at the time, Olivia was pure of heart and mind when she had her first sexual encounter with her husband; however, I contend that her first sexual encounter seriously traumatized her, causing the experience to ultimately feel like rape instead of pleasure. In Christianity not only the degree of unawareness about human sexuality but also the rejection of sexual pleasure for the most part has been an indicator of the extent of a person's faithfulness to God (De La Torre 2007). Too often the Church's concept of pleasure has split the body from the spirit—the forbidden (body) from the embraced (spirit) (Rivera 2010). Isasi-Díaz (1992) contends that too often, the Church and society alike have defined pleasure as a forbidden sensation if it has to do with the body and sexuality. For this reason she calls for the need to rethink pleasure and what it means for the body as a whole—the physical and the spiritual—for this can "cure the trauma most women, not only Hispanas/Latinas, suffer" (Isasi-Díaz 1992, 52).

In a conversation with a colleague about Latinas and sexuality, he shared with me a story that clearly demonstrates the trauma Isasi-Díaz (1992) speaks about.

Susana grew up in a traditional Mexican Catholic household where sex and sexuality were never discussed, and she honorably complied with every expectation that her family had of her as she grew and matured.

When she became engaged, she had questions about what was going to happen on her wedding night but did not dare to ask anyone, much less her own mother. When the wedding day finally arrived, Susana was excited because she was going to marry the man she loved, but she was hesitant at the same time because she had no idea what to expect on her wedding night. She thought to herself, today for sure my mother is going to tell me what to expect. She became very anxious as the time neared for the ceremony.

Finally, to her surprise, instead of her mother her godmother walked into the room where she was getting dressed and asked all the other women to leave the room. Susana felt somewhat relieved, for finally somebody was going to talk to her about what to expect. To her dismay, Susana's godmother told her that on her wedding night all she had to do was to get under the sheets, pray, and close her eyes and *"dejar lo que tenga que pasar"* (let happen what needs to happen). She felt let down and scared at the same time. Instead of getting answers to her many questions, she felt more scared and more confused than before. This was the only information she received on sexuality, and it came only moments before her wedding ceremony.

Consequently, instead of looking forward to her wedding night, she was fearful—for her godmother never told her why she needed to close her eyes and pray or what was going to happen. According to Susana, she had done everything right, followed all the moral rules and family expectations, and could not understand why information about sex and sexuality was kept from her when she most needed it. Though Susana's experience was far from joyful, she has been able to transcend the silence in which the topics of sex and sexuality are enveloped. Reflecting back on her experience with her daughter in mind, she said, *"Ya no más, hasta aquí"* (no more, from here on), meaning she was not going to let this happen to her daughter.[28] Susana's account, like Olivia's, is a case of potentially pleasurable experience turning into the type of trauma Isasi-Díaz suggests is the result of the silence about sexuality and sexual pleasure in the Church and society. At the same time, Susana's testimony suggests that what women learn from within this Catholic imagination is not static but always in flux and open to reinterpretation.

As some of the women reached adulthood and got married, they continued to suffer the consequences of silence about the body as they were getting ready to be mothers for the first time. Josefa (age 77) became pregnant with her first child at the age of 18. Throughout her pregnancy she believed that she was going to give birth through her belly button, for that was what her mother had told her. A couple of weeks before Josefa gave birth, an elderly woman who was a midwife asked her if she was prepared for the birth of her child. Seeing Josefa's confusion, the elderly woman proceeded to explain the birthing process to her. When Josefa heard that she was going to give birth to her child vaginally, she was terrified, and began to cry. During the interview she told me

> Well, how do you think I felt? That my child was going to be born out of a place so filthy. I thought my child was going to be born from my belly button. No, no, I cried and cried all night.[29]

Josefa had never been told by her mother or anyone else how babies were born. At the time *Las Damas* were growing up, children were unaware how babies were born, and their mothers found creative ways to obfuscate where babies come from. Artemia (age 67), the woman who was abducted as a child, had a similar experience. She grew up thinking that babies came from frogs. In our interview Artemia shared about the day she went with her mother to the river to wash clothes and found a frog. She took the frog to her mother and told her that she was now going to have a sibling since she had caught a frog. She said that her mother smiled and said nothing. Unfortunately, Artemia also had a traumatizing experience when she became pregnant by her abductor. Throughout her pregnancy she was very confused, because she thought to herself, "*si los bebés vienen de las ranitas, ¿cómo, entonces, una ranita entró dentro de mí?*" (If babies come from frogs, how then did a frog get inside me?). Scared and confused, she did not want to have her child because she thought she was going to die in the process of giving birth. In her words,

> I thought that my stomach was going to rip open and that was how my child was going to be born, until the mother of my husband told me that my child was going to be born from a little hole and [in shock] I said no. I cried all day and all night.[30]

Though her experience was full of confusion, fear, and silence about sexuality, Artemia was not only one of the most outspoken women I interviewed but also self-identified as feminist. For example, unlike the other *Damas*, she was the only one who openly admitted to having used birth control when she was younger.

Rosario (age 65) and Esperanza (age 68) were the only women from the group that were born and raised in the United States. Nonetheless, each had different views about sex. Rosario's grandfather married her off at the age of 13 to a 20-year-old man whom she did not know. She and her husband had a total of 12 children. Many years after her husband died, for the first time in her life, she fell in love at the age of 65. She was dating at the time of our interview. She had met her boyfriend (a man approximately in his 70s) at the local senior center. When she told me about her boyfriend, she mentioned to me that she wanted to be clear that "*nada malo pasa entre nosotros*" (nothing bad happens between us); in other words, the relationship was not sexual.

Even to this day, Rosario holds the teachings of her grandparents and great-grandparents about women's "proper" behavior. She shared with me that when her boyfriend asked if she could be his girlfriend, she told him that he had to first talk with her aunt and uncle (who were in their 80s and also attended the senior center) and ask for permission to date. Once her aunt and uncle had had a long conversation with her suitor, they approved of the relationship, and Rosario and the man began to date. Rosario told me that one of the reasons why the uncle approved of the relationship was because her suitor told her uncle "*yo soy un hombre pasiado. Yo quiero bien a su sobrina y la voy a respetar*" (loosely translated: I am *pasiado*, I am serious about my love for your niece and I will respect her). *Pasiado* is a colloquial term that means that the person has had multiple sexual encounters. To say that a woman is *pasiada* means something completely different from when the term is used to refer to a man. When used to describe a woman it is a degrading term that places the woman in a virgin–whore dichotomy where her sexual agency is categorized as sinful and she is labeled a "whore." However, if a man is labeled as *pasiado* this connotes that his sexual activity has given him the type of life experience that allows him to have a broader and more centered perspective of life as a result of fulfilling his sexual appetite. By using the term *pasiado* to describe himself, Rosario's boyfriend meant that he had had multiple sexual relationships and therefore he had fulfilled his sexual appetite. Therefore, because he was *pasiado* he was serious about his relationship with Rosario and he was going to respect her. By respect he meant that his intention was not to have a sexual relationship with her. I asked her if she planned to marry him. Rosario interrupted me by saying that her children have encouraged her to marry her boyfriend, but she cannot because in the eyes of God and the Church you only marry once. For the first time in her life she chose a man to love, yet feels she cannot marry him because she had been previously married.

Not all *Damas* abided by the expectation to remain virgins until marriage. Esperanza (age 68), who never married and never had children, shared that even though her mother taught her about the importance of remaining pure until marriage, she had sex out of wedlock, but she did not give details of how or why it happened. Was her sexual encounter consensual? Unfortunately, this is a question that remains unanswered.

Conclusion

Women's perceptions of their own bodies across all three cohorts had deep cultural and Catholic underpinnings that have historically restrained women from their right to know their own bodies. In the experience of *Las Damas*, the way they carried and perceived their bodies was highly structured and required a well-defined etiquette. Breast-binding, strict dress codes, and silence about the menstrual cycle socialized *Las Damas* into a type of womanhood that denied them the freedom to embrace their embodiment without shame. To be a good girl meant being an obedient Catholic who never asked questions about the body, and questions about sex and sexuality were by extension absolutely off limits. For *Las Madres*, although the type of etiquette and silence about puberty was there, it was not present to the degree that it was for *Las Damas*. In both cohorts this silence about menses led to misinformation and deep distress. For *Las Mujeres*, though in a few cases there was silence around the topic of menstruation, what they emphasized the most in the interviews and focus groups were the age-old sexist notions about women's place in the home and the policing of their virginity by their mothers.

Up to this point in the book we have seen some of the contradictions the women across cohorts experienced early in their life. The home was a sacred space where some of the families came together to pray the rosary. The walls took on the quality of ancient Mexican codices that reflected a family's devotion with images of Our Lady of Guadalupe, Jesus, and other sacred figures, and home altars transformed an ordinary corner of the house into a family's chapel. At the same time in the home, the "back stage" of their lives, silence about puberty, submission to their father's authority and showing respect, were valued over all as part of the feminine character. In essence, the home was both a life-giving and death-bearing space at the same time. Frank discussion or an acknowledgement of natural maturation of girls' bodies into women was not possible. However, this changed somewhat for the younger women; as we recall from the previous chapter, Neida and her mother had a healthy relationship where sex and sexuality were openly discussed.

Overall, despite the silence into which they were socialized in their early years, as the women matured, private direct talks with *La Virgen* allowed them to expand their Mexican Catholic imagination. Ultimately, they were able to carve out some space within this kyriarchal society for thinking about their evolution into women. The Guadalupe of their childhood, the one they learned to love and see as mother, continues to accompany them as they transition on to adulthood. And as they mature, how they relate to *La Virgen de Guadalupe* becomes more holistic and complex.

6

Our Lady of Everyday Life

SEPTEMBER 16, MÉXICO'S Independence Day, is one of the highlights at the local senior center where I conducted the study that informs this book. As I walk in, the DJ is setting up and the seniors are coming in. Some are unaccompanied, others are in couples or groups. They make their way slowly like ocean waves on a sunny summer afternoon. Their smiles, laughter, and joy quickly fill every corner of the center, drowning the possibility of sadness. Some of the women are wearing colorful dresses or traditional Mexican blouses with embroidered flowers, while others appear more casual. Some of the men are wearing nice dress pants, *guayabera* shirts, and even cologne. As Pete (who was Pedro up until yesterday when he became a US citizen; according to him, he is now Pete) walks in, he turns off his cell phone. When I ask him why, he replies with a mischievous giggle,

> Because I want to dance and have a good time, and this way I don't hear when my wife calls me to go pick up our granddaughter from school. You see, I do invite her to come, but she refuses because she says that this place is for old people.[1]

All the seniors are ready for the big dance scheduled from noon to 3:00 p.m. As I make my way through the room, I see Paloma (age 80) quietly sitting on a corner, dressed in a smile that overpowers all the color in the room. She asks me to sit next to her and her husband, who is dressed in khaki pants, a dark brown suit jacket, shirt, and a bowtie. She tells me that they are looking forward to the celebration, although they will not be able to dance because Paloma's husband is in a wheelchair. She asks me how my interviews are going, and I tell her that they are moving slowly, but moving nonetheless. Then she adds,

Well let me tell you that for me she [*La Virgen de Guadalupe*] is like, well for us, she is God's mother. For us she is almost the same, yes, the same. We always say "God is first" but we never abandon her; she is our holy mother. She is like my mom because I do not have mine anymore.[2]

Paloma's interpretation of Our Lady of Guadalupe as the mother of God resonates with official doctrine in which Mary is the *theotokos*—God bearer—in Greek, which in Latin translates to "mother of God." However, for Paloma, she is not only God's mother but her mother as well. To other Latinx Catholics, her way of understanding what *La Virgen de Guadalupe* means in her life—Paloma and God share the same mother—would not sound surprising. However, to a nonreligious person or a non-Latinx, Paloma's assertion might sound irrational, for how to think one's biological mother could be replaced by *La Virgen de Guadalupe*? If we recall from my research trips with Goddess GATE, the first time I accompanied a group of U.S.-born *Mexicanas* who insisted on spending half the day at the Basilica. They wanted to be in communion with who they called their mother—*La Virgen de Guadalupe*. The second time I joined a group of white women. For them, a couple of hours at the Basilica was more than enough. Clearly, the sense of closeness that both groups of women felt toward *La Virgen de Guadalupe* had race and ethnic underpinnings.

After the dance I went home and took notes and revisited the ones I already had written. Paloma's words resonated not only with what I had heard from the other *Damas* but *Las Madres* and *Las Mujeres* as well. In childhood, the women first learned to love *La Virgen* from their mothers and grandmothers.[3] Growing up, they celebrated her feast day by dressing in indigenous outfits, setting up home altars, and partaking in family and community celebrations on December 12. They learned early on to see Our Lady of Guadalupe as their heavenly yet accessible mother—topics I addressed in Chapter 2.

As the women's Mexican Catholic imagination continues to develop over their lifetime, it is increasingly expressed through the five senses. That is, being Catholic for them is not only about material items deemed holy, it is also verbalized and expressed in very intimate forms in the private and public spaces they occupy. For example, they use popular verbal expressions such as *Santa Madre de Dios* "holy mother of God," *Ave Maria purisima* (Hail most pure Mary), or asking for a blessing from a grandmother as depicted on the cover of this book. Using sacramentals such as rosaries, medallions, scapulars, or prayer cards, or caressing a statue of a saint, using holy water and then making the sign of the cross, allows women to come in contact with the sacred through touch. The smell of fresh flowers that have been uprooted only to nurture and be nurtured by the family's prayers, pleas, and gratitude is a reminder of the presence of and relationship to the divine in their daily lives. The taste of special foods like tamales on the feast day of *La Virgen de Guadalupe* and on Christmas connote the familial, and home. Holy images at home are anchors to their eyes and spirit, reminding them that they are not alone but in communion with saints. As they mature and further develop a Mexican Catholic imagination, *La Virgen* continues to be part of their lives. The way they relate to her becomes more holistic and complex, which brings up a question: According to the women in this study, what is *La Virgen de Guadalupe*'s relationship to Mary of Nazareth?

In catechism classes and in their own families, *Las Damas, Madres,* and *Mujeres* were taught that *La Virgen de Guadalupe* is the Virgin Mary in the image and likeness of a mestiza (Spanish-Nahua) woman, and this came through in most of the interviews. The responses of *Las Damas* and *Las Madres* did not depart from what their mothers and the Church taught them about Our Lady of Guadalupe's relationship to the Virgin Mary. In fact, their responses came without hesitancy. The typical answer was *"pues claro que son la misma, así nos enseñaron"* (of course they are the same, that is what we were taught). Given that they were raised in families that adhered closely to traditional Catholic values and teachings, as we read in Chapter 3, it is not surprising that the responses of *Las Damas* and *Madres* aligned with Catholic views of Our Lady of Guadalupe's relationship to the Virgin Mary. What about *Las Mujeres*? How do they think about *La Virgen de Guadalupe* and the Virgin Mary? They were not necessarily satisfied with what they were initially taught, and they had their own interpretations that placed *La Virgen de Guadalupe* and the Virgin Mary at the intersection of generation, race, and *lo cotidiano* (daily life).

The responses provided by *Las Mujeres* for the most part departed from how *Las Damas* and *Las Madres* thought about Our Lady of Guadalupe's relationship to the Virgin Mary. The few *Mujeres* who stated that Our Lady of Guadalupe and the Virgin Mary are the same mentioned that this is what they learned in catechism and from their mothers and grandmothers. These *Mujeres* came from families that tended to be more conservative, and I did not see differences in responses to this question based on place of birth. Others, while they agreed that Mary and Guadalupe are the same, tended to hesitate before responding. In some cases, it was common for them to say that they knew that they were supposed to say that Our Lady of Guadalupe and the Virgin Mary are one and the same, but that in their hearts they felt that they are two separate virgins. Other *Mujeres* seemed confused when I asked the question and did not know what to respond. *Las Mujeres* who differentiated between Our Lady of Guadalupe and the Virgin Mary—the majority of the women in the cohort—said that they felt closer to *La Virgen de Guadalupe*, for reasons I outline below. For example, Dolores (age 19) said,

> I have a framed image of Mary, Joseph, and Jesus in my room, but I don't turn and pray to Mary, Joseph, and Jesus. I turn the other way and pray to *La Virgen*, you know . . . . Maybe it's the same thing, but to me she symbolizes so much more. Our Lady of Guadalupe is much more important to me than the Virgin Mary, and when I think of the Virgin Mary I see a white woman.

Dolores said that she could relate to Our Lady of Guadalupe because she is Mexican and according to her, the Virgin Mary is white.

Similarly, Teresa (age 20) says that she cannot relate to the Virgin Mary because, according to her, "Mary is so far removed from my experience that she is generic." I asked her what she meant by "generic," and she responded: "How the Virgin Mary is portrayed with light skin, white dress and blue mantle seems to me a very general basic image. You know what I mean, it's like I cannot relate to her." One explanation as to why the majority of *Las Mujeres* differentiate between the Virgin Mary and Our Lady of Guadalupe is that they are all college students and thus are more politically aware about issues of race, racism, and colorism (discrimination based on skin color).[4]

In essence, while Our Lady of Guadalupe and the Virgin Mary are the same for *Las Damas* and *Las Madres*, this is not necessarily the same for the majority of *Las Mujeres*. Our Lady of Guadalupe in the Mexican Catholic imagination of the youngest group of women is closer to them than Mary of Nazareth. In part this is because *La Virgen de Guadalupe* lives in and through people (Espín 1997). She is present in their lives via family and community festivities in her honor. Guadalupe has also been present in the form of images in their homes since they were very young—a topic addressed in Chapter 2.

What about God's relationship to *La Virgen de Guadalupe*? For the women across the three groups, Our Lady of Guadalupe and God coexist in a type of harmonious relationship. A Nahua analysis would argue that the way they see the Our Lady of Guadalupe–God relationship is similar to the Nahua concept of duality in which higher powers have a male and female aspect. However, what is important to understand is that the women relate to and see *La Virgen de Guadalupe* within a Catholic context—she is not an Aztec goddess. This raises the question: If Guadalupe coexists in a harmonious relationship with God, is she then greater than, equal to, or less than him? The rest of the chapter is divided into two sections that build upon one another: Motherhood—the Grand Equalizer, in which I address the question above, and the Complexity of Prayer.

Motherhood—The Grand Equalizer

Catholic theology teaches that God is greater than everything visible and invisible and thus greater than all saints, including Jesus' virginal mother, Mary of Nazareth. In the Catholic imagination that was introduced in México via colonization, God is male, almighty, and invincible. Such a social construction of God is limiting, for it does not allow people to see God as a compassionate giver of unconditional love—attributes that are understood as not only feminine but maternal.[5]

Missionary efforts removed these feminine attributes from God and instead projected them onto Mary, making her the "female face of God" (Rodriguez 1994, 152). For Rodriguez (1994), this interpretation of God is inaccurate because it removes "these [maternal] attributes from where they rightly belong: to God" (Rodriguez 1994, 153). She argues that careful attention to how Mexican Americans describe Our Lady of Guadalupe shows that the attributes they associate to Guadalupe are "closer to the Gospel's real God" (Rodriguez 1996, 26). Like Elizondo (1977, 1980, 1997), Rodriguez concludes that one way to understand Our Lady of Guadalupe is as the feminine side of God. However, Espín (1997) offers an alternative interpretation. He questions whether the way Mexican Americans see Our Lady of Guadalupe has more to do with how the Holy Spirit is conceptualized in Catholic theology. By making this claim, Espín is not arguing that Our Lady of Guadalupe is indeed the Holy Spirit, but that how she is understood and articulated among Catholic Latinxs has more to do with pneumatology (the branch of Christian theology concerned with the Holy Spirit) than with Mariology (the part of Christian theology dealing with the Virgin Mary). While resolving this issue is beyond my training and the scope of this book, in this chapter I address in depth the extent to which the doctrinal belief that God is greater than Our Lady of Guadalupe influences the way the women across all three cohorts view her in relation to God.[6]

The women in all cohorts refer to God and Jesus interchangeably. They understand both religious entities as part of the Holy Trinity: Father, Son,

and Holy Spirit. For them, God becomes tangible in the form of the cruci-
fied Jesus, *el Niño Dios* (baby Jesus), and the Sacred Heart of Jesus. Though
I discuss this earlier in the book, I emphasize it once again in this chapter
because the relationship between God (in these various forms) and Our
Lady of Guadalupe within a Mexican Catholic imagination transgresses the
hierarchy in which Church doctrine places them. That is, within the larger
Catholic imaginary, God the Father is above all else, followed by Jesus the
Son and the Holy Spirit. Mary the holy mother of Jesus occupies a space
outside this Trinity and plays a supportive role in the life of Jesus. However,
within the women's Mexican Catholic imagination, the relationship of
God, Jesus, and Our Lady of Guadalupe to each other is far more complex.

Las Damas

In general, *Las Damas* adhere more to the traditional view of Our Lady of
Guadalupe in relation to God. For *Las Damas*, God is greater than *La Virgen*,
but this is usually followed by an affirmation that Guadalupe also occupies a
high status because she is, as they say, "*la madre de Dios*" (God's mother). For
Las Damas, she is not God or the Aztec goddess Tonantzin, and they claim
that they do not adore but rather venerate her. For most of them, Guadalupe's
motherhood status is what makes her equivalent in power and influence
and therefore worthy of the same respect. However, other responses aligned
with the traditional view of God being greater than Guadalupe. This was
usually followed by an emphasis that this is what the Church, their mothers, and in some cases fathers taught them. However, they affirm that this
does not make Our Lady of Guadalupe any less important, as Paloma (age
80) said at the beginning of this chapter. What I observed is that the closeness of *Las Damas* to Catholic teachings makes them less inclined to supply
a rationale for their belief in Guadalupe's place in relation to God. In the
same way, the less rigorous Catholic training that *Las Madres* experienced
early in life, coupled with the separation of families due to migration, led
them to be open to interpretations outside Catholic doctrine. As we saw in
Chapter 3, with migration come many changes, including a degree of separation from more traditional Catholic views and practices.

Las Madres

The majority (12 out of 15) of *Las Madres* believe that *La Virgen de Guadalupe*
and God are equal. However, at least one of *Las Madres* takes it a step

further. Gabriela (age 37) believes not only that Guadalupe and God are equal but also that Guádalupe is a goddess, separate from the male concept of God. She bases her explanation on the emotions she feels *La Virgen de Guadalupe* transmits to her.

> I see her as a goddess because I feel peace when I am in her presence. [I feel] a lot of peace and tranquility and [this] gives me more faith. I feel she is with me and she does not abandon me. She transmits to me [the feeling] that everything that sometimes gets out of my hands will be all right. This is when I get closer to her, and I feel that peace . . . when I talk to her, I feel more faith.[7]

Gabriela had never heard of Tonantzin, the Aztec goddess associated with Our Lady of Guadalupe, yet for her Guadalupe is a goddess. Candelaria (age 35) conceptualizes her argument of who Our Lady of Guadalupe is in relation to God in the following way: "One can say that they are equal. She is his mother, and you see us mothers perceive our children as equals to us. We feel their pain and they feel ours."[8]

Candelaria's response is surprising, given the tendency to think of parents as above their children, not equal to them. But Candelaria understands the relationship between God and *La Virgen* based on how she perceives her relationship with her own children. Candelaria feels her children's pain and they feel hers, and this is what makes the relationship egalitarian. However, unlike Gabriela, Candelaria subsequently told me that although she perceives Our Lady of Guadalupe and God as equal, *La Virgen de Guadalupe* is not a goddess; she is the mother of God. Among *Las Madres* who consider Our Lady of Guadalupe and God to hold the same status, it is precisely Guadalupe's motherhood quality that places her on par with God since, as they explain, "*es por ella que Dios—su hijo— está aquí*" (it is because of her that God—her son—is here). As I demonstrate next, *Las Mujeres* think of *La Virgen de Guadalupe* and God in very similar ways.

Las Mujeres

Like *Las Madres*, for the majority of *Las Mujeres*, *La Virgen de Guadalupe* is equal to God because, according to them, she is his mother and as such has the same status as God. For Neida (age 19), who came to the United States at the age of 10, God and Our Lady of Guadalupe are equal because each has a different influence on people. Three of the 15 women took their answer a step further, and (like Gabriela from *Las Madres* group) said that she is "like another god." However, in their case they did think of *La Virgen de Guadalupe* as Tonantzin, and they said that they learned about this connection in the Chicanx studies courses they had taken in college. For *Las Mujeres*, the status of mother is worthy of utmost respect and love; if *La Virgen de Guadalupe* is the mother of God and their own heavenly mother as well, this elevates her to the same status as God.

Their articulation of Our Lady of Guadalupe in relationship to God arises from two social contexts that provide *Las Damas, Madres,* and *Mujeres* a type of Guadalupan "catechesis" that emerges from *lo cotidiano*. The first context takes place in the "back stage" (Goffman 1959); that is, in their family where they first learn about *La Virgen de Guadalupe* through devotional practices, the topic of Chapter 2. Second is the front stage or public sphere, which in this case is church life. This second context includes going to Mass (though this practice is less common among *Las Mujeres*), parish devotional practices, and catechism classes.[9] However, for *Las Mujeres* there is an additional social context—college. In this third context, *Las Mujeres* have access to Chicanx studies courses. In these courses the predominant interpretation of Our Lady of Guadalupe is that she is the Aztec goddess Tonantzin. Such interpretation is largely based on Chicana feminist analysis of Our Lady of Guadalupe as explained in Chapter 1. This often results with younger generations, in this case *Las Mujeres*, concluding that *La Virgen de Guadalupe* is Tonantzin.

Overall, when *Las Mujeres* find themselves in need, they tend to turn to both God and Guadalupe. However, for matters that have to do with women, they turn to Our Lady of Guadalupe. As Dolores (age 19) states, "You turn to her because she is your mother and will always be there. She is a mother who has love and compassion for her children." Among the youngest group, the women consciously choose to seek *La Virgen de Guadalupe* as opposed to God for certain matters.[10] *La Virgen* not only gives them hope but also tells them to have faith in themselves. In the eyes of *Las Mujeres, La Virgen* is a mother who calls her daughters to action—she is there to help them, not do things for them. I suggest that in part this has to do with their exposure to different philosophies in college. For Manuela (age 24),

She is there and gives me comfort, power, and strength. Though she is covered, I have never thought of her as a submissive woman.

She is a symbol of a better tomorrow. She is always there like a mother would [be], you know. You turn to your mother in the worst of times and in the best of times, you turn to your mother because you know she will always be there.

For Anita, the outspoken Chicana who was scolded by her grandmother for talking openly to her mother about her menstrual period, *La Virgen de Guadalupe* is a mother who calls her daughters to action.

She tells me to never forget my roots. Just as she appeared to an indigenous person, she also tells me to not forget where I come from and that I, too, am from indigenous roots. She tells me to just preserve my roots, you know. Especially 'cause you see in a country like the US, you see a lot of children with Latino parents that don't have a drop of culture in them. I think her message to me is to just pass down that legacy and make sure that children are aware [of] where they come from.

The Guadalupe of *Las Mujeres* does not model passive behavior. While Mexican culture through *Marianismo* may transmit these messages, this does not mean that the women in my study see her that way. Furthermore, Manuela makes reference to *La Virgen*'s vestment; she says that being completely clothed does not suggest that Our Lady of Guadalupe is submissive. Similarly, the rest of *Las Mujeres* said that because *La Virgen de Guadalupe*'s vestment covers her completely and her hands are clasped together it does not mean that she is passive. Unlike Chicana feminist artists who dress their representation of Guadalupe in more contemporary clothing (e.g., *Walking Guadalupe* by Yolanda López produced in 1978 and *Our Lady* by Alma López produced in 1999) for *Las Mujeres* she is powerful as is.[11] Our Lady of Guadalupe is not only a Catholic symbol for them, she is also a cultural and national one; she is, as Esperanza (from *Las Damas* group) says, "*café con leche.*"

Essentially, a fused integration that could only come out of a "well-stirred" *café con leche* lens moves them to perceive no hierarchical distinctions within the concept of divinity. In other words, the *café con leche* concept explains a way of seeing that is more open to fluidity, to the extent that (as we will see in the following section) *La Virgen de Guadalupe* does not necessarily need a special time and place for the women to be in communion with her.

The Complexity of Prayer

With a few exceptions, *Las Damas*, *Las Madres*, and *Las Mujeres* express that they pray both to God and to Our Lady of Guadalupe, for they consider the two to be important figures in their faith. All respondents across cohorts, with the exception of one, pray at least twice a week. Intrigued by the importance that prayer has for all cohorts, I asked the women to describe some of the prayers they say to *La Virgen*. All three cohorts indicate that they say to her the Hail Mary and the Lord's Prayer—a prayer usually reserved for God. Besides these two prayers, *Las Madres* and *Las Damas* cohorts mention saying the rosary, praying to the Holy Spirit, reciting the Nicene-Constantinopolitan Creed, and saying other prayers that they developed themselves. For *Las Mujeres*, their prayers consisted of the Hail Mary and the Lord's Prayer. In addition to these prayers, some of *Las Madres* pray the rosary at least once a week; others say they pray the rosary twice or three times a week. The way that the women across the groups define prayer resonates with how prayer was defined in colonial times, meaning literally saying prayers.[12] For example, the women across the three groups described the traditional Catholic prayers as a structured practice that involves concentration and requires time and space apart from the routine of daily life.

Las Damas

Las Damas pray to *La Virgen de Guadalupe* and to God every day. They also pray the rosary at least twice a week. According to MariChuy (age 78), "*no hay una mañana o noche que no le reze a La Virgen*" (there is no morning or evening that I do not pray to the Virgin); Josefa (age 77) said, "*el primer bocado es con rezos*," meaning she never eats breakfast without first praying. Ester (age 76) begins her prayer ritual with a prayer to the Holy Spirit, part of which she recites during our in-depth interview:

Espíritu Santo, tú que iluminas mi camino, tú que siempre has estado siempre conmigo, tú que me has dado el don del perdón, quiero agradecerte por todo. Quiero reafirmarte [el Espíritu Santo] que nunca me separaré de ti. No importa cuán [sic] grande sea mi deseo material [de hacerlo].

(Holy Spirit, you who illuminates my path, you that has always been with me, you that has given me the gift of forgiveness, I want to thank you for everything. I want to reaffirm you [Holy Spirit] that

I will never separate from you, no matter how great is my material
desire [to do so].)

Ester says that she prays to the Holy Spirit because "he is very powerful"; just like God and Our Lady of Guadalupe, she says that the
Holy Spirit is also present in her life. A theological analysis of how
she understands this relationship is beyond the scope of this book
but I wonder how Catholic theologians would interpret her response?
After this prayer, Ester then moves on to special prayers to Our Lady
of Guadalupe, which include the Hail Mary, the Lord's Prayer, and the
Nicene-Constantinopolitan Creed. In Catholic doctrine, the last two
prayers are typically reserved for prayer directly to God, although the
Lord's Prayer is part of the rosary.

The inclusion of the last two prayers as part of Ester's Our Lady of
Guadalupe prayer ritual is an example of the relationship between God
and *La Virgen de Guadalupe* in the Mexican Catholic imagination of *Las
Damas*. For them, Our Lady of Guadalupe and God are equally important; it makes no difference if you are praying the Hail Mary, the Lord's
Prayer, or the Nicene-Constantinopolitan Creed to her. The perception
of *La Virgen de Guadalupe* as the mother of God is one of the common-
alities in the experiences of all *Las Damas*. "Not because we pray to God
first means that we do not have *La Virgen* in our minds, we never forget her, we would never do that, she is our mother" (Ester, age 76).[13]
What is more, Ester does not see her as an Aztec goddess or a cover up
for Tonantzin—she sees her as the mother of the Christian God. If we
recall from the introduction, Ester is the woman who reached under
her blouse in front of everyone and pulled out a prayer card of Our Lady
of Guadalupe. *La Virgen de Guadalupe* is indeed in the everyday life of
Las Damas. *La Virgen* goes with them in their prayers, thoughts, and in
prayer cards that they literally hold on to very closely.

Besides praying in the morning and evening, *Las Damas* often pray
in the middle of the day. Some share that often, when they pray in the
middle of the day, a phone call or someone knocking on their door
interrupts them; by the time they come back to continue praying, they
have already forgotten where they left off and must start the process
from the beginning. *Las Damas* are positive that *La Virgen* does not
mind this, because she knows how busy life is. In Roberta's (age 79)
words,

> Sometimes when I pray the phone rings and I begin to chat and when I hang up and want to return where I left off in my prayers, you are not going to believe me—I forget. [Laughing she tells me,] I am old, so I begin all over but *la virgencita* understands me.[14]

Moreover, the prayers that *Las Damas* tend to say stem from special petitions or requests that come about throughout the day. Angelita (age 70), who in her younger years was a key lay leader in her parish community, says that she sometimes receives calls from parishioners who ask her to pray for them or a loved one. Other *Damas*, who were not as actively involved in their parish communities as Angelita was, share the same experience. However, in their case, the prayer requests come from their grown children, grandchildren, or other close relatives and friends. While the requests for prayers happen occasionally, *Las Damas'* role in the family and community resembles that of *rezadoras* (women who pray). In Latinx communities, some older women, who the people believe have a stronger religious faith and devotion, serve as intercessors before God by praying for special requests or for certain individuals. This practice is an example of the central role of older women in Mexican families and communities.[15]

Las Madres

With a few exceptions, all of *Las Madres* pray to God and Our Lady of Guadalupe equally. *Las Madres* pray every day, either in the morning or at night, when they are getting their kids ready for school or for bed. Three of *Las Madres* tell me that the Hail Mary and the Lord's Prayer are the only two prayers they know, and that they rely on prayer books on some occasions. Raquel (age 34) uses her first communion prayer book to pray.

Only one of *Las Madres* prays with both her husband and children; the rest pray alone or with their children. Candelaria (age 39), who prays with her children, says that her husband never joins her and the children for prayer because he does not have time or prefers to watch Spanish soap operas (*novelas*) on TV, but she is hopeful that one day he will. Julia's (age 24) husband never joins the rest of the family for prayer either. However, she says that her husband's devotion to *La Virgen de Guadalupe* is strong, but that he tends to hide it. In a hopeful tone, however, Julia affirmed that *"le da vergüenza pero está empezando a cambiar"* (he is embarrassed, but little by little he is beginning to change). I argue that this sense of being embarrassed to pray is perhaps influenced by the gender expectations of men to be physically and emotionally strong and thus not in need of praying.

While some of *Las Madres* pray when their husbands are at work and the children in school, prayer time for others is a mother–child practice—a time when, together with their children, they pray to God and *La Virgen* both. Most *Madres* pray with their children right before they put them to bed because the mornings are too hectic. For example, Julia (age 24) prays with her children at bedtime.

> Every day before putting my children to bed I pray to *La Virgen*. I would like to try it in the morning but sometimes I do not even remember to thank God for a new day. I get up at 6:00 a.m. to bathe and change my daughter. And then the other child gets up later. Only at night is when we have a time for us to be together.[16]

Whether they pray in the morning or in the evening, the devotional triangles (composed of the child, mother, and *La Virgen de Guadalupe*) form. The devotional triangles within which *Las Madres* were introduced to Our Lady of Guadalupe continue to be the main configuration *Las Madres* rely on to introduce their own children to the devotion to Guadalupe, thus replicating the triangle with every new generation. *Las Madres* reveal that at least for them, motherhood is the essential relationship for devotion and fundamental to their prayer practices. Just as their mothers introduced them to prayer practices, they now do the same with their children.

Examining the exceptions to regular prayer to *La Virgen de Guadalupe* reveals more about the complexity of prayer in these women's Mexican Catholic imagination. Sandra (age 21) said that she never prays to *La Virgen de Guadalupe*. She respects her, but says that she does not worship her like she worships God. In our interview, however, she paused and said that there had been one or two occasions when she consciously made an exception and chose to pray to Our Lady of Guadalupe and not to God, but it was done for a very special reason. What circumstances move some women to believe that *La Virgen* is more likely than God to listen to and answer certain prayers? Gender plays a significant role in how women relate to religious images and to whom they choose to pray.

When Sandra became pregnant with her first child, her parents did not like the person with whom she was involved. This led her to consider having an abortion, for according to her it was the easiest solution. She went to church and prayed to God. However, she felt that God could not be as understanding of her situation because He was male; this is when she prayed to *La Virgen de Guadalupe*. Sandra felt that Guadalupe as a woman and mother could advocate to God for her and ask for her forgiveness. Sandra ended up not having an abortion, and gave birth to her son.

Sandra found herself in a life situation where she felt that God could not help her and chose to pray to Our Lady of Guadalupe because as a woman and mother, she could not only understand her situation but would not judge her.[17] The act of gendering prayer is an aspect of their devotion that I saw consistently. *Las Madres* perceive God as male and judgmental, but they believe that Our Lady of Guadalupe, on the other hand, is understanding. They feel *La Virgen de Guadalupe*'s gender and maternal status allow her to understand women's issues; besides, she would never turn down her children (i.e., *Las Madres*).

Las Mujeres

Though *Las Mujeres* pray to God and *La Virgen de Guadalupe*, it is not to the degree that is for *Las Damas* and *Madres*. What the three cohorts have in common are the prayers that they recite: the Lord's Prayer and the Hail Mary. When they pray, they pray to God and to Our Lady of Guadalupe equally. Two exceptions are Rosita (age 20), who was born in the United States, and Elena (age 21), who immigrated to the United States at the age of eight. These two tend to pray more to God and think of *La Virgen* as an intercessor. In Elena's words, "Our Lady of Guadalupe is the mother of God. She is more of an intercessor. God is the one with all kinds of power. I learned this from my parents." Rosita said that she learned to see Our Lady of Guadalupe as an intermediary from her parents and in catechism.

I did not find place of birth to be a determining factor of praying patterns among *Las Mujeres*.[18] The fact that Elena was born in México, where devotion to *La Virgen de Guadalupe* is very strong, does not necessarily make Elena more inclined to pray to her. Instead, my findings reveal that Elena and Rosita hold close traditional Catholic teachings, which place God above all else—a doctrine that they said they received in catechism classes and at home. In this respect, Elena and Rosita's experience with prayer is closer to *Las Damas*, who adhere very closely to traditional Catholic teachings. Though Rosita and Elena were born on different sides of the border, they both experience life as first-generation working-class Mexican-origin

women living in the United States. This, I contend, is one significant reason why their praying patterns are so similar.

The religious dimension of these young women has a very particular language, that of their parents—Spanish. As discussed in Chapter 3,
Las Mujeres learned their prayers from their mothers and from Spanish-
language catechism classes. As a result, they continue to pray in Spanish
in their young adult years. As Dolores (19) put it, "Así fue como me los enseño
mi mami de chiquita, yo no se rezar en inglés" (That is how my mom taught
me the prayers when I was little, I do not know how to pray in English).
Therefore, when these young women pray, they choose to do so in Spanish
because "it feels more natural" to them. Pilar (age 24), like Rosita (20), says
that when she prays every night she does so in Spanish because "it feels
more comfortable because that is how [she] was taught by [her] mother."

It is common for the women across the cohorts to use the phrases
"rezar a La Virgen" (praying to the virgin) and "pedirle a La Virgen" (asking the virgin) or "platicarle a La Virgen" synonymously. I went back to
Rodriguez's (1994) study on Our Lady of Guadalupe and noticed that in
the narratives of her participants, the women used the phrases "praying to
La Virgen" and "talking to La Virgen" interchangeably as well.

When I initially came to this research I defined praying as the act of
reciting traditional Catholic prayers. It was with this definition in mind that
I asked all the women whether for them there was a difference between
praying and talking to Our Lady of Guadalupe. They were surprised by
my question, for they had never thought about how they communicate
with La Virgen de Guadalupe. My definition about prayer and their reaction
to my question reveal two things. First, my definition of praying was too
narrow. Second, rezarle a La Virgen (praying to La Virgen) for them meant
less about saying specific prayers and more about the quality of relating to
La Virgen de Guadalupe. Their prayers have a familismo horizontal (earth)–
vertical (heaven) quality. They emanate from lo cotidiano and reach out to
La Virgen, which in turn they say gives them a sense of peace. The women
confide in La Virgen their worries and hopes. They ask for the protection
and healing of family and friends. Se apapachan—figuratively cuddle up—
to Our Lady of Guadalupe when they feel lonely, and they also trust her
enough to complain to her when things are going wrong.

When I asked them to tell me more about how they pray to Our Lady
of Guadalupe, they describe their way of praying as conversations with
La Virgen, and less as traditional Catholic prayers. Saying prayers to Our
Lady of Guadalupe meant for them reciting traditional Catholic prayers

learned from Church and their own mothers, such as the Hail Mary and Lord's Prayer. Praying to her, on the other hand, was about the relationship the women across the three groups developed with Our Lady of Guadalupe over the years, which emerges out of how they feel when they talk to her as opposed to the result of saying traditional Catholic prayers. A sense of familiarity is not limited to *La Virgen de Guadalupe*. They talk to God and Jesus in the same way—that is, in a manner that speaks to the familism quality of their Mexican Catholic imagination—but they are strategic as to who they choose to pray to for particular issues.[19]

Praying to *La Virgen de Guadalupe*

Our Lady of Guadalupe has been with *Las Damas* throughout their lives. She is their celestial mother who makes her presence palpable in the trials, tribulations, and joys of daily life. *Las Damas* pray to Guadalupe in the mornings and evenings; what begins as a traditional Catholic prayer develops into a conversation that they have with her throughout the day. Like Amelia (age 69), the other *Damas* say that they could never pray to Our Lady of Guadalupe without talking to her. They talk to *La Virgen* about their physical pains, about how they feel; they ask for the protection of loved ones, and for peace on earth.

Las Damas grew up with the belief, transmitted to them by their mothers, that Our Lady of Guadalupe is their ever-present heavenly mother; she never goes away. Therefore, it is no surprise that at this stage in their lives, when the children have left the house or they have lost a husband or loved one and consequently live alone or feel lonely, *La Virgen de Guadalupe* takes on a more complex meaning. Their Mexican Catholic imagination is informed by their own experience as Catholic women, and in some cases as mothers. Their belief that *La Virgen de Guadalupe* is their celestial mother, and a woman just like them, is particularly stronger in *Las Damas* compared to *Las Madres* and *Mujeres*. *Las Damas* see in Our Lady of Guadalupe someone with whom they have enough trust to put aside the formality and protocol that comes with structured prayer, and simply be themselves.

Esperanza (age 68), who never married, describes her relationship with *La Virgen de Guadalupe* in the following way:

> I feel really comfortable about saying whatever I want, even if it is nothing good, you know what I mean? Even if it is not a petition or

asking something, but just complaining, you know. I can go to her and complain to her, "I don't like this, I hate this," you know. Even get upset or get mad, you know; she accepts whatever I say or feel, you know, like a mother would. Any mother would listen to her children, right?

Some of *Las Damas* say that at certain times of the day they sit and simply talk to her. They talk to her about their day, worries, hopes, joys, and memories; they complain, plead, give thanks, and ask for advice.

Like *Las Damas*, most of *Las Madres* say traditional Catholic prayers, but they feel most comfortable praying to Guadalupe in a more conversational way because they could do so more frequently throughout the day. When I asked *Las Madres* how they pray to her, the common response was that they had never before taken the time to reflect on how they actually communicate with her. For example, when I asked Gabriela (age 37) if she prayed to *La Virgen*, she responded in a firm tone that she did. When I asked what she prayed, she paused for a moment and said, "*Me hiciste pensar. Te diré que realmente no sé cómo rezar. Más bien, hablo con ella y luego le rezo El Padre Nuestro*" (You made me think. I'll tell you I really do not know how to pray. Instead, I talk with her and then I say the Lord's Prayer). Gabriela's definition of prayer is restricted to traditional Catholic prayers, and she perceived her way of relating to Our Lady of Guadalupe as "not praying."

Like Gabriela, with the exception of two respondents who rely more on traditional Catholic prayers, *Las Madres* find themselves engaging in a conversational way of praying with Our Lady of Guadalupe. *Las Madres* think of the traditional Catholic way of praying as a structured practice that requires uninterrupted time and space set aside from everyday life. Given the busy nature of their lives—raising children, performing housework, and (for a couple) working outside the home—there are very few opportunities for praying in this way. With little time, their way of praying to Our Lady of Guadalupe takes on the quality of a conversation. Lupe (age 36) says that she devotedly says traditional Catholic prayers to Our Lady of Guadalupe about three times a week, but also simply speaks to her every day because it is so much easier, for traditional prayer requires that you stop your daily chores and set aside time and space. On the other hand, praying in a conversational way can be done at any time and place. This preference for conversational prayer over traditional prayers to *La Virgen Guadalupe* is an example of what happens when the doctrinal Catholic practice of prayer is contextualized in and shaped by *lo cotidiano*.

Some speak with *La Virgen de Guadalupe* while they are changing the baby's diaper, getting their children ready for school, cooking, cleaning, ironing, doing laundry, washing dishes, driving, and so forth. Others talk to her at the end of their daily household chores when they take some time to rest before their children come home from school and husbands/partners from work. According to *Las Madres*, Our Lady of Guadalupe does not mind their irregular traditional prayers or conversational prayers, for as a mother she knows that *los quehaceres de la casa* (housework) has to get done. *La Virgen de Guadalupe* for them is indeed "Our Lady of Everyday Life."

While all of *Las Mujeres* say traditional Catholic prayers to Our Lady of Guadalupe in Spanish, in their conversational prayers (when they talk to her) some speak to her both in English and Spanish. Some women, like Neida (age 19) who says traditional Catholic prayers and talks to *La Virgen de Guadalupe* every day, had not realized until our interview that they tend to say traditional prayers in Spanish, but their conversational prayers to Our Lady of Guadalupe are in both languages interchangeably. As Neida says,

> That's what's weird: *los rezos son en español* [the prayers are in Spanish] but when I talk to her sometimes I mix it up. *Cuando hablo* [when I talk to her] sometimes my Spanish changes over and I speak to her in English.

Furthermore, *Las Mujeres*, just like *Las Damas* and *Madres*, are aware that Our Lady of Guadalupe does not talk back, at least not in the way people do, but instead does so at the level of feeling. That is, the sense of comfort and peace they feel after talking to her is one way they say *La Virgen de Guadalupe* speaks back. In Manuela's (age 24) words:

> Even though she doesn't respond back to me, still you know "oh, this is going on, help me, school is . . . " You know, it's more like a conversation. I don't sit there and pray.

Las Mujeres describe the verbal relationship that they have with Our Lady of Guadalupe as reciprocal. It does not matter to them that *La Virgen* does not literally speak, because they experience her presence in a way that feels tangible for them.

Las Mujeres feel that their conversational prayers to Guadalupe are often far more effective than traditional prayers. According to them, they can say the Lord's Prayer and other prayers that they have been taught in childhood a hundred times, but most of the time the prayers turn into a recitation with very little feeling attached. According to them, prayers such as the Lord's Prayer and the Hail Mary do not leave any room for special petitions, as explained by one of *Las Mujeres*:

> When I was a young child my parents and my catechism [classes] taught me *El Padre Nuestro* and *Santa Maria*, you know, but I'm like, "I'm asking for a specific thing. Where do these prayers let me fit in my specific concern? I'm trying to pass a math test, you know." (Martha, age 29)

The conversational prayers that *Las Mujeres* have with *La Virgen* tend to center on issues that have to do with college life, as the above example illustrates: passing an exam or finishing a term paper. *Las Mujeres* define themselves as "practicing Catholics," although some have not attended Sunday Mass since they have been in college.[20] Fourteen of the 15 young women say prayers such as the Hail Mary and Lord's Prayer, but they also talk to her every night. *Las Mujeres* reach out to *La Virgen de Guadalupe*—not necessarily so that she can solve their problems, but to find strength as they reflect, before her image, on their troubles. Their devotion to Guadalupe does not lead to passivity but to action. For example, they know that if they want to pass an exam, besides asking *La Virgen de Guadalupe* for help they also have to dedicate the time necessary to their studies.

For *Las Mujeres*, *La Virgen de Guadalupe* is their heavenly mother who protects them and watches over them. For *Las Madres*, she is not only a mother figure but also something of a peer who, like them, is familiar with the joys and troubles that come with motherhood. For *Las Damas*, Our Lady of Guadalupe is a heavenly mother and a woman just like them. Most importantly, she is the ever-present mother to whom they can literally talk and confide in throughout the day, particularly when they feel alone.

Conclusion

My findings reveal that in the Mexican Catholic imagination of the women in this study, *La Virgen de Guadalupe* and the Virgin Mary are the same for *Las Damas* and *Las Madres* (with the exception of one), but not necessarily for *Las Mujeres*. Also, Our Lady of Guadalupe for the women across all cohorts is the mother of God, and they use the terms God and Jesus interchangeably. What is more, Our Lady of Guadalupe's motherhood status places her next to God, making her equal.

Their conceptions of Our Lady of Guadalupe raise a number of theological questions: Is she indeed the feminine face of God? If Our Lady of Guadalupe shares equal status with God, what is her relationship to the Holy Spirit? How do the women's articulations of *La Virgen de Guadalupe*'s motherhood support, depart from, or challenge theological explanations of motherhood and God? A theological analysis of the women's grassroots theological assertions about God, Our Lady of Guadalupe, and the Virgin Mary is beyond the scope of this book and my training, but I argue that they have direct implications for Latinx Catholic theology—particularly Latina feminist theology.

If we recall, when I asked Gabriela (*Las Madres*) how she prays to *La Virgen*, she replied: "I don't know how to pray." Her answer at first glance seems simple. However, analyzing it closely reveals the complexity of her response. It moved me to reflect on how I initially defined praying. It allowed me to see that when scholars apply concepts, definitions, and theories to lived experience, there needs to be openness to the opportunities that come about when our analytical lenses are challenged. Based on what the women across the groups shared, I contend that Gabriela does know how to pray. Like the women in this study, talking to *La Virgen* is a type of prayer. The prayers of *Las Damas, Madres,* and *Mujeres* to *La Virgen de Guadalupe* have a conversational quality and are enveloped in a sense of companionship in *lo cotidiano* (daily life) they feel she emanates. Similarly, Roberto Goizueta (1995) analyzes the inherently relational and embodied quality of the ways Latinxs understand Jesus in their lives, and in the Pentecostal tradition, Sammy Alfaro (2010) found that for Latinx immigrants, Jesus is a divine companion in their everyday lives.

Guadalupe as *una madre que está siempre presente* (an ever-present mother) is a characteristic I observed in all three cohorts, but the extent to which they express this sense of companionship significantly varies across the three groups of women. *Las Damas* show an increasingly complex and layered devotional relationship to *La Virgen de Guadalupe*. They also express a stronger feeling of companionship toward her. Possibly this has to do with the maturation of their devotion as a result of a longer life. For *Las Damas*, the experience of losing their own mothers (and husbands in some cases) seems to have created in them a sense of loneliness and emptiness that, in their perception, can only be filled with their faith and devotion to *La Virgen*: "She is like my mother because I do not have mine anymore" (Paloma, age 80). Or as Esperanza (age 68) put it: "She is my mother, my confidante, and I don't feel like I need anybody." Other *Damas* shared about how they intentionally set time apart during their days to *platicar con La Virgen* (talk with *La Virgen*).

At this stage of their life, *La Virgen* is literally seen as their ever-present mother—the one who is there with them because their own birth-mothers have died. The status of mother that *Las Damas* attach to Our Lady of Guadalupe is strengthened by their life experience as Catholics, as women, and as mothers (in some cases). Moreover, Guadalupe is always present in the lives of *Las Damas* as they go about daily life. They talk to her about their day, their worries, their hopes, and their memories. They talk to her, complain, plead, give thanks, and ask for advice.

Though the relationship to Our Lady of Guadalupe grows more lay-ered throughout life, as the experience of *Las Damas* suggests, the younger cohorts still share a common core of relationship to *La Virgen de Guadalupe*, though somewhat different due to their stage in life. *Las Madres* and *Mujeres* think of *La Virgen* as their mother, but the conception they have about the meaning of the term *mother* is different in each case. For example, *Las Madres* relate to Our Lady of Guadalupe as daughters and mothers—they share with her the experience of motherhood. *Las Madres* talk to *La Virgen* in ways similar to *Las Damas* but to a lesser degree, per-haps because of their busy lives as mothers of young children and wives. In the interviews, they emphasized that *La Virgen de Guadalupe* under-stands them, because, like them, she is a mother.

For *Las Mujeres*, Our Lady of Guadalupe is their heavenly mother, the mother that they inherited from their own mothers and grandmothers through the devotional triangle within which they were introduced to her—that of *La Virgen*, their own mothers, and themselves. *Las Mujeres* have not experienced motherhood, and therefore they do not relate to her in this way. They spoke of Guadalupe's companionship more in terms of how they can reach out to her in times of need (i.e., before taking an exam). One explanation might be that compared to *Las Madres*, and specif-ically to *Las Damas*, their devotion is at an early stage of maturation. What is more, their perception of *La Virgen de Guadalupe* being there if they need her is to some extent similar to how generally young people think of their caretaker/s. That is, they might not see them during the day due to school obligations, but they know they can reach out to them if the need emerges. If indeed *La Virgen de Guadalupe* is Our Lady of Everyday Life, how do the women feel she manifests herself in times of crisis?

7

Perceptions of Our Lady of Guadalupe's Relationship to Feminism

"THE TIME IS NOW"

Introduction

When the women at the senior center first found out that I was doing a study on *La Virgen de Guadalupe*, they told me that the one I should speak with was Rosario (age 65), because she was not only very knowledgeable about *La Virgen* but also a woman of deep faith. To be honest, when I first met Rosario I felt intimidated by her—not because she was aloof, but because she was always very proper and carried herself with elegance and grace. She was not outspoken like the other women at the center. I never heard her laugh out loud; on the contrary, she was quiet and always sat at the same table with her aunt, uncle, and the man who (as I later found out) was her boyfriend.

She was always dressed in beautiful long dresses and shawls. Some shawls were white with embroidered flowers at the ends, and others were plain but rich in color. Sometimes she wore a flower on her head that complemented her earrings, which swayed at the rhythm of her walk as they caressed her beautiful cinnamon-colored skin. Her black hair was always nicely swept up into a French twist just like the ones worn by the movie stars of the 1940s.

After a few days I finally got the courage to talk to her. I slowly made my way up to where she was sitting. Rosario looked at me, and her gentle smile melted my heart and made me feel welcome. I introduced myself and told her that I was writing a book about *La Virgen de Guadalupe*. She suggested that we go to the adjacent room where it was quiet because *lotería* was about to start. I asked her to tell me about herself, and she opened up right away, as if she were talking to an old friend.

> I was born in a horse corral in Texas. My mom abandoned me and left me at the corral. I never met her until I was an adult, and that is why I have no affection for her, because she wasn't there when I was little. But as my grandmother would say, "*La Virgen* will always be with us."[1]

Her grandmother's words, as we will learn, had a lasting impact on Rosario. Recall that in Chapter 2, Rosario also shared that her great-grandmother told her to always remember that *La Virgen* will always protect her, the family, and children—that *La Virgen de Guadalupe* will always give her strength and never abandon her.

When I asked her if *La Virgen* had ever granted her a miracle, she quickly said yes and added "*ella es muy milagrosa*" (she is very miraculous). I proceeded to ask her what she meant by her statement. Her expression quickly changed from happy and relaxed to pensive and reflective; then she sighed. At that moment I knew that this miracle was a life-changing experience for her.

In this chapter I quote Rosario and other women extensively to demonstrate the ways horizontal (or earthly) and vertical (or heavenly) relationships intersect in their Mexican Catholic imagination. I argue that it is at this axis that *La Virgen de Guadalupe* arises and calls them to be proactive. I feature the women's voices to a greater extent at key junctures in the analysis because that allows for a more encompassing perspective in this study of lived religion, demonstrating how, why, and at what points people call upon that which they consider sacred in daily life. This less-filtered methodological approach allows readers to engage more directly with the voices and experiences of the person whose story is being featured.[2]

Rosario was 13 when her two grandfathers married her off to a 20-year-old man whom she did not know and with whom she was not in love. He was a stranger, but she felt she had to respect her grandfathers' decision, for according to her they were acting in her best interest. She does not share about the wedding ceremony or wedding night; instead, she proceeds to say that she and her husband had a total of 12 children, but that they never lived together as a family. Puzzled, I ask why. She responds that he would only come by from time to time, and every time he visited her, he left her pregnant. I ask her if he was ever physically abusive; her immediate response is *"hasta eso que no, nunca me golpeó"* (actually no, he never hit me); after a minute's pause, in a quiet somber way she adds, *"bueno nunca hasta la última vez que lo vi. Eso pasó aquí en Estados Unidos"* (well, not until the last time I saw him. This happened here in the United States). I was not prepared to hear what she was about to tell me.

> He had threatened me in the past, but I never thought he would do something to me. One day, I got home tired from the cannery and I closed the front door and lay down on the couch. My husband showed up at my doorstep, and since he could not open the front door, he went in through the bathroom window. Next thing I knew, for I had fallen asleep on the couch, he was standing next to me, and I had blood all over me: he had cut my stomach open, and my guts were coming out . . . . I was nine months pregnant with twins. All I had time to do is to put my children and myself in the hands of *La Virgencita*. I got a gun I had under the couch and I shot him, I don't know how I did it. I was really afraid but *La Virgencita* gave me the strength, and I shot him. He had cut open the head of one of the twins, and the leg of the other one. The first one died, and the second survived . . . . My husband ran to get away, but the police found him, and he went to prison. Yes, my *Virgencita* is very miraculous, very miraculous. I have a lot of faith in her.[3]

Decades have passed; the son who survived is now a grown man, and he still bears the scar on his leg. Rosario's mental and physical scars have remained, but the way she carries herself is a testimony to her resilience anchored in her Catholic faith and devotion to *La Virgen de Guadalupe*. To this day, she attributes her survival and that of her child to *La Virgen*.

Rosario's story of physical violence suggests that Our Lady of Guadalupe figures into how women in this study understand and respond to physical and psychological domestic violence.[4] While not all the women in the study have experienced physical violence, they do have opinions on how *La Virgen de Guadalupe* might support women in these situations. Analyzing how these women's understanding of *La Virgen* informs their responses to domestic violence reveals much about their understanding of feminism and the workings of lived religion in their Mexican Catholic imagination.

Domestic Violence

To place Rosario's experience into perspective, 76% of intimate partner physical violence victims in the United States are women (National
Coalition Against Domestic Violence 2015). During their lifetime, approximately one in three women have experienced some degree of domestic
violence by an intimate partner, and "1 in 7 women have been severely
injured" as a result (National Coalition Against Domestic Violence 2015).

Alcohol abuse and domestic violence are further complicated when the
victim is undocumented. In addition to legal status, race, class, and gender
oppression, language barriers and minimal social networks further mar-
ginalize victims. Most cases of domestic violence, unsurprisingly, go unre-
ported; often victims do not seek out help because they fear deportation.[5]

In the midst of these destructive social forces among some of the
women in this study, La Virgen de Guadalupe becomes a potential, accessible resource for confronting the physical and psychological abuse in their
lives. As we have seen in Rosario's case, Our Lady of Guadalupe is called
on to give women the strength and courage they need to be proactive when
their lives or those of their children are threatened.[6]

A meta-analysis of research on pregnant women and domestic violence found that the prevalence of physical domestic violence during pregnancy is 13.08%.[7] Unfortunately, like Rosario in Las Damas cohort, this
was the case for Candelaria (age 39) in Las Madres group. When I first saw
Candelaria one Sunday morning after Mass, there was something about
her that stood out for me but I was not quite sure what it was. The look
on her face was somewhat somber, as if part of her was removed from
the present moment. She and her children were regulars at Sunday Mass.
Her children, stayed after Mass to socialize with the other teens, but she
always left right away with her youngest child. One day I said hello and
introduced myself. As we began talking, she told me that one of her children had mentioned to her that I was doing a book on La Virgen and that I
was looking for women who would like to be interviewed. She told me that
if I wanted, she could put me in contact with women at the workshops she
attends at the local community center. She also said that I could interview
her if I wanted. I thanked her. In the following weeks I held a number of
focus groups with some of the women, which I followed with in-depth
individual interviews.

Candeleria asked me to come over to her home for the in-depth interview. When I got there, she welcomed me and offered me something to

drink. It was 10:00 a.m. on a Tuesday, and she was alone with her 2-year-old child. Her husband was at work and the older children at school. We sat in the living room while her child played with some Lego toys. I asked her to tell me a little about herself. She began sharing general information, but as the conversation unfolded and she became more comfortable with me, she opened up more.

Before continuing with her story, it is important that we revisit Artemia's experience (*Las Damas* group) discussed in Chapter 4 because it provides a backdrop to Candelaria's story. Artemia was raised to be respectful and obedient in ways that affected her later in life by impairing her ability to escape from her abductor. Similarly, Candelaria was raised by both of her parents to be respectful, particularly to men. She was taught to not talk back when other people are talking. To be obedient and remain silent was a sign of respect; this, according to her parents, was a reflection of her integrity as a person of faith—a good Catholic girl.

Toward the end of the interview I asked her if *La Virgen de Guadalupe* had ever granted her a miracle. As in Rosario's case, I was not ready for what Candelaria was about to reveal.

> Because of how I was raised, when I got married I would lower my head when my husband insulted me. I thought it would come across as disobedient if I talked back to him. He would tell me about the other women he was having affairs with and he would be very explicit, and I would do nothing but cry.[8]

This belief in the need to be obedient could partly be explained by the long tradition of the *hacienda* system and the set of expectations within this particular social order. Mexican anthropologist Rosío Córdova Plaza (2003), in her book *Los Peligros del Cuerpo: Género y sexualidad en el centro de Veracruz*, contends that the image of the *hacendado* (landholder)—the strict and draconian father who knows what is best for his children—is the prototype of the peasant family in México, where even to this day obedience on the part of women and children is a directive and not a choice in many small villages and towns.

When Candelaria and her husband lived in México, one of her husband's friends came to their house to visit. He was upset because his wife had cheated on him. When her husband and his friend started to drink, his friend began telling her husband that Candelaria was probably just like his wife, that all the women were the same. As soon as his friend left, with no reason, Candelaria's husband began to punch and kick her, accusing her of being just like his friend's wife. He grabbed her by the hair and dragged her through the house, threw her against the cement wall and hurt her abdomen, back, and head. She was three months pregnant with their third child, but he did not seem to care. Candelaria cannot recall if she fainted or not, but she does remember that she did not know how to fight back and remained silent. She was terrified: "*Me sentí como un animalito maltratado. Pensé que me iba a morir, pero gracias a Dios y a La Virgen, no me morí*" (I felt like an abused little animal. I thought I was going to die, but thanks to God and *La Virgen* I did not die).

Her situation took a turn when she arrived in this country. She found out that near where she lived there was a community center that offered many services, from a food pantry to free clothes, and various workshops. She enrolled in a series of workshops that were designed for Latina mothers with young children. The workshops addressed issues of nutrition, self-care, and self-esteem among other topics. One of the things that she remembers most is how they taught her to not tolerate abuse, that there was help available for women in these types of situations, and that this was a free country. It was at these workshops that for the first time she realized all the damage her husband had done to her.

In our interview she shared about the first argument they had here in the United States; it was also the last time he hit her. This time she was five months pregnant with their fourth child. She recalls that when her husband started arguing, she took a deep breath and counted to 10, just as they taught her at the workshops. However, that did not help—she felt she could not defend herself. The workshops alone, at least for Candelaria, were not enough to change her situation.

The abuse continued as he told Candelaria that before she joined him in this country, he had a lover for four years. He told her that the other woman was a good person, that she would give him gifts, and that she worked outside the home unlike Candelaria. He relentlessly tormented her by telling her that the only thing he had to pay for was the room where she gave him what he wanted, and that she would make love with the lights on. Minutes later he began complaining because dinner was not ready. Full of rage, her husband threw her hard against the wall, just as he used to do in México. Candelaria told her daughters to go directly to their room and to lock themselves in; this was something that she told them every day when her husband came home from work, in an attempt to avoid any opportunity for him to get upset. She then told herself, "*Ya no voy a tener miedo . . . . Estoy libre aquí [en este país]*" (I am not going to be scared anymore. . . I am free here [in this country]). It is at this point that what she learned at the workshops and her own faith in *La Virgen* catalyzed one another.

> I prayed to Our Lady of Guadalupe to give me strength [gasping for air and raising her voice] to be able to yell back at him. I prayed to her so that I could be me. This was something impossible for me to do, but I held on to Our Lady of Guadalupe. I told myself, "She will give me strength and I will tell him exactly how I feel." I went to my daughters and told them, "Let's pray to *La Virgen* before you go to bed." A woman who was a distant relative and lived with us back in México once told me to pray Psalm 140 every time I had problems with my husband. The psalm talks about the evil man . . . who can cause harm and how he can be appeased. I know the prayer by heart. It says:

> > Deliver me, Lord, from the wicked; preserve me from the violent,
> > From those who plan evil in their hearts,
> > Who stir up conflicts every day,
> > Who sharpen their tongues like serpents,
> > Venom of asps upon their lips.

> > Keep me, Lord, from the clutches of the wicked;
> > Preserve me from the violent,
> > Who plot to trip me up
> > The arrogant have set a trap for me;
> > they have spread out ropes for a net,
> > laid snares for me by the wayside. (Psalm 140:1–4)[9]

The psalm is a direct prayer to God, yet Candelaria directs it to *La Virgen de Guadalupe*, explaining that "*Rezé este salmo con mis hijas y con mucha fe en La Virgen*" (I prayed this psalm with my daughters and with so much faith in *La Virgen*). Her evocation of this psalm demonstrates the fluidity of the Mexican Catholic imagination: a prayer to God can also be a prayer for Our Lady of Guadalupe.

In the middle of praying the psalm, her husband called her to go back to the kitchen, but she told him to wait until she and her daughters finished praying. Impatient, he went to the room where they were praying; he got her and threw her against the wall, then hit Candelaria in the face with his fist. But she got up this time and remembers telling *La Virgen de Guadalupe*:

> "The time is now." I told him [raising her voice and changing her tone], "I do not know what is going on with you. I am not the same. I am a different person. I am now here in the United States and I know my rights. I want you to respect me and if you have something to say, say it with manners."[10]

Taking off his belt, her husband threatened to hit her, but she told him that if he hit her she was going to call the police. Her oldest daughter, crying, immediately intervened: "*yo le hablo, mami, yo le hablo*" (I'll call, mom; I'll call; I'll call). Candelaria told me that her daughter's desperate voice to call the police sounded as if she had been waiting for her to confront her husband in this way. Her other children were crying unstoppably, and she felt her unborn child move inside her womb.

> I pray to God with all my heart and he always listens to me. "I ask you in the name of God and *La Virgen* to change." He told me, "If you do not shut up I will break your mouth." Then I felt my stomach trembling and my lower abdomen began to hurt badly. I told him, "Because of you I could lose my child." I did not feel good. My hands were shaking, my mouth, all of my body. I felt like the world was crumbling down on me. Then my oldest daughter told him "Shut up!" That is when he told her, "Call the police if you want and you will see what I am capable of doing."[11]

He then threw their 15-year-old daughter on the bed and was about to hit her when Candelaria yelled "*A mi hija no*" (not my daughter). Candelaria was terrified; she felt the child she carried in her womb begin to move rapidly. She began to count to 10 once again, just like they had taught her in the self-esteem workshops, but this time she called upon *La Virgen de Guadalupe* as she counted—something she did not do the first time: "*Ay Virgencita ayudame, te necesito*" (my dear virgin help me, I need you). She then grabbed her 175-pound husband from the back, lifted him up, threw him on the floor, and yelled back at him for the first time in 16 years of marriage: "*a mi hija no le pegas*" (you are not going to hit my daughter). Candelaria continued:

> My daughter tells me "Mom, it was *La Virgen*." My children have strong faith in God and *La Virgen*. I tell my children, *La Virgen* has

helped me so much. If it would not have been for her, I would have not had the strength that day and things would be the same.[12]

Though her husband sometimes resents the fact that she's more assertive now, life has changed. "*Ahora, él es diferente, es más cariñoso. Ya no dice cosas malas. Digo que fue La Virgen*" (Now, he is different, he is more affectionate. He does not say bad things anymore. I say that it was *La Virgen*).

Reflecting on all the abuse she endured all those years, she tells me, "*Ahora que miro hacia atrás, me doy cuenta de que hice lo mismo que mi mamá. Así es como me criaron*" (Now that I look back, I realize that I did just as my mom did. That is how they raised me). Now she realizes that she tolerated her husband's abuse because she learned from her mother: "*Mi mamá sufrió mucho con mi papá*" (My mother suffered a lot with my dad). Her father, like her husband, was an alcoholic, and she witnessed him many times physically abusing her mother. She also recalls asking her mother the same question her own daughter asked her so many times: "*¿Si mi papi te hace sufrir por qué no lo dejas?*" (If my dad makes you suffer so much, why don't you leave him?).

Candelaria spent many days analyzing the incident; though she called upon God and *La Virgen de Guadalupe*, it is *La Virgen* whom she thanks every day. A few days after the incident she called her parents and told them what had happened. Her father congratulated her and told her to have more faith. Then her father added, "*hiciste lo que tu mamá nunca hizo. Ella nunca me enfrentó. Si trata de hacerte daño de nuevo, llama a la policía*" (You did what your own mother never did. She never confronted me. If he tries to hurt you again, call the police). According to Candelaria, "*Mi papá también piensa que fue un milagro en todo el sentido de la palabra. Para que mi esposo cambiara drásticamente, tenía que ser un milagro. Antes de ese milagro, era un infierno vivir con él*" (My dad also thinks that it was a miracle in all senses of the word. For my husband to change drastically, it had to be a miracle. Before that miracle, it was hell living with him).

After this interview she invited me to her youngest child's birthday party, where I first met her husband. This is one of the challenges of doing field-work: at that moment, I had to pretend that I knew nothing about his history of abuse toward his wife and children. With a big smile that could fool anyone, he greeted and welcomed me. Candelaria told him that I was her new friend from church. This was also the day I found out how she and her husband first met. Looking at him as he was hanging the piñata with a rope, she told me:

As I mentioned in my interview, my father was an alcoholic. One of his drinking buddies was the man who is now my husband.

I remember seeing him [husband] walking down the street drag-
ging and hitting women—he was a womanizer. I would look out
the window and tell myself, not me. I had a boyfriend at the time,
he was a real sweetheart and we were both deeply in love. One day
at the local bar my dad got very drunk and he gave my hand in marriage to that man, all for a couple of drinks.[13]

Though Candelaria and her now-husband had never spoken, he had
told her father that he was interested in her. Since he was Candelaria's
father's "drinking buddy" and would often buy him drinks, Candelaria's
father agreed to give her hand in marriage. Unfortunately, some experiences repeat across generations. Recall that this was also Rosario's case.
In her situation, it was both of her grandfathers who gave her hand in
marriage.

In other cases like Vicky (age 31), who has two young children under the
age of 5, mental illness and not alcohol seems to spur abuse. Her husband
is bipolar, and when he does not take his medication his ability to relate to
others is severely affected. Vicky has an altar to La Virgen de Guadalupe, but
only she knows where it is. She told me that when her husband has a rage
attack, though he has never physically harmed her, he is verbally abusive
and throws things around the house. One time when he had a rage attack,
due to missing a dose of his medication, he became very upset. He began
throwing things around the house; and because he knew how much Our
Lady of Guadalupe meant to Vicky, he destroyed her altar to La Virgen.
Since that day, she keeps her altar hidden in a drawer, out of her husband's
sight. Vicky says that she prays to La Virgen de Guadalupe for her husband
to continue taking the medicine or to cure him. While she says that things
are better now, she did not share with me whether Our Lady of Guadalupe
had granted her a miracle directly associated with her husband's health
condition.

Though the other members across cohorts made no mention of ever
experiencing domestic violence, all the women take a stance against it.
The participants also concur that La Virgen does not tolerate violence of
any type against women. For example, Teresa (age 20), Leonor (age 22),
and Martha (age 29) from Las Mujeres cohort say that though they have
not experienced domestic violence in their own families, they believe
that Our Lady of Guadalupe can give women strength and courage to
liberate themselves from such oppressive situations. Anita from Las

Mujeres group also agrees that *La Virgen* can help women overcome abusive relationships, but she takes her analysis a step further: "I think she is a model for inner strength, but the act of actually doing it will have to be on the person." Anita, believes that faith alone in most situations is not enough. The faith in *La Virgen* must be strong enough to move the woman to take action, just as it moved Rosario to pull the trigger and Candelaria to lift and throw her husband on the floor.

All the women from *Las Damas* and *Las Madres* group also believe that *La Virgen de Guadalupe* is potent enough to empower women. However, Beatriz (age 34) from *Las Madres* group says that she thinks that Our Lady of Guadalupe can only help sometimes, as in the case of her sister who lives in México. She shared with me that her sister's husband is very abusive. The situation has reached a point that her sister has attempted suicide three times. Her mother took her to see a therapist, but her sister refused all the help and went back to her husband. Beatriz's example supports Anita's argument that faith needs to be accompanied by action. For example, in Rosario's case she asked Our Lady of Guadalupe to give her the strength, but she pulled the trigger. In Candelaria's example, the workshops alone were not helpful; it was at the moment when her devotion to *La Virgen* intersected with the survival tips she learned at the community center that she found the strength to lift and throw her husband on the floor. How do these women come to understand *La Virgen de Guadalupe* as a force that moves women to physically confront their husbands when their lives are threatened? Does some form of feminism play a role in this transformation?

Feminism in the Context of Las Damas, Madres, and Mujeres

I asked the women across the three cohorts if they had heard the term *feminist*; many of them had, with the exception of some of the women in *Las Damas* cohort. Not wanting to impose my own definition of feminism on those who were not familiar with the term, I told them in general that feminism advocates equality between men and women. I then asked *Las Damas*, *Madres*, and *Mujeres* if, based on their own experiences, they could share with me how they would define the term. Asking them this question further revealed to me what feminism means to them in the context of their own experience as Catholic women. Their answers allowed me to better understand how they articulate feminism, and how their past experiences and Catholic faith clearly informed their interpretations of the term.

Las Damas define feminism in terms of respect between women and men. One explanation is that Las Damas grew up in a Catholic culture in which obedience and respect for God, the elderly, men, and clergy was a way of life, and young girls were held more accountable than boys, as Chapter 3 demonstrates. It was a way of life in which the primary responsibility of women and girls was to attend to men's needs.

The way they now articulate respect differs from the definitions of respect into which they were initially socialized, allowing us to see how their Mexican Catholic imagination continues to be shaped with the passing of years and the life experiences that come with them. Furthermore, feminism for them means opposing the physical and mental maltreatment of women. It also means that men have the responsibility to help with some of the household chores, and some of Las Damas shared their own experience as examples of the latter. Ester, in a broken voice because her husband had recently died, told me that every day when she came home from the cannery, her husband would have a salad waiting for her.

> He always made sure I ate when I came home from work. We had a good life. My husband would help with the house chores when I was at work. He cooked rice and made tortillas for the whole family. [Crying she added] How am I not going to miss him?[14]

Ester's example demonstrates that unequal gender expectations were not always the norm, and some men chose to transgress them.

Furthermore, Las Damas placed a particular emphasis on education and said that women have the right to get an education and pursue a professional career before having children. Las Damas, with the exception of one, did not have the opportunity to attend school beyond elementary school; their stance on education and by extension professional career is another example of how they transgress the gender expectations into which they were socialized. Although feminism is generally understood as equality between genders in the family, political, and economic spheres, Las Damas departed from this interpretation of feminism as it relates to one social institution in particular—the family. Las Damas believe that while men should help out around the house, both men and women should occupy some traditional gender roles. For example, according to this generational cohort, women (and not men) are responsible for instilling moral and religious values in their children. As Juanita (age 82) put it, "*La mamá es responsable de criar a los niños. Ella es la que enseña los valores a los niños y la fe en Dios y en nuestra Santa Madre*" (The mother is responsible for raising the children. She is the one that teaches [children moral] values and faith in God and our Holy Mother).

All of *Las Damas*, however, seem to agree that in the past women were much more marginalized and that this was wrong. According to them, the Church and Mexican culture have had equal influence on the unequal treatment of women and cannot be separated one from the other, thus reinforcing Esperanza's concept of *café con leche* as a metaphor of the mixing of religion and culture. Irma (age 76), recognizes that compared to her experience and that of her generation, women now occupy higher social status: "*Las mujeres antes no tenían voz, podían decirles 'quedate allí' y [ellas] se quedadan, casi como animalitos. Ahora las cosas no son las mismas. Las mujeres tienen más voz*" (Women did not have a voice before, you could tell [them] "stay there" and [they] would stay, almost like a little animal. Things are not the same today. Women have more voice). Irma used the metaphor of "*animalito*" (little animal) to describe women and, if we recall, Candelaria (*Las Madres* cohort) referred to how she was treated by her abusive husband using the same term: "*animalito*." The comparison of women to "little animals" was one metaphor they used to illustrate to me the extent of the denigration of women.

Las Damas are also aware of the rigid androcentric social system in which they were raised and learned to be women. Josefa (age 77) admits that women's voices were not heard or respected either, and believes that women need to be proactive in order to be respected. In other words, it is women's responsibility to make themselves heard. In Josefa's words, "*La mujer debe hacerse escuchar, es malo quedarse callada*" (A woman needs to make herself heard, it is not good to keep quiet). Clearly, agency is key for *Las Damas*.

Like *Las Damas*, *Las Madres'* descriptions of feminism are directly tied to agency and to a sense of awareness of gender inequity. While some of *Las Damas* and *Las Madres* would not call themselves feminists, some of their core beliefs align with some feminist principles. *Las Madres* believe that women should have equal career opportunities and access to education, but they place a stronger emphasis on equality within the home. They also draw more on personal experience to illustrate their opinions of feminism. With the exception of two, *Las Madres* do not work outside the home, and this explains their focus on equality within the home. In this generation we begin to see gender roles increasingly changing within the home, and according to them this is an outcome of their migration to this country. *Las Madres* compare the gender roles they embodied in México to the ones they adopted in the United States. When Julia (age 24) lived in México with her husband she always kept quiet, and her husband was the one who made all the decisions, big and small. Since migrating to the United States and taking classes at the local community center, she speaks up; she and her husband make family decisions together.

Similarly, María (age 36) attributes her feminism in part to the classes she is taking at her local community center. In her words,

> I am not the same one as before. Taking classes at the center has helped me a lot, especially to be much stronger. It has helped me to be assertive with my husband, with my children, with my responsibilities. Before, I was very submissive and I cried for everything. For everything! Before, I had many problems with my husband, and my family. My marriage was practically destroyed.[15]

The women who are involved at the local community center say that since taking the classes they have personally changed for the better. Their husbands do not make all the family decisions any longer; they demand respect from their husbands, and they do not cry or stay quiet like they did in the past.

Candelaria (age 39) clearly is one of *Las Madres* who benefited from such workshops. However, her story also indicates that it was a combination of the workshops and faith in *La Virgen de Guadalupe* that ultimately helped her put a stop to the abuse she had endured all those years. Candelaria now considers herself a feminist.

> I am a feminist when I defend my rights as a woman. When we have to make a decision for the sake of our children. Like for example when he does not want to do something and I manage to make him see things, like when my daughter wanted to go camping with the other children of her school.[16]

Despite their current sense of equality in the home, like *Las Damas*, the definition of feminism for *Las Madres* is selective. For example, they are self-conscious about when they choose to be more assertive and when to let their husbands take the lead. For instance, Faviola (age 46) says that she believes that women are mentally stronger than men and are better at organizing and coordinating, but that she does not consider herself 100% feminist because there are times when her husband makes family decisions and she is the one responsible for cooking and cleaning.

For *Las Mujeres*, being a feminist is about being comfortable with who you are, no matter what people may think or the role you may hold in society. For these women, as long as they are at peace with themselves, worrying about what people may say is not their concern. This cohort of women feels more autonomy and less need to comply with society's traditional gender role expectations. However, that does not mean that they all see themselves as feminists.

While some advocate equal career choices and opportunities for both men and women, others, like Pilar (age 24), do not identify as 100% feminists. However, for Pilar and other *Mujeres* who think like her, this does not necessarily mean that they feel disempowered or do not exercise feminism at times. Pilar, for example, says that she considers herself a feminist only at times, and that her feminism takes precedence over her Catholic faith, but she emphasized to me that this "does not necessarily mean that Our Lady of Guadalupe and Catholicism are pushed away completely." This sense of being able to exercise their feminist agency without compromising their Catholic faith is strongly mediated by their understanding of *La Virgen de Guadalupe*.

> No matter how many mistakes you make you can always come back
> and it is that unconditional love that we feel *La Virgen* feels for us.
> It's just something that you feel when you go to Mass and it's like
> you're not perfect but she stills loves you. When I took a women's
> studies class we were talking about the struggle that women go
> through here in the United States and the whole birth control and
> abortion issue. When I wrote a paper for the class I chose not to be
> a Catholic and I wrote about what the book said, and yeah. So I felt
> guilty about it, but yeah, I did it.

Pilar is an example of how the women in her cohort unbind their bodies, sexuality, and religious beliefs from the more restrictive aspects of Catholicism. Furthermore, her choice to "not be Catholic" when she wrote her paper on birth control is a form of "oppositional consciousness" (Sandoval 1991). This consciousness is both manifold and flexible: manifold because it is a result of multiple oppressions that women experience based on race, class, gender, and sexual orientation; flexible because women underscore a specific characteristic of their identities according to the social space they occupy at any given time (Sandoval 1991). Clearly, Pilar chose to frontload her feminist beliefs over her Catholic faith. However, what is important to emphasize is that whether *Las Mujeres* consider themselves or their actions feminist or not, or they choose to deemphasize their Catholic identity at certain times, they still identify as Catholics.

Do You Consider Our Lady of Guadalupe a Feminist?

Given that *La Virgen de Guadalupe* is a source of strength for all three cohorts, do they see *La Virgen* as a feminist? Twenty-six percent of *Las Damas*, 20% of *Las Madres*, and 53% of *Las Mujeres* consider Our Lady of Guadalupe a feminist. According to them, Our Lady of Guadalupe appeared to San Juan Diego to bring justice, and this includes gender equality. For the 26% of *Las Damas* who consider *La Virgen* a feminist, they think of her as an advocate of justice and equality for all, and this alone is what makes her a feminist. To support their opinion of Our Lady of Guadalupe's feminism they made a reference to her apparition story as evidence. They emphasized that *La Virgen* wants equality for all, men and women, just as she did for San Juan Diego and the rest of the Nahua people of the time. However, even though I asked if they could tell me more, the explanation of why they consider Our Lady of Guadalupe a feminist did not extend beyond this point, because they felt that they could not speak for *La Virgen de Guadalupe* beyond this description of her feminism.

Table 7.1 Question asked: Is Our Lady of Guadalupe a feminist?

Cohort	Yes	No	Guadalupe is not a feminist, but she believes in gender equality
Mujeres	53% (8)	13% (2)	33% (5)
Madres	20% (3)	40% (6)	40% (6)
Damas	26% (4)	33% (5)	40% (6)
Complete sample	33% (15)	29% (13)	38% (17)

Note: Numbers in parentheses = number of respondents.

Similarly, the 20% of *Las Madres* who consider Our Lady of Guadalupe a feminist say that *La Virgen* is an advocate of gender equality. However, *Las Madres* elaborated on what they meant by their assertion that *La Virgen de Guadalupe* is a feminist. According to them, *La Virgen* supports the division of household labor between husband and wife, and she does not tolerate psychological and physical abuse against women. The emphasis on violence against women was a predominant theme among *Las Madres*. What Meche (age 42) had to say reflects the beliefs of *Las Madres* who consider Our Lady of Guadalupe a feminist. In her words:

> If she sees that women are being humiliated, she would not be in agreement. That is why she appeared, so that there would be equality on earth. I think that in this way *La Virgen* is a feminist. Men should not be more powerful than women. That is how I see her.[17]

However, Candelaria, who considers herself a feminist, does not see Our Lady of Guadalupe as a feminist, but she does believe that *La Virgen* advocates gender equality.

For *Las Mujeres* who consider *La Virgen de Guadalupe* a feminist, her strength makes her a feminist. Neida (age 19), for example, thinks that Our Lady of Guadalupe "has special power to help women stand up for themselves." Other *Mujeres* think that Guadalupe is a feminist because she did not just tell him "to sit and pray," but she sent San Juan Diego to talk to the bishop. Similarly, for Anita (age 21) Our Lady of Guadalupe represents strength and power; as such, she is "a feminist symbol." In sum, Our Lady of Guadalupe epitomizes hope, struggle, affirmation, and respect for women, and due to this perception of *La Virgen*, 33% of the total sample of women across cohorts considers her feminist.

By comparison, 33% of *Las Damas*, 40% of *Las Madres*, and 13% of *Las Mujeres* did not see Our Lady of Guadalupe as a feminist. *Las Damas* said that she was too traditional to be a feminist. *Las Madres* believe that she is not a feminist because *"antes no se usaba eso del feminismo"* (feminism did not exist during her time), when *La Virgen de Guadalupe* appeared to San Juan Diego. Similarly, *Las Mujeres* maintain that *La Virgen* is traditional and, as such, not a feminist. This group of respondents did not expand on their perception of Our Lady of Guadalupe as not a feminist.

However, there were others that, although they do not see Our Lady of Guadalupe as feminist, elaborated on their response by adding that just because Our Lady of Guadalupe is not feminist does not necessarily mean that she is not an advocate of equality (see Table 7.1). For these women, who actually constitute the majority of the overall sample (38%), *La Virgen de*

Guadalupe is a loving mother who does not tolerate injustice, and because of this she is an advocate of gender equality in and outside the home. *La Virgen* for them advocates equality between men and women because she loves her children and does not make distinctions between genders. These women also made reference to Our Lady of Guadalupe's apparition story as evidence that she advocates equality, but they did not see it as Our Lady of Guadalupe taking on a feminist stance.

One of the great advantages of using ethnographic methods in the study of lived religion is that it allows one to get at the complexity of people's world-making. I, for example, found that the lived experience of the women in this study complicates religious and feminist boundaries of what *La Virgen de Guadalupe* is and is not. Among the women that do not see Our Lady of Guadalupe as feminist or as an advocate of gender equality is Esperanza (age 68, *Las Damas* cohort). When I asked her if she perceived *La Virgen de Guadalupe* as a feminist, she was quick to respond: "No way, José, don't put that label on her; she would die. If you are a feminist, you are all the way over there. No way, don't put that label on her."[18]

For Esperanza, "all the way over there" means that *La Virgen de Guadalupe* is not like the women who seek equality between men and women across social institutions. She firmly believes such equality is impossible to achieve: "I could never be a man, women can never be equal to men." From her response one might infer that she believes that women are weaker and do not have what it takes to be on par with men. However, she means quite the contrary. When I asked her to elaborate, she continued:

> I could never be a man; women can never be equal [to men]. Women have so much going for [us] . . . we are more intelligent, open, scouts, [and] we have compassion. *Los hombres se cierran* [men close themselves off]. We are so much stronger—*si queremos tenemos el control* [if we want we can have control]. *Nosotros tenemos control* [We have control]. *Adam, se hubiera puesto los pantalones* [he should have tightened his belt (i.e., been firm)] and said no to Eve. Don't we have control over them? [laughing] We are conniving little things. We are so much ahead of them.

If we recall from Chapter 4, Esperanza was taught that obedience to men was not an option but a way of life. When her father would ask for a glass of water she not only had to bring it to him, but she had to cross her arms at the chest and remain by his side in case he needed something else. Though Esperanza has remained deeply Catholic, she has transgressed the rigid gender role into she was socialized. Her view of women—not equal to men, because women are so much more—is a testament to her evolving Mexican Catholic imagination.

Furthermore, Esperanza's remarks highlight the subtleties of the women's Mexican Catholic imagination and the articulations of equality and feminism that emerge at the axis of their vertical and horizontal relationships. While women like Esperanza do not consider themselves and *La Virgen de Guadalupe* feminist, this does not necessarily mean that they think of themselves and *La Virgen* as all-accepting and all-enduring women. Esperanza considers Our Lady of Guadalupe a strong and determined woman for, as she put it, "*La Virgen* taught God [in the person of Jesus] how to walk and pray. She taught him everything; how could she not be strong?"

What is Your Opinion of Birth Control for Women?

Esperanza's response brings to light the complexity of the women's Mexican Catholic imagination, allowing me to see how their intricate ways of knowing inform their articulation of Our Lady of Guadalupe and why they do or do not see her as feminist. Wanting to know more about the malleable quality of their Mexican Catholic imagination, I asked all three cohorts about their thoughts on birth control. I chose this particular issue because of the controversy that surrounds that topic in Catholic communities.

Table 7.2 Question asked: Do you agree with the use of birth control?

Cohort	Yes	No	No, but I understand why some women choose to use it
Mujeres	100% (15)		
Madres	100% (15)		
Damas	20% (3)	20% (3)	60% (9)

Note: Numbers in parentheses = number of respondents.

The self-perception of *Las Mujeres* and *Las Madres* as feminists significantly informs their opinions on the use of birth control, but the responses of *Las Damas* were much more complex (see Table 7.2). In essence,

Las Mujeres and *Las Madres* all approve of the use of birth control for reasons including protection against sexually transmitted diseases and prevention of unwanted pregnancies. As for *Las Damas*, three of them are
against any type of birth control, with the exception of the rhythm method
approved by the Catholic Church. Another three, on the other hand, openly
approve of the use of birth control for women. As Artemia (age 67) put it,

> I do like [birth control methods]. I used them and I did not offend
> anyone. If we had not used them, we would have had seven, eight
> children. I think that birth control methods do not kill anyone nor
> are they harmful. Who are you offending? Sex is one thing and
> children are another. It is a lot more beautiful if they are planned.[19]

The two main reasons that they give in favor of birth control are that
it helps prevent sexually transmitted diseases and that the high cost of
living prevents couples from appropriately caring for multiple children.
Artemia's life has come full circle, from a frightened 14-year-old who
was snatched from her mother by a much older man, to a woman who
is still deeply Catholic but also assertive. Confidently and unashamedly,
she told me that when her first husband died, she remarried and used
birth control because she wanted to have sex for pleasure rather than
procreation with the man she chose to love. The other nine *Damas* said
that they did not use birth control and do not necessarily approve of it
because it goes against the teachings of the Church, but they understand that times have changed. Once again we see that even though *Las
Damas* grew up at a time when women's sexuality was a forbidden topic,
they now show some openness to new ways of thinking about women's
sexuality.

   The self-perception as feminists (as they define the term) of some of
Las Mujeres, *Las Madres*, and *Las Damas* and their opinions about birth
control add more empirical evidence to the existing arguments about the
binary quality of the relationship between religion and women's decisions regarding their bodies. Previous research demonstrates that religion
does not influence women's decisions about their bodies. Mexican-origin
women do not simply follow Church doctrine when it comes to decisions about contraception.[20] Religion does not necessarily shape women's
beliefs about sexuality.[21] Sex/sexuality for Mexican immigrant women is a
personal matter, while religion is a spiritual affair.[22] Furthermore, when

it comes to matters of the body and sexuality, young Chicanas make their own decisions apart from what the Catholic Church teaches about modesty and morality.[23] However, there is one question that remains unanswered. Do the ways women think about their bodies and sexuality influence their lived religion and, more specifically, how they understand *La Virgen de Guadalupe*?

What Do You Believe is La Virgen de Guadalupe's Stance on the Use of Birth Control for Women?

Across the age cohorts the women described *La Virgen* in similar ways: as a strong, loving, unconditional mother, a fighter for justice, an advocate for women, and as a humble woman that does not tolerate injustice. But how far do the women in this study go in their perception of *La Virgen* as an advocate for women? I decided to explore this question by asking them about Our Lady of Guadalupe's stance birth control.

Table 7.3 Question asked: Is Our Lady of Guadalupe pro–birth control?

Cohort	Yes	No	Don't know
Mujeres	60% (9)	27% (4)	13% (2)
Madres	27% (4)	60% (9)	13% (2)
Damas	0% (0)	67% (10)	33% (5)
Complete sample	29% (13)	51% (23)	20% (9)

Note: Numbers in parentheses = number of respondents.

Contrary to the mandates of the Catholic Church, which only approves of the rhythm method, a significant percentage of participants across cohorts believe that *La Virgen de Guadalupe* is pro–birth control for women (see Table 7.3). Not surprisingly, 67% of *Las Damas* say that Guadalupe is against birth control, and 33% say that they do not know. *Las Damas* that responded that they do not know, say that they cannot think or answer for *La Virgen* because, as Olivia (age 57) says, *"hacerlo sería atreverme mucho"* (to do so would be intrusive).

Twenty-seven percent of *Las Madres* say Our Lady of Guadalupe approves of the use of birth control; 60% say she is against; and 13% say that they do not know what her stance is. Meche's (age 42) response reflects the opinion of *Las Madres* who think that *La Virgen de Guadalupe* approves of birth control.

> Even though the Catholic Church disapproves of it, I think that she would understand that it is necessary in order to have smaller families and be able to afford raising children. Before women used to have 10 children or more, and it was difficult to raise them. I do think that she would approve.[24]

Sixty percent of *Las Mujeres* believe that *La Virgen de Guadalupe* is for birth control; 27% say she is against; 13% say they do not know. One explanation for the high percentage of *Mujeres* who think that *La Virgen de Guadalupe* approves of birth control is that they are all attending college and thus exposed to feminist beliefs about women's right to choose to use birth control. The response of Manuela (24) illustrates how women in *Las Mujeres* cohort unbind *La Virgen* from Catholic teachings on birth control. In Manuela's words, "Our Lady of Guadalupe would be pro–birth control if [she were] detached from the Church." The Church under this view is a sort of religious corset that binds *La Virgen*'s feminist autonomy. The Church is constraining for all women, including Our Lady of Guadalupe.

Overall, 29% (accounting for all cohorts) of the total sample believes that Our Lady of Guadalupe is pro–birth control for women. While this percentage may seem low, what is significant is that women at the grassroots believe in a *La Virgen* who not only symbolizes strength but also departs from the more conservative decrees of the Catholic Church in matters of women and their bodies while remaining deeply Catholic. Clearly, for some of the women, their perceptions of feminism and birth control influence their lived religion as it pertains to *La Virgen de Guadalupe*.

Early on in childhood, these women learned from their own mothers that Our Lady of Guadalupe is a loving, understanding, and nonjudgmental mother. This view of *La Virgen* as the celestial mother who would never abandon her daughters moves them (to varying degrees) to transgress the limiting views of women's bodies into which they were initially socialized. As they transcend these views, their Mexican Catholic imagination becomes more inclusive. This rearticulated imagination does not clash with their perceptions of their own bodies in relationship to their Catholic upbringing and to real life issues; they are part of the *café con leche* quality of life.

Conclusion

In sum, of the women across cohorts that do consider themselves feminists, feminism to them means gender equality at home, work, and in education. It also means mental strength, resilience, and autonomy as it pertains to choosing to use birth control or not. However, the stories of Rosario and Candelaria that opened this chapter point to the complexity of feminism within the Mexican Catholic imagination as experienced by the women in this study. At the beginning of the chapter I asked: Does some form of feminism play a role in Rosario and Candelaria's transformation? Rosario does not consider her self a feminist, but Candelaria does. This raises an important question: Because Rosario does not consider herself a feminist, can it still be argued that shooting her husband is a feminist act while not imposing this label on her? This remains an open question for debate. Candelaria, in contrast, considers herself a feminist, but her feminism differs from Chicana feminists' definition of that term because generally Chicana feminism does not consider religion as an intersectional force that might move women to take a stand against domestic violence.

Significantly, the fact that some of the women across cohorts, like Rosario and Candelaria, do not see *La Virgen de Guadalupe* as feminist does not necessarily mean that they think of her as a submissive and suffering mother. Quite the opposite is true: they see her as a symbol of love, strength and resilience. Their description of feminism and the characteristics that the women across cohorts assign to *La Virgen* reveal a type of feminist consciousness that wrestles with and sometimes transgresses Catholic orthodoxy but remains, for them, Catholic.

Wanting to learn more about how their interpretations of feminism unfold within their Mexican Catholic imagination and devotion to Our Lady of Guadalupe in particular, I asked the women what they thought of Chicana feminists' artistic representations of Our Lady of Guadalupe. The next chapter's exploration of their opinions on Chicana feminist representations of *La Virgen* reveals more about how they think of feminism in relation to *La Virgen de Guadalupe*.

8

Why Do They Paint Her This Way?
She Is Our Mother

Introduction

As I packed my computer, the projector, and the video camera, memories of my *abuelita* (grandmother) came to my mind. I remembered sitting on her lap as she told me the story of *La Virgen de Guadalupe*. She loved telling me the story, and the tone of her voice as she narrated the story made it come to life, so it seemed to me as though I was hearing it for the first time. As I prepared to interview the women participating in my research study, the rapid palpitations of my heart and the migraine pain I felt building suddenly brought me back to the present moment. I was getting ready to conduct my first focus group with *Las Damas*. I could not wait to hear what they had to share about their devotion to *La Virgen*, and at the same time I wanted to slow down the clock. I was very nervous because the focus groups involved a slide show presentation of Chicana feminist representations of *La Virgen de Guadalupe*. As I discussed in Chapter 1, Chicana feminist interpretations tend to depart from traditional representations and have caused controversy when displayed in other venues. I headed out the door—all this debating back and forth about whether to include this piece in the investigation or not had made me late.

This chapter analyzes how *Las Damas, Las Madres,* and *Las Mujeres'* understanding of *La Virgen* informs their responses to Chicana feminist representations of Our Lady of Guadalupe, revealing much about their understanding of feminism and the workings of lived religion in their Mexican Catholic imagination. Their opinions of Chicana feminist representations are complex, and as uplifting as they are critical. Some will agree and others disagree with their views, but in spite of the intellectual battles over who has the right to interpret *La Virgen*, what is important to recognize is that we cannot ignore the opinions of women who "live" a Guadalupan devotion.

As we have seen throughout the chapters, according to the women across cohorts, *La Virgen de Guadalupe* is present in their daily life in moments of joy, fear, anxiety, and sorrow. If she is indeed "Our Lady of Everyday Life" for these women, how then would Our Lady of Guadalupe look if she were actually to appear to them? *Las Damas* and *Las Madres* said that Our Lady of Guadalupe would look the same as in traditional representations, and that they could not imagine her otherwise because they are, as one woman put it: "accustomed to seeing her in a certain way." *Las Damas* answers to my question ranged from "I cannot imagine her different" to a simple yet firm "no." While *Las Madres* had similar responses, they added more descriptive details. In one of the focus groups I conducted with *Las Madres*, in a brisk tone one woman interrupted and quipped, "*¿Verla usando una minifalda o shorts? No*" (To see her wearing a mini-skirt or shorts? No). The rest of the women in the focus group laughed in agreement. Another quickly replied by saying, "*No me importa pensar si se vería diferente, no*" (I do not care to think if she would be different, no). The responses of *Las Madres* across the focus groups I conducted carried emotions of bewilderment; seen from their social location, I was asking an illogical and improper question.

Las Mujeres were more detailed in how they imagine Our Lady of Guadalupe would look if she were to appear to them. While there were *Mujeres* that could not imagine *La Virgen de Guadalupe* in any other way, and their firm tone of voice made it clear, others said that *La Virgen* would be wearing *huaraches* (sandals) or would simply be barefoot. Other *Mujeres* focused on her hair and said that she would be wearing her hair in two long *trensas* (braids), or she would be wearing her hair in a simple ponytail. Yet others focused on her clothing and said that her dress would be slightly shorter, maybe to her ankle, and her mantle not as long, and she would be wearing little hoop earrings. Their responses to my question allow me to see the ways *La Virgen de Guadalupe* visually enters and inhabits their worlds. This made me wonder how they would perceive Chicana feminist representations of Our Lady of Guadalupe.

Responses to Chicana Feminist Representations
of La Virgen de Guadalupe

Before analyzing the responses from the three cohorts to Chicana artistic interpretations of this religious icon, a recap of the context and purpose of this artistic and political project may be useful. In their attempts to decolonize and empower women, Chicana feminist artists selectively engage with Mexican popular Catholic practices, Native American and Mexican pre-Columbian religions, and iconography to create a type of hybrid spirituality that is healing, socially agentic, and politicized.[1] In particular, they have reinterpreted the image of Our Lady of Guadalupe and offered feminist representations of her.

Unfortunately, when Chicana representations of Our Lady of Guadalupe make news headlines in Spanish-language TV networks, the discourse tends to be framed in a dichotomous paradigm that fails to capture the complexity of responses such images provoke among believers. Here I refer to the women who, like Las Madres and Las Damas, have no access to scholarly conferences or access to feminist theological writings and Chicana feminist studies, and thus do not participate in the public project of intellectual knowledge-making on Our Lady of Guadalupe. I also refer here to young Mexican-origin women like Las Mujeres, who come from Catholic traditional families and have been exposed to Chicana Studies in college. To what extent do they see themselves represented in feminist artistic interpretations of La Virgen de Guadalupe? In the voices I feature in this chapter, I include Rosario (Las Damas) and Candelaria (Las Madres), whose stories of domestic psychological and physical abuse were the focus of the previous chapter. Given their near-death experiences, faith, and resilience, do Rosario and Candelaria find Chicana feminist rep-representations empowering? While there is literature on why Chicana artists are moved to represent Our Lady of Guadalupe, we know very little about how ordinary women think of these representations.[2]

Thus, I conducted a series of small focus group discussions followed by individual interviews. The focus groups that I conducted included a slide show presentation of Chicana feminist representations of Our Lady of Guadalupe. The purpose of this aspect of the research was to find out about their collective thoughts on the ways Chicana artists represent La Virgen. In the individual interviews that followed, we revisited the images and I asked each woman to further comment on the representations. The slide show contained eleven Chicana feminist representations of Our Lady of Guadalupe.

To launch these focus groups, as I mentioned earlier in this chapter, I prompted the women to consider how they would describe Our Lady of Guadalupe. Once they shared their thoughts, I replied that, just like them, other women understand *La Virgen de Guadalupe* in various ways, and through their paintings attempt to personify these attributes. If they were not familiar with the Chicana/o movement, as in the case of *Las Madres* and *Las Damas*, I made a general introduction as a way of contextualizing Chicana art within this larger history.³ What follows are their general opinions of all the Chicana feminist representations of *La Virgen de Guadalupe* that formed part of the slide show. I presented each image and had them comment on it. I decided to not provide information initially on the individual representations, because I wanted to know their first impressions. After they commented on an image, I provided more information on it as we continued the focus group discussion. The focus groups revealed clear collective thought patterns. For example, among *Las Damas* and *Las Madres*, as soon as one the women objected to the image, the others followed either by making comments or simply nodding their heads in agreement. However, *Las Mujeres* were more likely to voice their opinions even if it meant going against what others were saying. One explanation might be that they attend college and the classroom culture encourages students to voice their opinions.

Las Damas

Just as I had suspected, the focus group discussions were rich and at times uncomfortable for everyone, including me. The women usually began criticizing the images right away. On other occasions there was complete silence in the room. Some *Damas* were very outspoken; others looked at the images in disbelief; and yet others turned their eyes away from the images and stared at the floor. Their silence felt like an eternity to me, and I could not help but ask myself, what had I done? Had I insulted them and their faith in *La Virgen de Guadalupe* by showing them these images? The comments of *Las Damas* in regard to the paintings were based on occasional quick glances at the images as they were too uncomfortable to stare at them. In one of the focus groups, one of *Las Damas* got up from her chair and approached me and, upset, told me: *"eso no se hace muchachita, ella es nuestra madre,"* meaning, "you do not do this young lady, she is our mother." She thought I had painted the images. When I mentioned that I did not paint any of the images she calmed down, but remained somewhat upset.

It was at these moments of anger, confusion, and misunderstanding that I regretted including this piece in the research. Part of me felt as though I had made a big mistake, yet another part of me felt a strong responsibility to document their thoughts, as harsh as they might seem, on the Chicana feminist representations of *La Virgen*. I decided to tell them the reason why I was showing them the images. I explained that while we know much about what propels Chicana feminist interpretations of *La Virgen de Guadalupe*, we know very little of what women like them have to say. And their opinions are far too important to be ignored. Once I made my intentions clear, they were a little more at ease, and the group dynamic shifted. It no longer felt like I was imposing the images on them, but rather that *Las Damas* were the authorities on the views and opinions of ordinary women on these representations. In fact, I also observed this change in attitude among *Las Madres* and *Las Mujeres* when I told them the reason why I was presenting these images to them.

Las Madres

Las Madres, like *Las Damas*, perceived the representations of *La Virgen* as disrespectful. As I showed the images, some opted to remain silent and shake their heads in disagreement and others were vocal, but there was tension in each of the focus groups nonetheless. One difference between *Las Damas* and *Las Madres* was in the degree of detail in their opinions. Like *Las Damas*, some mentioned that the representations showed a lack of respect not only to Our Lady of Guadalupe, their holy mother, but also to the faithful. *Las Madres* had strong views on the images that ranged from anger to confusion, as I demonstrate below. However, they were more open to hear why Chicana feminist artists represented *La Virgen de Guadalupe* in these ways.

Las Mujeres

Since I had already interviewed *Las Madres* by the time I conducted the interviews with *Las Mujeres*, I added an additional method to those focus groups. Like in the two previous cohorts, I began the focus groups by having them comment on the images; this was followed by the stories behind the image. In our discussion afterwards, I read to them some of the quotes from *Las Madres* and asked them what they thought about what *Las Madres* had to say about the representations. The young women said that they understood why *Las Madres* would perceive the images as disrespectful, but they would not go as far as seeing, for example, "Our Lady" by Alma López as an image of a sex worker. When commenting on what *Las Madres* had to say, *Las Mujeres* made reference to their own mothers and grandmothers and said that they understood *Las Madres*, because like their mothers and grandmothers, they are traditional. In the next section, I analyze what they had to share about two images in particular: "Walking Guadalupe" (1978) by Yolanda López, and "Our Lady" (1999) by Alma López. I highlight the women's discussion of these two images because they provoked the most revealing reactions. I argue that these reactions illustrate how the women's relationships to *La Virgen de Guadalupe* along the vertical (or heavenly) axis and along the horizontal (or earthly) axis are shaped by race, class, gender, religion, sexuality, and generation, and this in turn informs their larger Mexican Catholic imagination.

"Walking Guadalupe" (1978)

In 1978 Yolanda M. López produced a mixed-media collage titled "Walking Guadalupe." The image depicts *La Virgen de Guadalupe* as traditionally portrayed, with a couple of exceptions: her dress and mantle are calf-length, and she is wearing slip-on high-heeled shoes (see Figure I.3). This representation caused international uproar when *Fem* magazine, a Mexican feminist magazine, had "Walking Guadalupe" as the cover for their June–July 1984 special issue on Chicanas. Not surprisingly, the Church was the first institution to object publicly, followed by ultra-conservative groups. The artist received death threats and the magazine was forced to remove their special issue on *Las Chicanas* from newspaper stands.[4] What was so troubling about the image and why? The opinions of the women provide some answers, at least from the perspective of ordinary Catholic women.

The opinions of *Las Damas*, *Las Madres*, and *Las Mujeres* regarding "Walking Guadalupe" overlap at various points. Therefore, instead of separating the opinions of each of the cohorts into subsections, the analysis that follows weaves their opinions. The three cohorts liked the representation to the extent that it corresponded with the traditional image of *La Virgen de Guadalupe*. They pointed out that they liked her face, her hands in the position of prayer, and the color of the mantle and dress. In short, they liked the representation from the waist up; however, from the waist down, they disagreed with aspects of the image. *Las Damas* and *Las Madres* did not like the length of her dress and mantle, and her legs; and all three cohorts disliked the shoes. Rosario (*Las Damas* cohort), for example, said: "*No entiendo, ¿por qué la pintan así? Es nuestra madre*" (I don't understand, why do they paint her this way? She is our mother). Rosario could not comprehend why someone would represent *La Virgen* with a shorter dress and mantle and wearing shoes. Like the other *Damas*, she considers *La Virgen de Guadalupe* her mother, and as a mother *La Virgen* deserves full respect. *Las Damas* and *Las Madres* objected to the length of her mantle and dress because the hemline was at calf-length. Their comments once again made me nervous, because if they were uncomfortable with this image, I knew that they were going to object to Alma López's image that could be considered more revealing.

After *Las Damas*, *Las Madres*, and *Las Mujeres* expressed their dislike of the shoes *La Virgen de Guadalupe* is wearing in this representation, I told them that the artist's intention was to counter the stifling roles that women have in society. I also shared with them that one of the messages the artist is trying to convey is that *La Virgen* needs movement. I added that according to the artist, the length of her mantle and dress, and being carried by an angel in traditional representations, prevents *La Virgen* from moving. In one of the focus groups with *Las Damas*, one replied: "*La Virgen de Guadalupe se mueve a través de nuestra fe, ella no necesita un manto o vestido corto*" (Our Lady of Guadalupe moves through our faith, she does not need a short mantle and dress). Similarly, *Las Madres* expressed that Our Lady of Guadalupe moves through those that have faith in her. Candelaria (*Las Madres* cohort), for example, said: "I can see what the artist is trying to communicate, but *La Virgen* does not need to be painted in a different way. She moves through the faith that we have in her."[5] Later in the individual interview, Candelaria told me that she based her opinion on her own lived experience with domestic violence. If we recall from the previous chapter, Candelaria said that *La Virgen de Guadalupe* gave her the strength to lift her husband. *Las Damas* and *Las Madres* critiqued the length of the dress and mantle in light of how they think faith materializes.

Clearly, the way *Las Damas* and *Las Madres* understand Our Lady of Guadalupe's movement differs from that of the artist. For *Las Damas* and *Las Madres*, *La Virgen* moves through people's faith. For Yolanda M. López, who in previous interviews has stated to not have a devotion to Our Lady of Guadalupe and thus her perspective is strictly artistic, *La Virgen*'s movement had to be physically represented.[6] *Las Mujeres* simply said that they do not think *La Virgen de Guadalupe* needs to show her legs and wear shoes to move. *Las Damas, Las Madres*, and *Las Mujeres'* answers reveal how they come to understand their faith in light of their life experience.

Another aspect that *Las Damas, Las Madres*, and *Las Mujeres* disliked was that she was wearing shoes, and all three cohorts critiqued the type of shoes depicted in the image. In one of the focus groups with *Las Damas*, one woman took it a step further and asked: "*¿Qué tan lejos puede ir con esos zapatos?*" (How far can she go wearing those shoes?). Another *Dama* quickly responded, "*Pos [pues]no muy lejos*" (Well, not very far). *Las Madres* supported their critique of the shoes with their own experience wearing that type of shoe. As Vicky (age 31) said: "*He usado ese tipo de zapatillas y después de usarlas un rato se sienten incómodas*" (I have worn that type of shoe and after a while they are uncomfortable).

There was an additional aspect of the image that some of *Las Madres* focused on that I did not hear from *Las Damas*. Some of *Las Madres* focused on her weight and expressed that this aspect of the representation of *La Virgen de Guadalupe* bothered them: "*En esta imagen, ella está bien gorda y sus piernas están gordas también, y así no es como es ella, La Virgen es delgada*" (In this image she is really fat and her legs are fat too, and this is not the way she is, *La Virgen* is slender). Other *Madres* went a little further and said that they disliked this representation because "*La Virgen se ve bien gorda y ella no es así, ella es bonita*" (La Virgen looks too fat and she is not like that, she is beautiful). Clearly, there is a degree of internalization of idealistic body image expectations for women at work in their articulations of "Walking Guadalupe." I read to *Las Mujeres* some of these comments. They were shocked about what *Las Madres* had to say, but they also added that this is exactly what their own mothers would probably say about the image.

Las Mujeres went further, attributing their critique of the shoes to their own feminist stance. For example, Elena (age 21) said, "I don't think *La Virgen* likes wearing *tacones* [high heel shoes]. You know I am thinking in my feminist point of view." In general, *Las Mujeres* said that while they did not necessarily agree with the image, they understood why some women might find it offensive. Some did not find the representation empowering. Yet, there were others who saw nothing wrong with the image and found it inspiring. In Anita's (age 21) words:

> By adding the feet and the legs, you know, women can identify with her. She walks just like we walk. She can do it herself you know she

doesn't need the angel to hold her up. She doesn't need anybody to
do anything for her.

If we recall, Anita identifies as a Chicana and this in part explains why she
is able to see Yolanda M. López's message through the depiction of Our
Lady of Guadalupe as "Walking Guadalupe." The next image, "Our Lady"
by Alma López, elicited even more diverse opinions across cohorts.

"Our Lady" by Alma López

"Our Lady" (1999) by Alma López represents *La Virgen de Guadalupe* wearing a two-piece outfit made out of bright, colorful roses. Her eyes and posture convey an assertive stance. Her veil is the dismembered Aztec goddess
Coyolxauhqui, and at her feet is a woman posing as the angel and her
breasts are exposed (see Figure I.4). As mentioned in Chapter 1, during
Holy Week a museum in Santa Fe, New Mexico exhibited "Our Lady" as
part of a larger exhibit titled "Cyber Arte." The exhibit made many people
angry, for according to them, Alma López had committed a sacrilegious
act. Alma López, however, was perplexed, for no one asked her why she had
represented *La Virgen de Guadalupe* in this way. Raquel Salinas, the woman
posing as *La Virgen*, was raped when she was a teenager and she was made
to feel ashamed by those closest to her. Therefore, posing as *La Virgen* was
her way of healing her spirit and reaffirming her body and sexuality.

I will never forget *Las Damas'* expression when they saw the image,
"Our Lady." They looked at the image; they looked at me, at each other,
and turned their eyes away from the image. Rosario was one of the first to
comment: "*¿Por qué hacen eso con Nuestra Madre?*" (Why do they do that to
Our Mother?). Artemia, who was in the same focus group, added: "*A mi
da tristesa que la tomen como juego. 'Pos si no es una Barbie 'pa que la vistan
y desvistan*" (It makes me sad that they play with her image. She is not a
Barbie for them to dress and undress). The comments in the other focus
groups were similar to Artemia's and Rosario's.

Some of *Las Damas* expressed sadness because, as Paloma (age 80) put
it, "*Las muchachas de hoy han perdido el verdadero significado de La Virgen*"
(Young women today have lost the true significance of *La Virgen*). Other
Damas focused their attention on the angel, and critiqued the angel
because the woman's breasts were exposed. These objections are not too
different from the ones made in Santa Fe. Some viewers of this image
may think: What is the big deal? Breasts are part of the female and male

body and there is nothing wrong; we should celebrate our sexuality with pride. Those who tend to be more conservative might be thinking: "*Las Damas* are absolutely right. Alma López's representation is wrong." If we recall from Chapter 5, when *Las Damas* were coming of age, breasts were something that had to be concealed. Therefore, in their eyes, the fact that the angel had her breasts exposed was not only wrong but went against how they learned to perceive this part of their bodies. The constructions of gender into which *Las Damas* were socialized, particularly during puberty, desexualized the female body, and this became the lens through which they interpreted "Our Lady."

After I told them the story of Raquel the model, in each of the *Las Damas* focus groups there was silence, and they looked at each other and slowly they began to speak again. Though they understood the trauma Raquel had experienced, they still disapproved of the way she posed for "Our Lady." Artemia, who like Raquel suffered trauma, went up to the camera that was recording her focus group, but not before asking one of the women sitting next to her "¿como me veo?" (how do I look?), and looking directly at it said: "*Eso no se hace. Eso no se le hace a una madre. ¿Tu pintarias a tu propia madre así?*" (You don't do this. You don't do this to a mother. Would you have painted your own mother in this way?). Artemia was clearly upset.

Las Madres, like *Las Damas*, perceived the image of "Our Lady" as disrespectful of *La Virgen*. One stark difference between *Las Damas* and *Las Madres* was in the degree to which their opinions were explicit. For example, some said that more than empowering women, the image carries the potential to arouse men, and therefore it is wrong. As for the angel, like *Las Damas*, they thought it was improper to expose the breasts. However, *Las Madres* placed less emphasis on the angel than did *Las Damas*. One explanation for this is the difference in generation. *Las Madres* came of age at a time women's breasts were not as heavily policed as in the time of *Las Damas*. There was one focus group exchange in particular that sums up the opinions I heard among *Las Madres*.

According to Gabriela (age 37), the representation was sexually suggestive, which, in her eyes, was offensive. For Eva (age 44), "*La mujer de la pintura parece una prostituta que trabaja en las cantinas*" (The woman in the painting looks like a prostitute who works bars). I then interjected and proceeded to tell them the story behind the painting, as I had done with the other focus groups, but this did not make a difference for *Las Madres*. For the women, the representation was not only insulting; some felt that the woman who posed as "Our Lady" looked like a sex worker, and by extension, as Eva put it, "a *Playboy* figure."

According to Beatriz (age 34), the image was like a logo for something that is not good; besides, she insisted, *La Virgen de Guadalupe* is completely covered, and in this representation she exposes her body. Laura (age 37) in a nervous tone said:

> For me . . . well . . . now knowing the story . . . one thinks a little . . . about the person . . . not of the painting . . . because [*La Virgen*] granted her a miracle and was able to show her body again. But about the person who did the painting and what she has to say . . . the message she gives is different. Because if my husband . . . if he were to see this picture where she is like this . . . no . . . it's because whoever sees this picture, I don't know . . . a young man he would get aroused . . . This is why I say it is not good . . . it is something of the devil. *La Virgen* is supposed to be something of God . . . something sacred. [The rest of the women in the focus group nodded their heads in agreement.][7]

Laura understood the woman's reasons for posing for the painting: *La Virgen* had granted her a miracle. What she could not understand was why López had decided to paint her in that manner, for according to Laura "she gives a different message." This message, from her social location, is one of "uncontrolled sexuality," and for this reason *La Virgen* in this representation "cannot be good." The theme of men's uncontrolled sexuality, and women's responsibility to conceal their bodies so as to not provoke men permeated *Las Madres'* interpretations of "Our Lady."

Candelaria (age 39) said that if she had the opportunity, *"le diría que hay otras formas de compartir su mensaje y no necesariamente vestirla con un disfraz"* (I would tell her that there are other ways of sharing her message and not necessarily dressing her in a costume). Candelaria's response reflects the tenor of *Las Madres'* analysis of the image. In sum, what for Chicanas is a representation of sexual agency and liberation, *Las Madres* saw as disrespectful.

One of *Las Madres* asked me with some puzzlement why the artists had chosen to represent *La Virgen de Guadalupe* as opposed to other images. I suggested that Chicana feminists argue that *La Virgen* must be liberated from the negative associations of acceptance, submission, and the colonization of women through which the Church in general tends to continue to oppress women. Mereides (age 47) interrupted me, disagreeing with me: "*Oh no. . . no way . . . .*" I asked if any of them had been told that they had to be like *La Virgen*, or if they had been told that *La Virgen de Guadalupe* was the model for women to follow? Laughing at my questions, Faviola (age 46) said "no," and was joined by the rest of *Las Madres'* assenting voices. In Faviola's words: "*No, a mí nunca me dijeron que tenía que ser como La Virgen de Guadalupe*" (No, I was never told that I had to be like *La Virgen de Guadalupe*). Mereides elaborated on her initial response and made the distinction between religion and Our Lady of Guadalupe.

> To follow the principles of your religion is something different. If you are a good Catholic, you follow the rules. But you are never going to see *La Virgen de Guadalupe* as an example to follow or try to be like her. She is original, she is special.[8]

Mereides makes a distinction between religion as an institution, with a set of rules to follow, and Our Lady of Guadalupe. For her, *La Virgen* transcends the set of regulations set by the Catholic Church. *La Virgen de Guadalupe* for her is original, and this makes her special, and she or anyone else cannot emulate this quality. I asked the same questions in the in-depth interviews, and the responses of the women across cohorts were similar to Mereides'. None of them had ever been told that they had to be like Our Lady of Guadalupe nor did they perceive *La Virgen* as a role model for women that represents submissiveness, passivity, and obedience for Mexican women.

Though these women received messages on obedience that were justified as a mandate from the Catholic Church (as I demonstrate in Chapter 4), at least in their experience, *La Virgen de Guadalupe* was never used as the ideal role model to follow. This is contrary to Chicana feminist assertions that Our Lady of Guadalupe is the idealized role model for obedience that Chicanas/Mexican American women are taught to emulate. My respondents' departure from Chicana feminist claims reaffirms the need for more nuanced ethnographic analysis of women's lives. I argue that this can only be done through an intersectional analysis of race, class, gender, sexuality, and religion. This would allow us to see when, where, how, and under what circumstances the symbol of *La Virgen de Guadalupe* is used to propel a type of obedience that represses women's agency.

The women's perceptions of Alma López's "Our Lady" and their answers to my question about *La Virgen de Guadalupe* as role model reveal the complexity and sophistication of their Mexican Catholic imagination. While they do not see *La Virgen* as a model to emulate, their stories of growing up Catholic (discussed in Chapters 4 and 5) reveal the intrinsic ways Catholic patriarchal perceptions of the female body, like water, find their way into shaping their Mexican Catholic imagination. On one hand, they disagree with Alma López's representation of Our Lady of Guadalupe and describe her in ways that are reflective of how they learned to perceive the female body. On the other hand, in spite of growing up in strict households, they do not assign oppressive attributes to Our Lady of Guadalupe. Analyzing how these women's understanding of *La Virgen* and women's bodies informs their responses to Chicana feminist representations of Our Lady of Guadalupe reveals much about the workings of lived religion in their Mexican Catholic imagination.

While the focus groups allowed me to learn about their collective ways of interpreting "Our Lady," the individual interviews revealed the complexity of how some women receive and interpret Chicana feminist representations of *La Virgen*. Some interpreted this in ways that ran counter to the general sentiments of most of the cohorts. It gave them the opportunity to share what they really felt about Alma López's representation. Of *Las Madres* that participated in the focus groups, there were two women, Sandra and Meche, who in the group sharing objected to the image as much as the rest of the *Madres* from their respective groups. However, when I interviewed them individually, they had different opinions. Sandra (age 21) made a distinction between the image of *La Virgen de Guadalupe* as we traditionally know it and the representations.

> If I see the painting from a religious point of view, I do see it as a lack
> of respect. If I see it from the perspective of art, then I see it more
> like what she did in this representation is part of her profession.[9]

One explanation could be that she was among the youngest of *Las Madres*.

In another focus group there was Meche (age 42), who was in complete agreement with the women who were saying that "Our Lady" looked like a sex worker. In our in-depth interview she thanked me for the opportunity to express what she really felt about López's "Our Lady."

> I wanted to say how I really felt about the representation, but out
> of respect for the other women in the group I chose to stay quiet.
> I was a prostitute, and to hear the other women criticize "Our Lady"
> because she looked like a prostitute hurt me.[10]

To understand Meche's reaction, it helps to know some particulars of her own story and the role of *La Virgen de Guadalupe* she saw in it. She became involved with a young man who was a few years older when she was 17. Out of this relationship she became pregnant twice; her partner never took responsibility for his children, and her family disowned her. Finding herself alone with two children, in her desperation and need for survival she became a sex worker. "*Sentí que no tenía otra salida, mis hijos tenían hambre. ¿Qué más podría haber hecho?*" (I felt I had no other way out, my children were hungry, what else could I have done?).

Unfortunately, the social stigma attached to what she saw as her only option to survive led to tragic consequences. One day, when she felt so ashamed of herself that she could no longer cope with the life that she was living, she attempted suicide, slitting her wrists with a knife. Fortunately, someone found her and took her to the hospital and Meche survived. To this day she cannot explain how she survived, but the one thing that she is certain about is that *La Virgen de Guadalupe* gave her a second chance at life. She is now 42 and happily married to another man.

In her explanation of her relationship with Our Lady of Guadalupe, Meche said: "*La Virgen es mi roca. Ella es muy amorosa, pero también exige que tengamos el control de nuestras vidas. Ella no es sumisa*" (*La Virgen* is my rock. She is loving, but she also demands that we get control of our lives. She is not submissive). Rejection and a sense of shame imposed by family led her to ultimately inflict violence on herself, but her faith in *La Virgen* moved her to become resilient.[11] Meche added:

> The women who have had a beautiful childhood cannot see *La Virgen* like I see her . . . they cannot relate to the painting because they have not suffered. I can see what Alma López is trying to say, and I completely agree.[12]

Meche not only understood Alma López's message, but the suffering she had experienced in life and her near-death experience allowed her in some way to see herself in "Our Lady." What is more, she added: "*Yo le añadiria otras cosas a la pintura*" (I would even add other things to the painting). I took this opportunity to ask her to describe to me her own representation of *La Virgen de Guadalupe*. She replied:

> I would paint her completely naked, with her arms open. She would not be ashamed of her sexuality. I would also draw around her, a

condom, birth control pills, a beer can, [a] syringe, and two young men fighting. My *Virgen*'s message would be one of pregnancy, gang, and drug prevention.[13]

If we recall from the previous chapter, Meche is one of the *Madres* who believes that *La Virgen de Guadalupe* supports birth control. Clearly, Meche's example demonstrates the range and complexity that exists among these women.

Las Mujeres also had much to say about "Our Lady." Like Sandra from *Las Madres* cohort, Dolores (age 19) from *Las Mujeres* cohort does not necessarily agree with Alma López's representation, but says that she is able to see what the artist is trying to project with the image. When I asked her what it is that helps her see what these artists are trying to represent even as she disagrees, she added:

> My mom and my abuelita are closed-minded, and they would not understand why Alma López is doing this. [. . .] I think that just the fact that I'm in college and you learn to be more open-minded and more receptive. You open your mind more and you learn not to be so traditional like, "oh this is the only way that it can be." There're so many ways to understand Our Lady of Guadalupe.

Like Sandra and Meche (*Las Madres* cohort), Dolores sees the possibility of many interpretations that differ but are not in conflict with one another.

Furthermore, *Las Mujeres*, like *Las Damas*, had strong opinions on the portrayal of the angel. In some cases some found the image of the female posing as "Our Lady" equally as offensive as the angel; in other cases, some thought that the angel was more offensive for having the breasts exposed. One would think that *Las Mujeres*, like *Las Madres*, would have less of an issue with the angel's breasts, but I found this not to be the case. One possible explanation is that their thoughts on the angel are reflective of the policing of their bodies that they experience as young women at home, as we learned in Chapters 4 and 5. As for the woman posing as "Our Lady," they all had something to say, and their answers revealed the range of mixed feelings they had about the representation: from the image reinforcing the sexualization and idealization of the Latina body to empowering Chicanas.

While most of *Las Mujeres* were not able to relate to "Our Lady," there were some exceptions. As this passage will demonstrate, this representation sparked reflections on struggle with ideal body images—as illustrated in one of the focus group exchanges among the women. Some considered it an affirmation of the beauty of the Chicana body—a beauty that should not be shamefully hidden under layers of clothes. Yet, there were other women who could not relate to the image because of her looks. Leonor (age 22) said: "the woman posing as 'Our Lady' has a perfect body shape, we Chicanas on the other hand have hips, and are fuller." Similarly Celene (age 20) said: "Yeah, she's pretty, she has a nice body and she looks really nice, but that is not how I look." Chavelita (age 23) added: "She is skinny. What about those of us that are not as slim as she is? The majority of us Latinas do not have that body. No, no, no." Anita (age 21) jumped into the conversation and said:

> I can relate to that image. Ashamed of my body, I tried all the diets you can think of, and none worked. My mother would take me to the mall and we would look at dresses; this was usually followed by, "*mija*, this dress would look good on you if you would just lose some weight." López's representation tells me that I should not be ashamed of my full figure. I find "Our Lady" empowering. I've been made fun of all my life about my weight. "*Que no era bonita. . . que era fea*" (that I wasn't pretty . . . that I was ugly) . . . People tell you ignore that, but when you are told that everyday, seven days a week it gets to you. All through high school I had eating disorders: bulimia, anorexia . . . you name it, I had it. To feel comfortable with your body is really hard, it took me a long time. López's representation tells me that I should not be ashamed of my body.

Later in the individual interview Anita told me that what Alma López did in "Our Lady" "was very risqué, but she does deliver a powerful message of women's empowerment." Among *Las Mujeres*, the image of "Our Lady" was perceived as both an affirmation and denial of the Latina body. What is more, the fact that some *Mujeres* disliked the representation of "Our Lady" because according to them it has a perfect body image is in some way similar to the argument made by *Las Madres* who considered "Walking Guadalupe" obese. Both perceptions of the female body image reveal the struggle some women have with society's expectations of women to fit the ideal body image.

Undeniably, many of the women from the various cohorts disapproved of these images. However, the perspective of Anita and Meche on López's representation supports feminist analyses that argue that these Chicana artists re-image *La Virgen* in ways that speak to women's self-empowerment.[14]

Conclusion

Looking back, I am glad I stepped outside my comfort zone and showed the slide presentations, because these ordinary women's reactions add to the body of knowledge of how various women receive these images. Furthermore, the diversity and range of their responses illustrate that Mexican Catholic imagination is shaped at the axis of their vertical (heavenly) and horizontal (earthly) relationships. Their testimonies suggest that a vital part of that axis is the way it is influenced by intersectionality. In other words, how they understand Chicana feminist representations of *La Virgen de Guadalupe* is influenced by the intersectionality of race, class, gender, sexuality, generation, education, and religion, and the degree of influence of each of these categories on their views. Moreover, life-changing experiences among individuals can also influence their perceptions of Chicana feminist representations of *La Virgen de Guadalupe*.

A close analysis of the intersection of race, class, gender, sexuality, generation, and religion reveals why some women were more open to Chicana feminist representations of *La Virgen* than others. The women share the same demographic attributes: race, class, gender, sexuality (all identified as heterosexual), and religion, but differ in generation and level of education. From this, one might conclude that the latter two factors explain the difference in opinions. This is not necessarily the case, however. For example, not all of *Las Mujeres* agreed with "Our Lady." For some of *Las Mujeres* (like *Las Damas* and *Las Madres*), Our Lady of Guadalupe's image does not need to be reimagined to personify her love and resilience. Therefore, generation and level of education do not seem to influence how they think of Chicana feminist representations. What, then, is the influencing factor?

The factor that seems to explain whether some women were able to be more accepting of the representations is the degree of malleability of their Mexican Catholic imagination—again influenced by the many components of intersectionality. While Rosario (*Las Damas* cohort) and Candelaria (*Las Madres* cohort), who like Meche had near-death experiences, found "Our Lady" offensive, Meche (*Las Madres* cohort) did not, and neither did Anita (*Las Mujeres* cohort). Meche, like Anita, considers herself a feminist. What is more, Meche and Anita's stories highlight the creativity that is part of the Mexican Catholic imagination—a type of creativity that takes the significance of *La Virgen de Guadalupe* and applies it meaningfully to Chicana feminist art while remaining deeply Catholic.

Conclusion

SHORTLY AFTER I first began this project, I took a pilgrimage to the Basilica in honor of *La Virgen de Guadalupe* in México City. It was near dusk, and people continued making their way to the Basilica to see *La Virgen*. Some people walked, and others made their way on their knees. Parents carrying babies, people in wheelchairs, children, teenagers, adults, older people, and entire families. Some had made long, arduous pilgrimages that lasted anywhere from a couple of days to several weeks. The continuous flow of people was overwhelming. Never in my life had I experienced the living faith and devotion to *La Virgen de Guadalupe* of thousands of people all in one place.

There was hardly any space in between people, and all seemed to move at the rhythm of smooth ocean waves on a summer night, but it was December 11—the day before the feast day of *La Virgen de Guadalupe*—and the temperature was 50 degrees and rapidly dropping with the passing of the hours. The atrium was past its capacity level. Some people made the pilgrimage with friends from their towns or communities, and others came alone. Class differences were visible. Some people were well dressed, with thick warm coats, and others had holes in their shoes. Though these different social classes pointed to contrasting life experiences, there was this sense of connectedness in the air as though we were all part of one big family coming to visit our heavenly mother. If I had to describe the feeling, I would say that it felt like I was in the womb of the world.

As I waited for the clock to strike midnight, I noticed that many of the pilgrims had fallen asleep in the atrium; some had blankets, sleeping bags, or cardboard that served as makeshift mattresses. It was getting colder by the minute; by now, the temperature had dropped to 35 degrees Fahrenheit. I looked at my watch—11:55 pm, and many were still asleep. I was puzzled: "Aren't they going to get up to listen to Mass?" I asked myself.

In the United States, it is the custom of many Catholic Mexican-origin families to tune in to one of the Spanish-language channels right at midnight on December 12 to listen to a special Mass being broadcast live from the Basilica in México City—*La Misa de Gallo*. This Mass attracts many viewers who listen attentively and await the concert that follows, which features some of the most popular Mexican singers who serenade *La Virgen de Guadalupe*.

The clock struck midnight and nothing happened. I was able to hear the Mass starting inside, pilgrims outside continued to make their way slowly into the atrium, and neither the people nor the cold seemed to bother those who were asleep. The next morning I was curious to find out why people did not get up to listen to Mass, so I asked one of the women. Surprised by my questions, she said:

'*Pos, no nos levantamos porque ya habíamos cumplido nuestra promesa a La Virgensita . . . de venir a verla.* [We did not get up because we had already fulfilled our promise to *La Virgencita*—to come and see her.]

She then continued:

Mi esposo y yo caminamos todo un día y una noche, no tenemos nada más que ofrecerle a La Virgensita nomas que nuestra fe y el polvo que nuestros zapatos recogieron en la peregrinación para venir a visitarla. [My husband and I walked one full day and night, we have nothing more to offer to *La Virgensita* but our faith and the dust that our shoes collected on our pilgrimage to come visit her.]

Though I identify as a Catholic and *La Virgen de Guadalupe* holds a special place for me, at first I was not able to understand why people would skip Mass. "Isn't that disrespectful to the Church?" I asked myself. My confusion stemmed from my memories as a child attending Mass and my mother pinching me every time I dozed off. In the process of completing this study, it all began to make sense to me. Even at the Basilica, a holy ground representative of the institutional Church, the lived religion of the people transgresses the expectations of the Catholic Church for its faithful, such as attending Mass.

Moved by the staying power of *La Virgen de Guadalupe* I witnessed at the Basilica, I wanted to know more about her significance, and the women in this study allowed me to see that their devotion is part of something bigger. Initially, I did not know what to call it or how to describe it.

Through their life histories, however, I came to understand the significance of *La Virgen de Guadalupe* as part of a phenomenon I call in this
book the *Mexican Catholic imagination*.

Mexican Catholic Imagination Defined

According to Andrew Greeley, "Catholics live in an enchanted world." In
this world, the sense of connectedness to God and saints is materialized
in objects deemed holy (i.e., votive candles), and that points to a profound
sense of awareness "that inclines Catholics to see the Holy lurking in creation" (Greeley 2000, 1). What I learned from the women I interviewed for
this study led me to move beyond Greeley's suggestive definition to articulate patterns of meaning-making that emerged from their lived experience.
As their stories unfolded, key terms revealing aspects of how they enter
into relationship with the sacred emerged as central to what I came to
call their Mexican Catholic imagination. These terms include: *flor y canto*,
popular Catholicism, Spanish inflected, *café con leche, cotidiano* (daily life),
familismo (familism), vertical and horizontal relationships, and (fe)minism.

A key part of what brought those crowds to the Basilica in honor of
La Virgen de Guadalupe in México City on the night that I witnessed was
a foundation laid early in life. The women were socialized early into the
devotion to *La Virgen* within a "devotional triangle" composed of mother,
daughter, and Our Lady of Guadalupe. This devotional triangle became
the anchor of their connectedness to *La Virgen de Guadalupe* and initially
formed their Mexican Catholic imagination even before they fully grasped
an understanding of Our Lady of Guadalupe. This relationship was solidified through a *flor y canto* (flower and song) essence that drew on popular Catholicism to socialize the women in childhood into particular ways
of expressing devotion to *La Virgen*. *Flor y canto* is a Nahua concept to
refer to the profound poetic quality of the Nahua people's horizontal (with
other people) and vertical (with sacred entities) communications. For *Las
Damas, Las Madres*, and *Las Mujeres*, and people I met during my research
in México, *flor y canto* takes many forms. This includes the metaphors
people use to describe their relationship with *La Virgen de Guadalupe*, as
in the case of the woman at the Basilica who told me that she had nothing to offer *La Virgen* but her faith and the dust her shoes had collected
in her pilgrimage. It is also expressed in family, cultural, and religious
traditions embedded in national pride and communicated in a particular
language—Spanish.[1]

As the devotional triangle helped the women establish a vertical (or heavenly) relationship with *La Virgen de Guadalupe*, it intersected with their horizontal (or earthly) relationships with their mothers, and the experiences that come with *lo cotidiano* (daily life). These intersecting relationships (vertical and horizontal) have a *familismo* (familism) quality, crafting a type of connectedness to Our Lady of Guadalupe that is very similar to the love and respect they feel for their earthly mothers. However, the experiences that come with life and the relationships that emerge have a double-edged nature—they are life-giving and at times stifling. For example, popular Catholic traditions such as home altars and family and community Catholic practices helped strengthen the bond between mothers and daughters, and the sense of closeness that the women in this study felt with *La Virgen*. Other life experiences had serious consequences that came about as a result of rigid, gendered definitions of respect and obedience, which impacted girls and women to a greater degree than boys and men. Such experiences revealed that how some women act—including what they choose to accept or contest—is shaped by the intersection of race, class, gender, sexuality, and religion. My findings based on an intergenerational analysis of the life experiences of *Las Damas*, *Las Madres*, and *Las Mujeres*, point to generation as another important category of analysis. The intersections of all these categories that shape life take place at the axis of their vertical and horizontal relationships—though at varying degrees.

Significantly, another trait clearly evident in the Mexican Catholic imagination of the women featured in this study is the central and profound role *La Virgen de Guadalupe* continues to occupy in their lives. The concept of "chain of memory" provides an initial explanation. People are socialized into a "chain of memory" (Hervieu-Léger 2000), which brings them into a collective shared belief system. However, with time people begin to distance themselves from such belief systems and may adopt other religious or spiritual alternatives.[2] This is true in some cases, but there is something distinctive about devotion to *La Virgen de Guadalupe* that contributes to her staying power. Her significance cuts across generations, genders, and national, religious, and ethnic boundaries. People give her prayers and their gratitude, and even mundane offerings, as in the case of the woman I met at the Basilica—the dust that her shoes collected in her pilgrimage to see her mother, *La Virgen de Guadalupe*.

Psychologist Robert Jay Lifton's (1993) concept of the *protean self* helps to further explain *La Virgen de Guadalupe*'s staying power in the lives of the women in this study. According to Lifton, the protean self is the source of the ability to adapt to social changes without losing the part of the self that anchors one's being. One can think of the devotional triangle as the part of the self that anchors one's Catholic faith. From this grounded devotional space, women re-articulate what *La Virgen de Guadalupe* means to them and what she advocates as they themselves question, contest, and challenge gender expectations and family configurations that were passed on to them. As evidenced by the life stories analyzed in this book, this protean quality—this type of consciousness—that allows them to transgress gender roles and expectations does not suddenly emerge out of thin air. It evolves over time and is continuously shaped by the intersection of race, class, gender, sexuality, and religion, and generation.[3]

The staying power of their devotion to *La Virgen* is rooted in the devotional triangle (mother–Our Lady of Guadalupe–daughter) in which they were initially socialized and introduced to *La Virgen de Guadalupe*. As their devotion evolved, they learned from their own mothers to see *La Virgen* as their heavenly yet accessible mother who coexists alongside and not in competition with their birth mothers. This explains why some did not approve of Chicana feminist representations of Our Lady of Guadalupe, by arguing that this should not be done to *La Virgen*—"*nuestra madre*" (our mother).

What is more, instead of blindly accepting androcentric Catholic teachings or rejecting Catholicism altogether, *Las Damas, Madres,* and *Mujeres'* Mexican Catholic imagination allows them to transgress limiting notions of what a good Catholic woman should be, while retaining the aspects of Catholicism they found life-giving—all while continuing to identify as Catholics. This is most visible in two ways; first, in their relationship to *La Virgen de Guadalupe*, which is not fixed but fluid and deeply engaged in their process of self-awareness. For example, they do not take the Catholic Church's stance on birth control at face value. Second, it influences the extent to which they consider themselves and *La Virgen de Guadalupe* feminist, thus opening a new set of questions about the intersection of their devotion to Our Lady of Guadalupe and feminism within their Mexican Catholic imagination.

There were, however, limits to the extent to which their feminism transgresses the Catholic Church. For example, when I asked *Las Damas, Las Madres,* and *Las Mujeres* to comment on Chicana feminist artistic representations of Our Lady of Guadalupe, the majority across cohorts found the images challenging. While there were a few that were open to these interpretations, for the most part the women in this study did not see a need to reinterpret *La Virgen de Guadalupe*. They objected to the representations by arguing that the images were disrespectful to Our Lady of Guadalupe, their heavenly mother, and to the faithful.

Furthermore, Aída Hurtado (2003b) contends that there are "underground feminism[s]" that have yet to be studied and documented. This raises the question: Do the experiences of some of the women in this study point to some type of underground feminism? The women find empowerment in a Catholic Guadalupe. They see no need to draw on multiple religious traditions or associate *La Virgen de Guadalupe* with the Aztec goddess Tonantzin to find meaning in Our Lady of Guadalupe in their experience as Mexican-origin women.

The experiences of the women in this study indicate that this way of relating to *La Virgen* does not capture their lived religion or the type of consciousness they have developed. While the women, like Chicana feminists, do contest oppressive secular and religious social structures and creatively find strategies to live in two worlds (the United States and México) or the borderlands (Anzaldúa 1987), they nonetheless do so as Catholics, and it is their Catholicism that informs many of the decisions they make, like in the cases of Rosario and Candelaria. What might we call the type of agency that Rosario and Candelaria exercised? As we recall, Rosario (*Las Damas* cohort) shot her husband, and Candelaria (*Las Madres* cohort) lifted her husband and threw him on the floor. Significantly, neither one of them drew on a non-Catholic spirituality.

My deliberations on this question were added to by a term I remember encountering years ago. In 1999 I attended a conference on Latinxs and religion where sociologist Milagros Peña shared that one of her participants defined *feminismo* (feminism) as *fe en mi mismo* (faith in oneself). I became intrigued by her respondent's definition of feminism, particularly the use of *fe* (faith) in her definition of the term. Her definition is, in many ways, a highly personalized—even individualized—type of feminism, different from the way some forms of feminism are defined as a collective movement.[4] Ever since Peña shared this story, the term feminism as *"fe en mi mismo"* has intrigued me. What range of meanings does it imply? What can this interpretation contribute to the existing body of feminist research? Finally, what does *"fe en mi mismo"* say about the consciousness development of women who neither have access to feminist scholarly exchanges nor are activists in their own community?

When I first heard the term *(fe)minism* it caught my attention, but I did not know what to make of it. It was not until I interviewed Rosario and Candelaria that the term materialized for me in their experiences. The life histories of these women provided some answers to these questions. The type of consciousness development that I observed is highly complex. It suggests how the liberating acts of these women can be traced to Catholic devotionalism—one possible interpretation of Peña's respondent's definition of feminism *(fe en mi mismo)*. I observed that the type of underground feminism in which these women engage is (fe)minism where *fe* literally means faith. That is, the horizontal (their sense of their own agency, here in their lived earthly experience) and the vertical (their faith in the heavenly power of the Catholic *Virgen de Guadalupe*) intersect. In this intersection, a certain type of feminist consciousness emerges—what I call a (fe)minist consciousness—which allows them to develop strategies for transcending oppressive situations and limiting belief systems.

This (fe)minism is another aspect of their Mexican Catholic imagination. It is a type of feminism in which lived religion and a woman's sense of autonomy complement one another within their Mexican Catholic imagination. In this space, there are no contradictions; a woman can be a devout Catholic but in favor of birth control. A woman can perceive *La Virgen* as the Catholic mother she inherited but also believe Our Lady of Guadalupe shares equal status with God. For some women, *La Virgen* is a prototype of feminism because she not only ordered San Juan Diego to go talk to the bishop, but in doing so, she demanded equality and justice for the Nahua people. The women in this study have a deep devotion to *La Virgen* and see her as a loving and compassionate mother, one who gives them the strength not to endure but to act. Furthermore, I found that devotion to *La Virgen de Guadalupe* is not a selective process. That is to say, it is not put away and retrieved only in times of need; it is always present, but certain life situations seem to spur devotion and women's agency to materialize in the form of (fe)minism. (Fe)minism among the women in this study is not homogenous; women experience (fe)minism differently and at varying degrees. My intention is not to impose this term on the women; I find this term useful to theoretically explain my observations of how they make sense of their worlds from within their Mexican Catholic imagination.

(Fe)minism for some manifests itself as they make the choice to use birth control, because according to them, it is the mandate of the Church to provide for and raise healthy families. It manifests when women choose to take the necessary steps to end physical abuse, as in the case of Rosario and Candelaria, because *La Virgen* of their Mexican Catholic imagination does not tolerate violence against women. This not only applies within individual families, but to the US immigrant population at a macro level.

Pastoral Implications

Pastoral ministers working with Latinx immigrant communities must be aware of and honor the Catholic cultural practices and beliefs people bring with them from their home countries. Honoring such practices and beliefs, as yet another way of expressing the Catholic faith, can only strengthen the diversity and multicultural reality of the ever-growing US Catholic Church.

More specifically to Mexican-origin women, the way that *La Virgen de Guadalupe*'s message gets interpreted at the pastoral level has both a macro and micro dimension. At the macro level, her message is interpreted as one of justice for the most vulnerable, with a particular reference to the immigrant community in the United States. We see this type of message in Sunday Mass sermons and in particular on her feast day, December 12. At the micro level, pastoral ministers working with women should consider an interpretation of Our Lady of Guadalupe's message as one of pro-action in their pastoral counseling.

The message of pro-action could center on *La Virgen de Guadalupe*'s insistence that San Juan Diego go to the bishop and ask him to build a hermitage on Tepeyac Hill. According to the story, she insisted even after the bishop refused to believe San Juan Diego and in spite of San Juan Diego's suggestion that she send someone else. *La Virgen de Guadalupe* did not tell him to sit and pray, nor did she send someone else. Her message for women, as I heard it from *Las Damas, Madres*, and *Mujeres*, is one that calls them to be proactive, not passive, during difficult times or if they find themselves in abusive relationships. *Las Damas, Madres*, and *Mujeres* see in *La Virgen* a vital spiritual source that propels them to exercise agency on behalf of themselves and their children.

More specifically, non-Latinx pastoral ministers working with or counseling Latinas should pay close attention to the sacred (vertical) and secular (horizontal) relationships that shape their Catholic imaginations. And perhaps more challenging to pastoral ministers is to consider the sociological findings of this study about the lack of conflict many women feel about traditional Catholic Church teachings regarding birth control and their own perceptions about the benefits of it. Their opinions, as demonstrated in this study, are anchored in serious contemporary social and economic factors, which they connect to Church teachings about the importance of providing for and growing healthy families.

In essence, the life narratives of the women in this study call on lay and clerical pastoral ministers in the Catholic Church to reflect deeply on the negative implications of articulating the message of *La Virgen de Guadalupe*—and other Catholic beliefs, for that matter—in ways that are detrimental to women's humanity.

Limitations of the Study

This is an exploratory study, one of the first sociological studies on Catholic devotion to Our Lady of Guadalupe among Mexican-origin women. As such, it has some limitations. First, this study was done among heterosexual women. How different would my results have been had I interviewed lesbian women? Second, this study was conducted in Northern California, which raises the question of possible geographical differences. Third, the study was limited in size; a bigger sample would have allowed for much more complex patterns of devotion. What this study does represent is the lived religion of first-generation working-class Catholic Mexican-origin women from three different life experiences (young college women, mothers, older women) who continue to have strong ties to Catholicism, the Spanish language, and Mexican customs.

Implications for Further Research

Early on in childhood, women interviewed in this study were not merely passive recipients of Catholicism but were active makers of their Mexican Catholic imaginations. For example, they took what was taught to them about *La Virgen de Guadalupe* and gave it further meaning, or they contested rigid expectations for girls in creative ways. As women wove intricate webs of relationships between the sacred and *lo cotidiano* (everyday life), their Mexican Catholic imagination took on a *café con leche* quality. This indicates that by excluding religion as a category of analysis, we limit the depth of our research because, even if their interpretations of Catholicism depart to some extent from organized religion, they nonetheless have roots in it. Their stories demonstrate that the ways religion and sexuality intersect with race, class, gender, and other social categories have serious implications for our understanding of women's subjectivity and their mental and physical health. Therefore, treating them as separate categories in our research undermines our ability to grasp the fluidity and complexity of women's experiences.

I suggest that Chicana/Latina feminist social science research would benefit from an analytical framework that is more inclusive. That is, treating religion as a necessary category of analysis in the study of Chicanas/Latinas—in addition to race, class, gender, and sexuality—could allow for a deeper and more complex understanding of women's subjectivity. Doing so would allow us to better see how Latinas' horizontal relationships (formed with people) and vertical relationships (formed with what they understand as heavenly entities) intersect at critical moments in life. For Rosario and Candelaria, this intersection lead them to embody a (fe) minist type of agency. Their experiences reveal that not all feminist agency is secular; on the contrary, in some cases women's agency has religious (and not necessarily spiritual) underpinnings. This, I contend, has serious implications for how women's agency is explored in academia. Research on domestic violence and social movements, for example, would greatly benefit by integrating religion as a category of analysis; scholars may find that religion, to a certain degree, propels women's sense of awareness and activism. This methodological approach would allow scholars to have a more complex understanding of how women engage in feminist acts as people of faith—a faith anchored in organized religion but not limited by its teachings and beliefs.

In a like manner, their stories call religious studies scholars and theologians to unbind the female body from Church-sanctified beliefs about women's bodies and sexuality. I suggest that this requires openness from religious studies scholars and theologians alike to a critical analysis of how the intersection of race, class, gender, and sexuality influences and is influenced by religion as an institution and as a lived experience.

Direction for Future Research

This book analyzed a Mexican Catholic imagination as experienced by three groups of women, but there are many other variations among populations that raise questions for further research. Do these variations have things in common with other groups? If so, can we talk about a Latinx Catholic imagination? Are there aspects of their religiosity that Latinx ethnic groups and other religious traditions share in common and thus open the possibility for a discussion on a Latinx religious imagination?

Furthermore, how might the term *(fe)minism* be useful in describing other women's faith-based agency? Thinking more broadly, can (fe)minism help us explain what propels female-driven faith-based social movements? In addition, the interpretations of *La Virgen de Guadalupe* are manifold and complex. The politics of interpretation that emerge as people attempt to understand her complexity are yet to be fully analyzed.

Conclusion

From my personal experience, and from what I have heard from the women in this study and in the classroom in my years of teaching, I know that younger generations of women are too quick to judge older women; particularly, their mothers. As I close this book, it is my hope that the life histories of the women who confided in me encourage intergenerational dialogue among women about their own life experiences of becoming women. It is also my hope that the reader walks away with the awareness that women, as these life histories demonstrate, challenge and reject in creative ways the sanctification of shame, guilt, and *aguante* (endurance at all cost) by institutional Catholicism that are oppressive in many ways. For example, Ester carries the image of *La Virgen de Guadalupe* resting on her breasts—a part of her body that at age 13 she was socialized into believing was a temptation for men that she needed to bind and hide. This act of carrying the image reflects the staying power of *La Virgen* she inherited from her mother. However, the religious beliefs and practices she learned as a child and her life experiences have shaped what *La Virgen de Guadalupe* has come to mean in her life today. Ester, who is now 76 years old, has reclaimed and embraced her breasts within a *café con leche* Mexican Catholic imagination that she now understands to be healing, life-giving, and transgressive of the aspects of Catholicism that deny women's humanity. *La Virgen de Guadalupe* for these women is without doubt Our Lady of Everyday life.

Appendix

General Overview of Catholic Practices

	Las Damas Grew up in a pre–Second Vatican Council Catholic culture.	Las Madres Grew up in a post–Vatican Council Catholic culture.	Las Mujeres Grew up in a post–Vatican Council Catholic culture.
Dress code	Women and young girls were expected to wear dresses or skirts to Mass.	Dress code for women and girls became more flexible, and they were allowed to wear pants.	Were not aware that before the Second Vatican Council there was a dress code for women and girls.
Use of *mantilla*	An expectation.	A choice.	A choice. *Las Mujeres* were not aware that it was an expectation before the Second Vatican Council.
Rosary prayer	A daily family religious practice.	A weekly religious practice.	An occasional religious practice in the families of most of *Las Mujeres*.
Mass	A daily practice for those who lived in towns in which the local parish had a permanent priest.	A weekly family practice.	Was not a priority for those who lived on campus. However, *Las Mujeres* who lived at home were expected to attend Mass with their families.
Home altars	All of *Las Damas* had a home altar, but the altars varied in size.	Some of *Las Madres* had home altars, and others dedicated a space on one of the walls for a framed image of *La Virgen de Guadalupe*.	The families of the women had home altars or dedicated a space on one of the walls for a framed image of *La Virgen de Guadalupe*.
Language in which they pray or talk to *La Virgen*	Spanish	Spanish	Spanish

Las Damas *Demographics*

Name	Age	Place of Birth	Age at Time of Migration	Year of Migration	Number of Children	Marital Status	Education
Amelia	69	Monterrey, México	15	1951	8	Married	5th grade
Angelita	70	Guanajuato, México	14	1949	0	Single, never married	6th grade
Artemia	67	Durango, México	18	1956	2	Married	2nd grade
Ester	76	Michoacan	16	1945	7	Widowed	2nd grade
Esperanza	68	Texas	N/A	N/A	0	Single, never married	9th grade
Irma	76	Zacatecas, México	40	1969	8	Widowed	4th grade
Josefa	77	Jalisco, México	50	1978	13	Married	3rd grade
Juanita	82	Guerrero, México	21	1944	9	Widowed	1st grade
Luz Elena	55	Michoacan, México	35	1985	4	Married	6th grade
MariChuy	78	Jalisco, México	16	1943	6	Married	4th grade
Nora	65	México City	30	1970	4	Married	5th grade
Olivia	57	Chihuahua, México	14	1962	7	Married	6th grade
Paloma	80	Jalisco	12	1937	10	Married	3rd grade
Roberta	79	Zacatecas, México	19	1945	9	Widowed	4th grade
Rosario	65	Texas	N/A	N/A	12	Widowed, currently dating	3rd grade

Note: All are pseudonyms to protect the identity of respondents.

Las Madres *Demographics*

Name	Age	Place of Birth	Age at Time of Migration	Year of Migration	Number of Children	Marital Status	Education
Beatriz	34	México City	29	2000	5	Partnered	6th grade
Candelaria	39	Durango	35	2001	4	Married	6th grade
Catalina	25	Durango	12	1992	1	Partnered	5th grade
Eva	44	Michoacán	40	2001	3 kids over the age of 18	Married	6th grade
Faviola	46	Guanajuato	35	1994	3 kids over the age of 18	Married	6th grade
Gabriela	37	Guadalajara	19	1987	3	Married	8th grade
Julia	24	Tijuana	20	2001	2	Partnered	6th grade
Laura	37	Jalisco	18	1986	2 under the age of 18 and 2 over the age of 18	Married	8th grade
Maria	36	Zacatecas	21	1990	3	Married	6th grade
Meche	42	Guadalajara	20	1983	3 under the age of 18 and 3 over the age of 18	Married	6th grade
Mereides	47	Sinaloa	27	1985	1	Married	4th grade
Raquel	46	Colima	34	1993	1	Partnered	6th grade
Sandra	21	Durango	14	1998	2	Partnered	5th grade
Vicky	31	Hidalgo	23	1997	2	Partnered	6th grade

Note: All are pseudonyms to protect the identity of respondents.

Las Mujeres *Demographics*

Name	Age	Place of Birth	Age at Time of Migration	Type of College	Year in College
Anita	21	Los Angeles, CA	N/A	Public	4
Chavelita	23	Oaxaca	7	Public	4
Martha	29	Michoacan	13	Public	4
Mereides	22	Mexico	7	Public	4
Pilar	24	Watsonville, CA	N/A	Public	4
Yolanda	21	Paradise, CA	N/A	Public	3
Celene	20	Watsonville, CA	N/A	Private	2
Conchita	21	Michoacán	9	Private	3
Dolores	19	Veracruz	6	Private	2
Elena	21	México City	8	Private	3
Leonor	22	Santa Clara, CA	N/A	Private	4
Manuela	24	San Francisco, CA	N/A	Private	3
Nancy	25	Oaxaca	17	Private	3
Neida	19	Jalisco	10	Private	2
Rosita	20	San Jose, CA	N/A	Private	3
Teresa	20	San Jose, CA	N/A	Private	3

Note: All are pseudonyms to protect the identity of respondents.

Notes

INTRODUCTION

1. I use the terms Our Lady of Guadalupe, Guadalupe, *La Virgen* (the Virgin), and *La Virgen de Guadalupe* interchangeably throughout the book.
2. Marisa is a pseudonym to protect her identity.
3. While most of the women were born in México, others were born in the United States—some identified as Chicanas, and others did not. Therefore, I use the term *Mexican-origin* to refer to all the women in this study. For this same reason, in the subtitle of the book I refer to the women in this study as Mexican women in America.
4. Miguel De La Torre is one of the few scholars who have written extensively on the intersection of religion and sexuality.
5. Asencio 2010; Flores 2013; González-López 2005, 2009, 2015; Garcia 2012, 2015; Guzman 2013; Hurtado and Sinha 2016; Juárez et al. 2016; Romo et al. 2014, 2016; Zuniga 2015.
6. Hurtado 2003; González-López 2005, 2009; Zavella 1997, 2003.
7. Gutiérrez R. 2010; Gutiérrez D. 2012.
8. Ammerman (2007) makes a similar argument about the risks of excluding religion from social science analysis.
9. Scholars in the area of lived religion such as Ammerman 2007, 2013; Griffith, 1997; Hall 1997; Hervieu-Léger 2000; McGuire 2008; and Orsi 1996 have previously pointed this out.
10. Hervieu-Léger 2000.
11. I do not argue that there is one Mexican Catholic imagination, because a Catholic imagination is shaped by an array of social factors that not all Mexican Catholics necessarily share.
12. Greeley refers to people's indigenous interpretations of Our Lady of Guadalupe as "superstitious" (Greeley 2000, 14). However, the same could be said about any religious belief, institutional or not.

13. See also: Castañeda-Liles 2008; Chavez 2006; Elizondo 1977; Fernandez Poncela 2000; Goizueta 2003; Guerrero 2008; Lafaye 1976; and Poole 1995.

14. Orlando Espín, an established authority in Latinx popular Catholicism, describes popular (of the people) Catholicism as "foundationally dependent for its existence on the entire community, on the families within the community and, especially, on the older women within the families" (Espín 1997, 4). It is "popular" in the sense that it comes from the grassroots—the people.

15. Catholic Mexican-American theologian Virgilio Elizondo (2000) maintains that Mexican Catholicism reflects the *flor y canto* (flower and song) of México's indigenous past. In other words, it represents a type of Catholicism that is festive rather than somber and that has a poetic quality.

16. There are three ways in which familism is experienced: attitudinal familism (the sense of faithfulness individuals have for other family members, often prioritizing others' needs over one's own); behavioral familism (the activities and practices in which family members participate as a way to reinforce family ties); and structural or demographic familism (the physical proximity of the family network; Baca Zinn 1982; Segura and Pierce 1993; Stein et al. 2014). Baca Zinn (1982) makes a distinction between *structural* and *demographic* familism. Structural refers to multigenerational households—for example, grandparents living with a son or daughter and grandchildren. Demographic refers to the extent of the kinship network beyond the nuclear and extended families.

17. For an analysis of the family within the context of Latinx theology, see also: Goizueta 1995, Isasí-Díaz 1996; and Torres 2010.

18. See also Thomas Tweed 2010.

19. These vertical and horizontal relationships are what Geertz (1973) calls the "webs of significance" that continue to sustain the peoples' Catholic faith and devotion.

20. Some of the information may have been modified to protect the identity of the women who trusted me with their life histories.

21. Some of the 91 participants chose not to take part in the in-depth interviews because of lack of time due to school, family, or other obligations.

22. http://www.sjsu.edu/urbanplanning/communityplanning/Final%20Report.pdf.

23. Zinn 1978; Zavella 1993.

24. In the Catholic Church, a catechist is a person appointed to teach the principles of the faith. A lector is someone who proclaims the Scripture readings during Mass. Both positions may be held by laypeople as well as clergy.

25. Massey Douglas et al. 1997; White et al. 1990; Durand et al. 2001.

26. Griffith 1997; Ammerman 2013.

27. Hervieu-Léger 1997; Ammerman 2013.

28. McGuire 2008.

29. Orsi 1996.

30. McGuire in Ammerman 2007, 187.

31. Paying particular attention to moments in history that rupture daily life, Davie (2007) uses the iceberg analogy to describe the processes she calls *vicarious*

religion: "The notion of religion performed by an active minority but on behalf of a much larger number, who (implicitly at least) not only understand, but, quite clearly, approve of what the minority is doing" (Davie in Ammerman 2007, 22). In her view, scholars interested in the study of vicarious religion must search beneath the religious expressions—the part of the iceberg that is visible—and pay close attention to what is underneath. She illustrates her point by arguing that societies have a religious element that often goes unnoticed until a significant event takes place that leads people to rely on or find comfort in transcendent figures or symbols; for example, the tragedy of September 11, 2001.

32. Orlando Espín (1997) makes a similar claim in his introductory chapter.
33. Nakhid et al. 2015.
34. Mercer et al. 2015.
35. Griffith 1997.
36. For example, the study by Howe, Zaraysky, and Lorentzen (2009), which examines the devotion to *La Santa Muerte* among transgender sex workers in Guadalajara and San Francisco.
37. *Café con leche* literally means "coffee with milk."

CHAPTER 1

1. Though the *Nican Mopohua* is widely accepted as a true account by most Catholics, every argument supporting Guadalupe's apparition has had a counter-argument. Debates about her apparition are still ongoing. Some scholars argue that Guadalupe's apparition did in fact take place and that it led to the conversion of a high percentage of Nahua people. However, other scholars claim that the event was fabricated and that the devotion began with the *criollos* (people of Spanish descent born in what we now know as México) and not the Nahua people (Poole 1995). Still other prominent intellectuals in the field, such as Matovina (2005), focus on the devotion to this sacred symbol from a historical perspective.
2. For further reading on the consequences of the conquest I recommend Ramón A. Gutíerrez's book chapter "A History of Latina/o Sexualities" (13–37) in *Latina/o Sexualities: Proving Powers, Passions, Practices, and Politics*, edited by Marysol Asencio (2010), Rutgers University Press.
3. Pineda 2004; Berrú-Davis 2009; Sánchez 2009.
4. Correll and Polk 2014.
5. Pineda 2004; Sagarena 2009.
6. Gastón Espinosa (2014b) in his book *William J. Seymour and the Origins of Global Pentecostalism* introduces the concept of "Christian transgressive social space" to explain the ways William J. Seymour made of the Azusa street revival a welcoming Christian space for all.
7. Feline Freier 2009.
8. *New York Daily News*, July 3, 2008.

9. *Catholic News Agency*, March 27, 2009.
10. *The Huffington Post*, March 6, 2012.
11. Lalo Alcaraz, the cartoonist, sells his representation of Our Lady of Guadalupe on his website. The image is part of a series of cartoons he has titled "Estar Wars."
12. http://www.tienda.distroller.com.
13. For a more extensive read on some of the anti-apparitionist arguments see Castañeda-Liles 2008.
14. Chapter 5 provides an explanation of *Marianismo* in the context of the lives of the women in this study.
15. Espín 2013.
16. Elizondo 1997; Matovina 2009; Delgadillo 2011; Medina 2014.
17. Some scholars argue that *mestizaje* does not fully capture México's cultural and ethnic reality, because it does not account for the African roots of people of Mexican origin. For more on the subject, see Menchaca 2001. For an in-depth analysis of how theologians have articulated *mestizaje*, see Medina 2014.
18. Anzaldúa 1987; Aquino 1996; Elizondo 1997; Goizueta 2003; Matovina 2005, 2009; Delgadillo 2011.
19. Chicanx refers to the chosen sociopolitical identity of some politically oriented US-born people of Mexican origin. This type of agentic awareness is rooted in the Chicana/o Movement of the 1960s.
20. See, for example, Elizondo 1980, 1997; Goizueta 2003; Matovina 2005; Rodriguez 1994.
21. Castañeda-Liles 2008; Matovina 2009.
22. Timothy Matovina 2009; Virgilio Elizondo 1998. For a more comprehensive reading on the various theological claims about Our Lady of Guadalupe I recommend Timothy Matovina's (2009) article.
23. As *mestiza/os*, Elizondo (1998) argues, Mexicans are not either–or but both–and. Therefore, the point of departure of his work on Our Lady of Guadalupe has always been the lived experience of people who exist at the intersection of two ways of knowing (Elizondo 1980, 1998).
24. Elizondo 1997; Goizueta 2003; Rodriguez 1994.
25. Rodriguez 1994; Elizondo 1998; Goizueta 2003; Matovina 2005, 2009; Espín 1997; Loya 2002; De Anda 2011; Medina 2014.
26. Elizondo 1997; Rodriguez 1994, 1996.
27. Moving beyond Catholic traditions to Protestant ones, there has been a gradual expansion of theological interpretations of Our Lady of Guadalupe. Such scholarship problematizes the understanding of what Our Lady of Guadalupe means for non-Catholics and why she has such staying power among them. Nora Lozano Diaz's (2002) epic essay, "Ignored Virgin or Unaware Women," brings a new and fresh perspective. Going beyond Latina Catholics, Lozano Diaz contends that Our Lady of Guadalupe cannot be ignored in Latinx Protestant theology, particularly Latina feminist theology; even though Mexican American

Protestant women do not have a devotion to this sacred symbol, it is nonetheless part of their Mexican culture and therefore should be taken seriously by scholars. What is more, with non-Catholics and non–Mexican Americans as his main audience, Anglican theologian Maxwell Johnson's (2002) book *The Virgin of Guadalupe: Theological Reflections of an Anglo-Lutheran Liturgist* provides a Protestant theological reflection on the significance of Our Lady of Guadalupe as it draws from biblical texts on Mary. Scholars like Lozano Diaz and Johnson provide two accounts of how Our Lady of Guadalupe crosses religious boundaries. While this aspect of Guadalupe studies is beyond the scope of this book, it is an important question for future research.

28. Lara 2008b.
29. Castillo 1996; Castro Dopacio 2010; Gaspar de Alba and Lopez 2011; Delgadillo 2011.
30. Anzaldúa 1987; Delgadillo 2011.
31. Delgadillo 2011; Facio and Lara 2014; Zavella 2015.
32. *Curanderas* are faith healers.
33. According to Elizondo, in one of the conversations between *La Virgen* and Juan Diego, she tells him:

    Listen, my most abandoned son, know well in your heart that there are not a few of my servants and messengers to whom I could give the mandate of taking my thought and my word so that my will may be accomplished. But it is absolutely necessary that you personally go and speak about this, and that precisely through your mediation and help, my wish and my desire be realized. (Elizondo 1998, 10)

34. Castillo 1996.
35. Hurtado 2003; Zavella 2003; Gonzalez-Lopez 2005; Garcia, Romo, Nadeem, and Kouyoumdjian 2010; Adams 2011.
36. In "Guadalupe the Sex Goddess" (which later inspired Alma Lopéz to paint *Our Lady*), Sandra Cisneros (1996), like so many other scholars, contends that female sexuality is more often than not treated with great modesty.
37. For reading on Chicana interpretations of growing up Catholic, see Sewell 2002.
38. Trujillo 1991.
39. Trujillo in Castillo 1996.
40. Trujillo 1991.
41. Pérez 1998.
42. Medina in Trujillo 1998.
43. Anzaldúa spells "Tonantsin" with an "s," but this goddess's name is generally spelled with a "z."
44. Anzaldúa 1996.
45. Ibid.
46. León 2004; Overmyer-Velazquez 2005; Medina 1998; Perez, 1998, 2007.
47. Anzaldúa 1999, 106.

48. Elizondo 1997.
49. For an extensive analysis of Yolanda López's work, I recommend *Yolanda M. López* by Mary Karen Davalos, 2008.
50. Davalos 2008; Andión, Lizarazo, and Margarita 2007.
51. Davalos 2008. The quote which appears in Davalos 2008, is an excerpt from an interview of the artist by R. Cordova, May 24, 2002.
52. Coyolxauhqui is the Aztec goddess who was dismembered by her brother for attempting to kill their mother, the Aztec mother goddess Coatlicue. For a Chicana feminist interpretation of Coyolxauhqui's story, see Anzaldúa 1996.
53. Gonzales and Rodriguez 1997.
54. For further reading on ex-votos, see Pineda 2004; Zires 2014.
55. Feminist theologian Ada María Isasí-Díaz coined the term "*lo cotidiano*" in Latinx theology, which claims to do theology from the everyday experiences of the faithful. However, some scholars have critiqued Latinx theology as lacking substantial empirical evidence to support such claims (Vanderwood 2000).
56. In the tradition of feminist theologian Isasí-Díaz, Rebecca Berru-Davis's (2009) point of departure is *lo cotidiano* (the quotidian), from which she explores the devotion to Guadalupe in a community in northern California.
57. A *quinceañera* is the celebration of a girl's 15th birthday, which symbolizes her passage into womanhood. For further reading on *la quinceañera* see: Davalos 2003, 2008; Cantú 2000.
58. See also Matovina and Poyo 2015; Vasquez and Marquardt 2003.
59. Ruiz, who grew up with a devotion to Our Lady of Guadalupe, claims that the Virgin Mary (under the title "Virgin of the Americas") appeared to her first in 1989 and several times thereafter (Kristy 2005).
60. Gamboni 2009.
61. Peña and Frehill's (1998) study is foundational in documenting the national landscape of the religiosity of Latinas: Cuban, Puerto Rican, South and Central American, and Mexican. Their study consisted of focus groups and a survey in eight cities across the United States. It was the first study to provide significant and detailed statistical information on Marian devotion. Peña and Frehill found two patterns of religiosity—a social dimension and a personal dimension. The personal dimension, which is associated with popular religion, is also associated with the Virgin Mary.
62. Rodriguez (1994) had similar findings. Also, Espín (2013) claims that the Guadalupan Marian devotion among Mexicans has a pneumatological quality—that is, the characteristics that Mexicans give to Mary are similar to those associated with the Holy Spirit by Catholic theologians. For further reading on Espín's approach to Our Lady of Guadalupe, see Espín (1997).
63. Peña and Frehill 1998.
64. Sarah MacMillen (2011) found cyber-pilgrimages offer an alternative way to foment Guadalupan devotion by allowing the faithful to visit the Basilica of Our

Lady of Guadalupe who otherwise would not be able to do so (e.g., for health or financial reasons). For example, http://www.sancta.org is a website devoted to Our Lady of Guadalupe. From an apparitionist perspective, it provides information about her manifestation to San Juan Diego; people can leave special prayers, petitions, and virtual roses. However, MacMillen found that while the option to partake in a "pilgrimage" from home is a great alternative, certain elements are lost. For example, those who engage in a traditional pilgrimage to the Basilica are spiritually and physically immersed in the experience, in community with other pilgrims, whereas those who opt to go on a virtual pilgrimage have an individual experience with a virtual Guadalupe; the sense of communion with other pilgrims is missing.

65. Cherríe Moraga (1981) coined the phrase "doing theory in the flesh." For further reading on *lo cotidiano* (daily life) as the space from which to do grounded theology, I recommend Nanko-Fernández 2015; Espín 1997; and Isasí-Díaz 2004.

CHAPTER 2

1. *Café con leche* literally means "coffee with milk."
2. *Mija* is derivative of *"mi hija"* (my daughter) and it is a term of endearment. Usually used by someone older to address a young woman. However, some men misuse the term in a condescending way to refer to women.
3. See also McGuire 2007; Orsi 1996; Tweed 1997. Also, in México the term *santo de bulto* is used to refer to statuettes of saints.
4. Díaz-Stevens (1994) contends that religion among Latinxs has a "matriarchal core." Orsi (1996) makes a similar argument when explaining Catholic devotion among Italian immigrants.
5. See also Espín 1994, 2006; León 2004; Matovina 2002, 2005; Peña 2011; Pineda-Madrid 2006.
6. See also Cadena 1995; Martin 1992; Orsi 2010; Reese 2012; Torres 2010.
7. See also Hughes 2014.
8. Orsi (1996) uses the term *devotional triangle* to explain the Catholic devotion to Saint Jude among the daughters of Italian immigrants.
9. It would be interesting to see how mothers transmit the Guadalupan devotion to their sons. This aspect is outside the scope of my study.
10. Robert A. Orsi (1996) found the similar pattern in his study on the devotion to St. Jude.
11. See also Orsi 2011.
12. The English text is a loose translation of the original quote that reads as follows: *La Navidad es algo grande [para nuestra familia] y culturalmente también, y ella [Guadalupe] siempre es una gran parte de esa celebración.*
13. *Posadas* is a nine-day celebration beginning on December 16 and ending on December 24. The nine days represent the Virgin Mary's nine-month pregnancy

with Jesus. Each evening a group of people, along with two dressed as Mary and Joseph, go to a different house asking for lodging. The exchange between the group asking for lodging and the residents at each house is done through song. At the end of the exchange, Mary and Joseph, along with the people who accompany them, are welcomed. A rosary prayer and a party with songs, food, and a piñata full of candy and fruit typically follow.

14. The lyrics of these songs emphasize Our Lady of Guadalupe's connection to Mexican nationalism. For example in the song *"A Ti Virgensita"* the lyrics include: *Eres nuestro orgullo, y México es tuyo, Tu guardas la llave* (You are our pride, and México is yours, you keep the key). The lyrics for the song *"La Guadalupana"* say, *". . . para el mexicano. ser Guadalupano es algo esencial"* (. . . for the Mexican people to be a Guadalupan is something essential).

15. The English text is a loose translation of the original quote that reads as follows: *Todos creíamos y escuchábamos todo lo que [mi abuelita y mi mamá] nos decian.*

16. The English text is a loose translation of the original quote that reads as follows: *En su mayor parte fue mi abuelita quien me contó la historia de Nuestra Señora de Guadalupe. Siempre vi santos de bulto [e] imágenes de Nuestra Señora de Guadalupe en la casa. Siempre preguntaba sobre la Virgen, y mi abuelita era la que me hablaba de ella. Así aprendí la historia.*

17. The English text is a loose translation of the original quote that reads as follows: *Aprendí de mi mamá porque siempre nos hablaba de Nuestra Señora de Guadalupe. Ella nos hablaba de milagros, que ella sabía . . . De cómo se le apareció a Juan Diego y cómo llevaba las rosas al obispo. Ella le dijo que construyera un templo. . . . Ese fue el mensaje.*

18. The English text is a loose translation of the original quote that reads as follows: *La Virgen cuando uno "taba enfermo, yo me acuerdo [que] mi bisabuela me decía: todo a nuestro señor dale las gracias que vivimos y tenemos y [a] La Virgen para que [n]os de poder." Dice, "La Virgen nunca nos abandona. La Virgen donde quiera que andemos, anda con nosotros y nos protege. Protege a la familia, a nuestros chiquitos, a nuestras tierras." Así que si nosotros teníanos poquito de aquello ibanos y le rezabanos y ya otro día vinia poquito más.*

19. Orsi (1996) describes this type of transmission of devotion as a relational process, because it is dependent on and also strengthens the relationships already established between the child and adult.

20. See also Turner 2008.

21. I would like to thank my colleague, Frank Castillo, for his valuable comment on *altares.*

22. Her great-grandparents, grandparents, and her parents were all born in México. Rosario was born in a horse stable, and her mother left her with her grandparents who raised her.

23. This quote is a loose translation of the original one that reads as follows: *Nuestra Virgen era de piedra. Y a ella como ofrenda le poniamos frijolitos y arroz y le ponianos*

flores y eran puros Rosales. A ella nunca le faltaban rosales, de una manera o de otra siempre le llevábamos rosales, pero a ella nunca le faltaban.

24. In the larger context of the Catholic Church, the rose has also been associated with important biblical moments: Mary's immaculate conception, assumption into heaven, and coronation, as well as her sorrow for the crucifixion of her son (Granziera 2004).

25. There are two main types of altars in Mexican Catholic homes: altars in honor of a particular saint and altars in honor of those who have died. The first type of altar is either permanent or set up temporarily for the feast day of the patron saint being venerated. Altars are usually located in the main area of the home or in the bedroom of the matriarch (mother or grandmother). The second type of altar is usually set up days before the *Dia de Los Muertos* (Day of the Dead) and left for a few days after. Flowers, food, and drinks placed on the altar are symbols of the transcendental continuum between heaven and earth and between the living and dead. The purpose behind the offering of food and drink is twofold, depending on the type of altar. If the altar is in honor of a particular saint, then the offering of food and drink is typically either to give thanks or to ask for food abundance. If the altar is in honor of a relative who has died, then the food or drink offered is whatever was the favorite of the deceased. The food and drink in this case are a symbol of communion between the departed and the family.

26. Quote in English is a loose translation of the original one that reads: *Cada año como se viste el árbol de Navidad ahora . . . vestíamos el altar con bombillas pa' La Virgen.*

27. Orsi (1996), in his book *Thank You, St. Jude: Women's Devotion to the Patron Saint of Hopeless Causes*, also discusses how women of Italian descent are very particular when selecting a statue or image of Saint Jude.

28. Quote in English is a loose translation of the original one that reads as follows: *Mi papá [le]hacía un altar a La Virgen y ponía [en el] una imagen de la Última Cena. [Iba a la tienda y compraba] dulces de los buenos para La Virgen. Me encantaban estos tiempos porque yo le robaba los dulces a La Virgen del altar. Me encantaba robar los dulces porque él siempre compraba de los buenos, de los que él nunca nos compraba porque eran muy caros.*

29. Griffith 1997. Also, I recommend Hughes 2010 for further reading on the lived religion of Mexican origin people from México's conquest to present time.

30. See also Turner 2008 and Orsi 1996.

31. The English text is a loose translation of the original quote that reads as follows: *En aquel entonces, todo era diferente. Mira, en mi casa, todos eran muy Católicos. A mí, mi mamá y mi abuelita me contaron la historia de La Virgencita y 'pos también teníamos un altarcito e imágenes de La Virgen, el Sagrado Corazón, y el Santo Niño de Atocha. No había cuarto que no tuviera una imagen sagrada.*

32. For a theological analysis of the consequences of racism and discrimination subsequent to the Spanish conquest, see Aquino 1992, Elizondo 2007, and Rodriguez 1994.

33. For a historical analysis of how Our Lady of Guadalupe shaped the national consciousness of Mexicans, see Lafaye 1987.

34. The English text is a loose translation of the original quote that reads as follows: *Mi mamá, nos vistia de inditas con huaraches, rebozo, nuestras trenzas con listones, y nuestro morralito atrás. A mi me gustaba mucho porque casi todas las niñas íbamos vestidas ansina y le llevábamos flores a La Virgen. Era un día tan hermoso y alegre. A mi [me] gustaba mucho ese día porque mi ama y mi abuelita hacían champurrado y pan de maíz pa' todos. 'Mija, eran tiempos muy bonitos de mucha fé.*

35. In this cyber age, the act of pilgrimage has taken a whole new meaning. Some websites offer cyber pilgrimages to sacred sites. For more about this new pilgrimage trend, see MacMillen 2011.

36. The English text is a loose translation of the original quote that reads as follows: *Yo me acuerdo que cuando mi abuelita 'taba muy enferma, mi mamá nos llevo a mis hermanos y a mí a la catedral del pueblo un 12 de diciembre. [La catedral] quedaba siempre lejos, pero nos fuimos todos caminando. Mi ama iba descalza y decía que se lo ofrecía a la virgencita de Guadalupe pa' que sanara a mi abuelita. Luego, ya casi llegando, mi ama se fue de rodillas hasta el altar. Pobrecita de mi ama, ya casi no aguantaba, pero era tanta su fe, 'mija que pudo llegar. Yo tenía hay veras, como unos ocho años, eso fue en México. Eso nunca se me va a olvidar.*

37. For example, Peña (2011) argues that a small group of people praying to Our Lady of Guadalupe on the hill at Maryville Academy in Des Plaines, IL (Chicago area), which began in 1987, has now grown to be one of the biggest December 12 celebrations outside of México. Last year, over 150,000 people, young and old, made the pilgrimage to the site, making it the second most visited Guadalupe shrine after the Basilica of Our Lady of Guadalupe in México City. For other scholarly approaches to the Latinization of US Catholicism, see Cadena and Medina 1996; Diaz-Stevens 1994; Ebaugh and Chafetz 2002; Levitt 2006, 2007; and Peña 2011.

38. The pilgrimage is a one-way journey that ends at St. Patrick's Cathedral in New York City. For a photographic account of the Torcha Guadalupana run, see *Tepeyac en Nueva York* (Merino 2002). In this book, renowned Mexican photographer Joel Merino takes the reader into the trajectory of the 72-day journey of runners who carry *La Torcha Guadalupana* from the basilica in México City to Saint Patrick's Cathedral in New York City. He provides an excellent visual of the devotion and sacrifice of people who make the long journey through the various states of the Mexican Republic and United States as an act of advocacy for immigration and immigration reform.

39. For a reading on the different types of pre-Columbian theater in the Maya region, see "Teatro Maya Peninsular: Precolombino y Evangelizador" (Castillo 2001).

40. Taylor 2004.

41. Ibid.

42. For a more thorough explanation of the differences between pre-Columbian and Spanish performance practices, see Taylor 2004.

43. Espín 1992; León Portilla 1969; León Portilla and Kemp 1962; Rull Fernández 1986; Taylor 2004. For further reading on Aztec thought and philosophy, I recommend León Portilla 1969; León Portilla and Kemp 2000, 2012.

44. Flores 1995.

45. In San Antonio, Texas, the San Fernando Cathedral reenacts the *Via Crucis* on Good Friday (Elizondo and Matovina 1998; Matovina and Riebe-Estrella 2002). In San Jose, California, the popular theater group Teatro Corazón of Sacred Heart of Jesus Parish recreates the story of Our Lady of Guadalupe, drawing an audience in the thousands. What makes Teatro Corazón unique is that it not only reenacts the apparition at its home parish, it also performs the play at various parishes in the Diocese of San Jose and at two colleges: Santa Clara University and Saint Mary's College. The theater group is made up of families and individuals of all ages from the parish. San Fernando Cathedral and Sacred Heart Parish are two of the dozens, perhaps hundreds, of parishes across the United States that use popular theater as a means to *tradition* Catholic devotion to Our Lady of Guadalupe.

46. For further reading on Our Lady of Guadalupe, colonialism, and resistance, I recommend Sánchez 2009.

47. Espín (1997) makes a similar argument.

48. In his study of the Shepherds' Play (*Los Pastores*) in San Antonio, anthropologist Richard Flores (1995) also found that people (performers and audience members alike) associated the struggles enacted in the play with their own troubles.

49. The role of social media did not come up in the interviews. However, an analysis of the role of Facebook, Snapchat, Instagram, Twitter, and Pinterest as platforms where devotion is introduced or reinforced in a larger community of people would make a fascinating study.

50. The English text is a loose translation of the original quote that reads as follows: *Aprendimos sobre La Virgen de mi mamá y mi abuelita, pero también de las películas que salen en la televisión. Fue a partir de ahí que aprendí más acerca de ella.*

51. For further reading on the anti-apparitionist debates see Castañeda-Liles 2008.

52. We also see this happening in theology. According to Matovina (2009), theological works have focused on Our Lady of Guadalupe's choice to appear in México and what this means for *mestizaje* and national consciousness. In essence, the film industry, theological interpretations, and Mexican popular Catholic practices all helped solidify a Guadalupan Mexican consciousness.

53. Orlando Espín (1997) asserts, among Latinx families, women particularly older women, "are ministers and bearers of our identity."

54. Orsi 1996.

CHAPTER 3

1. *Mija* is short for *mi hija*, loosely translated as "my daughter." It is used as a term of endearment in this case; however, men often use it to infantilize women.

2. *"Pos que no encontraba mi mantilla. La busque y busque, pero nada. Yo no queria despertar a mis hermanos y ¿que crees 'mija? . . . " [riendose continua] "Fui a donde mi ama tenia las sapetas de trapo sucias 'pa lavarlas y que agarro una que estaba toda orinada . . . y que me la pongo en la cabeza y ansina me fui a la Iglesia. En la Iglesia la gente se me quedaba mirando, mirando, [y aunque estaba seca] yo pienso que podian oler la orina [en la] sapeta. Pero yo tenia mi mantilla," dijo y se empezo a reir, luego en un tono serio agrego, "'mija, era la devoción y la fe que uno tenia . . . en aquel entonces . . . la gente tenia mucha devoción."*

3. Church officials through the centuries and via their colonizing crusades spread the notion that an unveiled head was a canonical sin worthy of excommunication. Accordingly, women's public hair display in church services was considered a serious violation that carried severe consequences. This was one of the Catholic beliefs about women and the Church that was transplanted to Latin America through the colonizing efforts of Spanish missionaries, who brought with them Pre-Tridentine Catholic practices and beliefs.

4. The US government created the Bracero Program to compensate for the labor shortage caused by World War II. For a more detailed account, see Alba 2016.

5. Newcomer 2004; Young 2013, 2015.

6. Napolitano 2009; Young 2013, 2015; see also Becker 1987; Fitzgerald 2008; Gonzalez Navarro 2001; Meyer 2008; Purnell 1999; Tuck 1982.

7. Meyer 2008.

8. *Pues que crees 'mija que un dia se me pegaron las cobijas, y me levante tarde 'pa misa. Nombre, que me doy el levanton y que me visto depronto, me hize mi trensa y luego que nomas no podia encontrar uno de mis zapatos. Y yo busque y busque y nada. Mi mama y mi abuelita ya 'staban afuera esperandome y la iglesia quedaba al otro lado del pueblo. Bueno 'mija ¿que crees? 'Pos que me voy a misa nomas con un zapato. Es que asi era antes no podias faltar a misa porque era pecado y tenias que confesarte y "lo el padre te regañaba."*

9. *Siempre nos teniamos que confesar los domingos y a mi me daba miedo. Toda las semana me la pasaba apuntando todo lo malo que hacia como resongarle a mi hermano mayor o renegar por no querer hacer el quehacer de la casa. Todo apuntaba 'pa que no se me olvidara el domingo cuando me confesara. A mi me daba miedo de que una de las veces el padresito no me perdonara. Yo tenia como ocho años.*

10. Structured prayer is another central characteristic of Catholicism; for example, the recitation of the rosary has been central in Marian devotion since the 15th century; see Granziera 2004; de la Rosa 2005.

11. Similarly, in his study on the devotion to Saint Jude among the daughters of Italian Catholic immigrants, Orsi (1996) found that the pleas to the saint were mostly made on behalf of relatives.

12. Original quote in English—Esperanza was bilingual.

13. Henderson 2011; Fernandez and Gonzalez 2012; Peña 2014; Gonzalez 2015. See also Durand, Massey, and Charvet 2000; Massey, Durand, and Malone 2002; Tilly 1973.

14. *Desde que estabamos chiquitas mi abuelita y mi mamá nos juntaban a todos a rezar el rosario en la tardesita. Teniamos que parar lo que estabamos haciendo, a mi me daba mucho sueño cuando rezabamos el rosario, pero nomas se acababa y el sueño se me quitaba, como la vez?*

15. For further reading on the long-term consequences of NAFTA, see Weisbrot, Lefebvre, and Sammut 2014.

16. See Cravey 1998.

17. For further reading on the impact of NAFTA, see Fernandez-Kelly 2007; Gereffi, Spener, and Bair 2009.

18. For more on the femicides in Juárez, see Arrizón 2014. For an excellent theological interpretation of the femicides in Juárez, see Pineda-Madrid 2011.

19. For further reading on causes for migration, see Donato 1993; Durand, Massey, and Charvet 2000; Gabaccia 1991; Massey 2013; Segura and Zavella 2007.

20. *"No, ¿para que? ¿Has matado a alguien? ¿Has abusado de alguien? ¿Le has sido infiel a tu esposo?" Y yo le dije "No." Entonces el dijo, "Nomas habla con Dios y confiesate con el."*

21. *Y yo pienso que hay se rompe la creencia que uno trai porque en México cada Domingo te confiesas y comulgas y ahorita yo me siento hablo con mi Dios y comulgo pero siempre hace falta ese contacto con el Padre.*

22. See for example, Bacallao and Smokowski 2007; Falicov 2007; Wilkin et al. 2009; Bermudez and Mancini 2013; Rusch and Reyes 2013; Edelblute et al. 2014.

23. *Y yo le dije [al padre] es que yo quiero que mi niña se confiese lo más que pueda y dijo: ¿Te apuesto que tu tienes más pecados que ella? Y dije:: huyyyy pues dejame pensar yo entonces. . . . Me derrumbó. ¿Si me entiendes? Son cositas asi que lo van tumbando a uno.*

24. Public officials were given freedom to inquire about the legal status of those who appeared to be undocumented. For further reading on the impact of Proposition 187, I recommend Margolis 1995.

25. Heredia 2009. For further reading on the preferential option for the poor, see Gutierrez and Inda (1988; originally published in Spanish, 1971).

26. Many Californians opposed the proposition, including conservative Ron Unz, then a Republican gubernatorial candidate.

27. The preferential option for the poor is one of the seven themes in Catholic social teaching (USCCB 2005). Inspired by the Second Vatican Council, the first to make this commitment to the poor were the Catholic Bishops of Latin America (Medina 2005).

28. For further reading on *La Pastorela* (Shepherd's Play) as performance space to express ethnic identity and political rights, see *Los Pastores: History and Performance in the Mexican Shepherd's Play of South Texas* by Richard Flores, 1995.

29. Gendzel 2009.

30. Matas and Rodriguez 2014.

CHAPTER 4

1. The English text is a loose translation of the original quote that reads as follows: *Mis papás eran muy buenos padres, pero eso si muy disciplinarios. Mi papá,*

una vez nos dijo: "miren, mijas les voy a decir una cosa, nomás dos cosas que tienen siempre que recordar es el respeto. Mientras tú no te des a respetar nadie te va a respetar. Mientras tú no te respetes a nadie vas a respetar. La otra cosa es la obediencia." ¡Fíjate como nos tenían! Y mi papá decía: "porque el que no obedece va a tener sus pruebas." [De] eso acuérdense siempre [y] sean respetuosas y obedientes. Porque como le vas a decir a alguien que haga algo que tú no haces. Todo lo que cabe en la obediencia se debe respetar.

2. While some Damas had catechism classes at their local parish, others had informal instruction by one of the older women in their communities.

3. *Marianismo*, as defined by Stevens and Pescatello (1973), is a religious and "cultural template" (Zavella 2003) by which women are socialized to be obedient, all-accepting, all-enduring, and submissive—characteristics associated with the Virgin Mary, hence the term *Marianismo*.

4. The English text is a loose translation of the original quote that reads as follows: *"Buenos Dias le de Dios" le agarroa la mano [a mi bisabuelito] y le besas la mano, te incas y luego ya si te ibas a ir al mandado o algo "ya me voy apacito." Y ya te percina [persigna] él y ya te vas. Pero, era un respeto porque como él [era el] hombre de la casa [y] él tenía la autoridad.*

5. The English text is a loose translation of the original quote that reads as follows: *Hay 'mija en aquel entonces era un gran, gran respeto que uno le tenía a sus padres, abuelitos, y a Dios nuestro señor. Que esperanzas que uno les levantara la voz. ¡No, eso no se hacía! Un gran respeto, un gran respeto no como ahora.*

6. Esperanza (68) was the only *Dama* who spoke to me in English and Spanish when I interviewed her.

7. The English text is a loose translation of the original quote that reads as follows: *Dónde iba a desobedecer a mi madre o al hombre que ya me había llevado. En esa época, valía la honra más que la vida. Si yo hubiera estado un poquito más grandecita o hubiera tenido más alayas, yo me le quito a ese hombre porque hubo oportunidad . . . . Un día, [fui a visitar a Rita-mi cuñada] que vivía cerca, [más o menos] como un día de camino desde donde yo vivía . . . . podría haberme escapado pero no lo hice, porque tuve que obedecer.*

8. This is still the case even today.

9. In other instances young women were *robadas* (stolen) by their boyfriends when the young women's parents disapproved of the relationship. Again, this was done so that the parents would have no choice but to let their daughters marry in order to save the young women's honor.

10. Over 17 years ago, in a historical analysis of the Catholic Church, psychologist Pepe Rodríguez (1997, 139) contended that the type of role model the Catholic Church imposed on women was one of a woman who "is docile, and subservient to men even if by doing so she risks her own life."

11. Mexican anthropologist Rosío Córdova Plaza (2003) contended that the image of the *hacendado* is the prototype of the peasant family in México, where even

to this day obedience to authority (i.e., landowners and the Church) is expected from everyone in many small villages and towns. Part of the explanation for this could be traced back to México's hacienda system. Under this system, obedience was a key way in which secular and religious landholders controlled the agrarian class; obeying was not only an involuntary way of life but also a form of survival.

12. The English text is a loose translation of the original quote that reads as follows: *Fíjate que como cultura mexicana pues no, primero no tener novio hasta que tenía-mos ... después ya de estudiar de los dieciocho por allá. Después que nos cuidaramos. Y eso de tener novio pues implicaba mucho [y]menos tener relaciones, me entiendes. Entonces, este era un temor el que le metían a uno, ¿verdad? Porque tienes que respetar tu casa, tienes que estudiar primero y pues casi era una prohibición tener el novio hasta los 18.*

13. The English text is a loose translation of the original quote that reads as fol-lows: *Siempre mi ama ha sido estricta. Más bien, mi mamá era de carácter más fuerte hasta la fecha todavía. No me dejaba salir a fiestas y me sentía frustrada ... ella decía: "disque nos podía pasar algo malo."*

14. The English text is a loose translation of the original quote that reads as fol-lows: *Yo pienso que la religión y la cultura van muy ligadas las dos cosas. Como tu sabes en este caso típicamente en México somos muy religiosos, pero también la cultura es muy arraigada. La cultura Latina [y la] mexicana [son] muy arraigada[s].*

15. MEChA is a Chicanx student organization that traces its roots to the Chicanx Movement. As such it advocates social justice and socio-political empowerment of Chicanxs and Latinxs.

16. For further reading on young Chicana women's experiences growing up female, see Hurtado 2003.

17. For further reading on young Latinas and sexual agency, see Garcia 2012.

18. Concerns about protecting daughters and cultural values of virginity are not unique to this culture, but their deep rootedness in the Mexican Catholic tradi-tion gives them great force in shaping girls' lives.

CHAPTER 5

1. If we recall, Angelita from *Las Damas* group told me that she wanted to be inter-viewed in the kitchen so we could speak more comfortably.

2. For example, see Garcia 2012; González-López 2007.

3. For the history of *Marianismo*, I recommend one of the foundational stud-ies: Stevens and Pescatello 1973.

4. For a historical analysis of *Marianismo* in México, see Pastor 2010.

5. For additional reading on *Marianismo*, see: Carranza 2013; Cianelli et al. 2013; Hussain et al. 2015; Nuñez et al. 2015; and Villegas et al. 2010.

6. For a Chicana feminist reading on Our Lady of Guadalupe and *La Malinche* see, for example, Irene Lara's (2008) "Goddess of the Americas in the decolonial imaginary: beyond the virtuous virgen/pagan puta dichotomy."

7. The English text is a loose translation of the original quote that reads as follows: *Era algo tan diferente 'pa nosotros cuando ya entramos en señoritas 'veda . . . yo creo que yo entre a señorita como de trece años. Mi mamá nos hacia los brasieres y que no se nos miraran los pechos porque era malo enseñarle a los hombres los pechos, era pecado . . . apretados ansina . . . y yo comenzaba a mirarle a las démas que tu sabes como en la escuela . . . "a no ustedes tiene que 'tar ansina" . . . vez . . . y dicia yo . . . hay Madre Santa me dolía.*

8. The tradition of women's use of the *mantilla* could be traced back to Apostle Saint Paul's letters to the Corinthians where he states that it was a disgrace for women to attend sacred temples or prophesize with their heads uncovered. Women's public hair display inside sacred temples or when prophesizing was equated to having a shaven head, which was believed to be a disgrace to God. Accordingly, women's public hair display in church services was considered a serious violation that carried severe consequences. This belief was transplanted to Latin America through the colonizing efforts of Spanish missionaries who brought with them Pre-Tridentine Catholic practices and beliefs. For example, in the 19th century, Bishop Fray Nicolás García Jerez, Bishop of Nicaragua and Costa Rica and Governor of Nicaragua between 1811 and 1814, was among the gatekeepers of such mandates. He demanded that women who covered their head with a gauze *mantilla* or muslin so clear that, far from contributing to modesty and decorum, which according to him her sex must at all times embrace, only served to call attention to them as an idol of prostitution, a stumbling block, and spiritual distress (Lobo 2015). He ordered that women who chose to continue wearing transparent *mantillas* be thrown out of the Church and excommunicated. For further reading on this topic, see Lobo 2015.

9. De Troyer 2003.

10. Unlike European civilizations, that of the Aztec and Maya did not consider women's menstrual cycle filthy (Vieira Powers 2005). However, in Christianity women's menstrual cycle has traditionally been looked upon as a filthy body function. This belief is informed by a long-established set of religious and philosophical interpretations of the menstrual cycle as impure (Ranke-Heinemann 1990).

11. Women's menses are explicitly addressed in the Old Testament:

    When a woman has a discharge of blood that is her regular discharge from her body, she shall be in her impurity for seven days, and whoever touches her shall be unclean until the evening. Everything upon which she lies during her impurity shall be unclean; everything also upon which she sits shall be unclean. Whoever touches her bed shall wash his clothes, and bathe in water, and be unclean until the evening. Whoever, touches anything upon which she sits shall wash his clothes, and bathe in water, and be unclean until the evening; whether it is the bed or anything upon which she sits, when he touches it he shall be unclean until the evening." (Leviticus 15:19–24, New Revised Standard Version)

Unfortunately, conquest forced such beliefs upon people who celebrated rather than stigmatized this particular time in a woman's life. See also Raming, Macy, and Cooke (2004); and Gutiérrez 2010.

12. Female sexuality is a taboo subject among Latinxs (Hurtado 2003; Zavella 2003, 2008). One central reason is that cultural and religious emphasis on the importance of female innocence leads many Latina mothers not to talk about sexuality with their daughters (Zavella 2008; Hurtado 2003; Raffaelli and Green 2003). Among US Latinx college students, for example, the religious elements of culture have a strong, direct impact on attitudes toward sexuality (Ahrold and Meston 2010). This is not to say that silence about sex and sexuality and the societal anxiety that accompanies it are unique to any one particular culture (Avishai 2010). See, for example, Ahrold and Meston 2010; Sharma 2008.

13. Zavella 2008; Villar and Concha 2012.

14. In 2002 Mexican scholars M. L. Marván, G. Espinosa-Hernandez, and A. Vacio conducted a study among 750 premenarchal girls between the ages of 10 and 13, from 13 different schools in México City and Puebla, about their attitudes toward menstruation. Their findings indicate that the girls felt a sense of embarrassment about their menstrual cycle and a strong need to keep it a secret (see also Charlesworth 2001).

15. The English text is a loose translation of the original quote that reads as follows: *Me asuste pensaba que me iba a morir [y] yo le dije a mi nana y a mi bisabuela y luego se agarraron llorando, me llevaron al río, me lavaron [y] rezaron por mí. Me llevaron al altar de la Virgen de Guadalupe y me dijeron: "ya eres mujercita, pero fué todo," y no me dijeron nada más. Yo no sabía . . . pos [pues] no sabía, pero yo solita tuve que aprender.*

16. The term *enferma* is still used today; however, it does not carry the same degree of negativity that it did when the participants were coming of age.

17. The English text is a loose translation of the original quote that reads as follows: *Hay algo que me acabo de enterar y pos como ya tu estas casada creo que es importante que sepas pa' que no estés tan cerrada como yo. ¿Sabías que los hombres no se enferman? Yo no lo sabía, pero mi novio me lo conto ayer.*

18. Jean Franco, in her book *Las conspiradoras. La representación de la mujer en México* (1989), also discusses the various ways lay and religious women exercised their agency within the limits of México's patriarchal system at the time.

19. The English text is a loose translation of the original quote that reads as follows: *No, no que esperanzas, no se usaba, no se usaba . . . NOOO . . . Cuando yo me enferme, me dio un susto. Ya hacía ya un año que me había enfermado y no le conté a mi mamá, ni nada . . . Una mujer que [ha veces de buen corazón, porque eramos muchos niños, le] ayudaba a lavar la ropa [a mi mama], ella fue la que me dijo. Dijo: "te vas a enfermar y me das pa" lavarte tus . . . En ese entonces no había Kotex, era material . . . doblecito los hacían . . . con mi mamá no se usaba*

240

Notes

hablar . . . casi tu mami no te hablaba de eso. No se usaba como ahora las chiquitas ya saben todo hasta más que uno.

20. The English text is a loose translation of the original quote that reads as follows: *Eso le pasa a las mujeres, ya no eres niña ahora eres señorita y ya no puedes andar brincoteando. Ponte algo y no te bañes hasta que se te quite.*

21. The English text is a loose translation of the original quote that reads as follows: *Una vez andaba allí en la noche, 'taba yo jugando y me golpie andaba jugando al señor quemado y por ir por la pelota corriendo al subir la banqueta me di una en la pura barriga y al otro día así amanecí, así mala. i mamá, se dio cuenta y yo ni cuenta me había dado y [mi] mamá me empezó a decir, pero ese día nomás [nada más] antes no. Tenía once años porque hasta eso de eso si me acuerdo.*

22. The English text is a loose translation of the original quote that reads as follows: *A mi nunca . . . se me vino la idea de platicarles algo a mi mamá ni a mis abuelas porque en aquel tiempo uno no tenía esa libertad, ni de hacer preguntas, ni de decir lo que pensábamos o queríamos. Ellos disponían por uno. Cuando a mi me bajo la primera vez, me acuerdo que esa vez, yo le dije a mi papá lo que me había pasado. Y [mi papá] me dijo: "ay, eso no es nada, ponte algo y ya." Pero, yo entonces estaba muy asustada y muy preocupada. Yo me bañaba y me bañaba, me bañaba y no se me quitaba. Y entonces decía, pero ¿qué va a pasar? Hasta que me puse algo, porque en ese tiempo no había que ponerse, [y] que iba a la tienda a comprar, no. Y entonces me puse algo y así fui aprendiendo, yo sola.*

23. Elsasser, MacKenzie, and Tixier y Vigil (1980), in their collection of women's biographies of older Latinas, *Las Mujeres: Conversations from a Hispanic Community*, also found that women never knew what exactly was happening to their bodies when they first had their menstrual cycle, and learned on their own.

24. The English text is a loose translation of the original quote that reads as follows: *Cuando le dije a mi mamá como a los tres días nomás, le dio risa. Y me hizo sentir como hay que mensa. Si me entiendes, así como en esa vez sí me acuerdo que si me frustre porque me dije en vez de darme ánimos como que me puso hasta el suelo. Yo tenía quince años cuando me bajo. No sabía todavía.*

25. It is important to note that according to Koniak-Griffin et al.'s (2006) study among white mothers, mother-blaming was also very common. Furthermore, Bhopal (1998) found that South Asian women in East London were constantly blamed by their mothers-in-law for their children's misconduct. See also Franco 1989; Lagarde 1990; Alfaro Alvarez 2005; Garcia 2012.

26. Scholars of Chicana/Latina feminist studies have extensively documented the value of virginity in Chicanx/Latinx communities. Zavella 2003; Gonzalez-Lopez 2004, 2005, 2008; Hurtado 2003; Garcia and Torres 2009; Deardorff, Tschann, and Flores 2008 are some of the scholars whose research on sex and sexuality among Chicanas and Latinas have made significant contributions to the study of gender and sexuality in this ethnic group. In her research, Hurtado (2003, 36) found that "remaining a virgin was essential to being 'picked' as a wife"—a belief

that to her surprise prevailed throughout her interviews among young, college-educated, self-identified Chicanas.

27. Her mother did not want Olivia to experience the same silence she did when she started menstruating.

28. I am deeply grateful to my colleague Héctor Sánchez-Flores for sharing Susana's testimony with me.

29. The English text is a loose translation of the original quote that reads as follows: '*Pos [pues], ¿cómo crees que me sentí? Que mi hijo iba a nacer de un lugar tan sucio. Pensé que mi hijo iba a nacer de mi ombligo. No, no, lloré y lloré toda la noche.*

30. The English text is a loose translation of the original quote that reads as follows: *Pensé que mi estómago se iba a abrir y que así era como mi hijo iba a nacer, asta que la mamá de mi marido me dijo, que mi hijo iba a nacer de un ollito y [en estado de shock] dije que no. Pos [pues] luego me puse a llore y llore todo el día y toda la noche.*

CHAPTER 6

1. The English text is a loose translation of the original quote that reads as follows: *Porque quiero bailar y pasar un buen rato, y de esta manera no oigo cuando mi esposa me llama para ir a recoger a nuestra nieta de la escuela. Verás, la invito a venir, pero ella no quiere porque dice que este lugar es pa' los viejitos.*

2. The English text is a loose translation of the original quote that reads as follows: *Bueno, déjame decirte que pa' mí ella [La Virgen de Guadalupe] es como, bien para nosotros. ¡Ella es la madre de Dios! Pa' nosotros es casi lo mismo ¡Sí, lo mismo! Siempre decimos, "Dios es primero," pero nunca la abandonamos. Ella es nuestra santa madre. Ella es como mi mamá porque ya no tengo la mía.*

3. Orlando Espín (1997) contends that women, particularly older women, are the main transmitters of faith and devotion in Latinx families.

4. According to Espín (1997), the Latinx religious experience takes place and lives in the context of their marginalization; we cannot fully comprehend it without first acknowledging this experience.

5. Elizondo 1997; Espín 1997; Rodriguez 1994.

6. The women that Rodriguez (1994) interviewed were Mexican American middle-class and second-generation women. She found that the women venerated and felt a deep love and attachment to Guadalupe. However, "although [Guadalupe] is of primary importance to them, and they prefer to petition her before petitioning God, they understand that [she] is not God" (Rodriguez 1994, xix). Rodriguez adds that while the women she interviewed do not see Guadalupe as God, they nevertheless describe her using God-like terms. She concludes, in alignment with traditional Catholic theology, that what the women are doing is ascribing to Guadalupe the attributes that have been stripped away from the original concept of God. The assimilation process that comes with living in the United States for

generations is the explanation Rodriguez provides for the ways the women in her study understand Guadalupe in their own lives. I found her results fascinating. They prompted me to ask how Mexican immigrant and first-generation women see Guadalupe in relation to God.

7. The English text is a loose translation of the original quote that reads as follows: *La veo como una diosa porque siento paz cuando estoy en su presencia. [Siento] mucha paz y tranquilidad y [esto] me da más fe. Siento que está conmigo y no me abandona. Ella me transmite [el sentimiento] que todo lo que a veces se sale de mis manos va a estar bien. Cuando me acerco a ella, siento esa paz . . . Cuando hablo con ella, siento más fe.*

8. The English text is a loose translation of the original quote that reads as follows: *Se puede decir que son iguales. Ella es su madre, ves que nosotros las madres percibimos a nuestros hijos como iguales a nosotros. Sentimos su dolor y ellos sienten el nuestro.*

9. Catechism classes were common among *Las Madres* and *Las Mujeres*, but not among *Las Damas* for reasons I present in Chapter 3.

10. For similar findings among Mexican American middle-class women, see Rodriguez 1994.

11. See Castañeda-Liles 2008 for a further reading on how Chicana feminist artists represent Our Lady of Guadalupe.

12. For further reading on the subject of prayer in the colonial context, see Dolan 1985.

13. The English text is a loose translation of the original quote that reads as follows: *No porque le recemos a Dios primero significa que no tengamos a la Virgen en nuestras mente[s]. Nunca la olvidamos [y] eso nunca lo haríamos [porque] ella es nuestra madre.*

14. The English text is a loose translation of the original quote that reads as follows: *A veces, cuando rezo, suena el teléfono y empiezo a platicar y cuando cuelgo y quiero regresar mis oraciones. No vas a creerme, se me olvida[n]. [Riéndose me dice]Pos [pues]'toy [estoy] vieja, así que empiezo todo pero la virgencita me entiende.*

15. See also Espín 1997.

16. The English text is a loose translation of the original quote that reads as follows: *Todos los días antes de acostar a mis hijos, le rezo a La Virgen. Me gustaría hacerlo en la mañana pero a veces ni siquiera me acuerdo de darle las gracias a Dios por un nuevo día. Me levanto a las 6:00 a.m. para bañar y cambiar a mi hija. Y luego el otro niño se levanta más tarde. Sólo por la noche es cuando tenemos un tiempo para estar juntos.*

17. Similarly, Rodriguez (1994) found that the middle-class Mexican American women in her study prefer to pray to Our Lady of Guadalupe because of her identity as female and mother.

18. A larger sample of participants might show a different pattern.

19. In his article, "Mary's Rain and God's Umbrella," Tweed (2010) found that the artist he interviewed also has the same type of familial relationship with God and Our Lady of Guadalupe.

20. There were a couple of women who did not use the term "practicing Catholics" because they said that though they were baptized Catholic, they had not been to Mass in a while.

CHAPTER 7

1. The English text is a loose translation of the original quote: *Nací en un corral de caballos en el rancho en Texas. Mi mamá me abandonó y me dejó en el corral. Nunca la conocí hasta que ya era una adulta, y es por eso que no le tengo afecto, porque ella no estuvo allí cuando yo estaba chiquita. Pero como diría mi abuelita, "La Virgen siempre está con nosotros."*

2. Ammerman and Williams 2012 also discuss the importance of narrative in social science research on religion.

3. The English text is a loose translation of the original quote that reads as follows: *Él ya me había amenazado otras veces, y pos [pues] yo nunca pensé que me fuera hacer algo. Pero un día, yo llegué cansada de la cañería,, cerré la puerta de la casa y me acosté en el sillón. Mi esposo llegó y como no pudo abrir la puerta de enfrente se metió por la ventana del baño. Cuando menos pensé, pos [pues] 'taba dormida en el sillón, él estaba parado enfrente de mí y yo tenía sangre por donde quiera, las tripas se me salían. Me había abierto el estómago con un cuchillo. Yo tenía nueve meses de embarazo y esperando gemelos. No tuve tiempo de nada nomás [nada más] que de encomendar a mis hijos y a mí a La Virgencita. Luego, que agarró una pistola que yo aguardaba debajo del sillón y que le disparó, no sé cómo lo hice. Yo tenía mucho miedo, pero La Virgencita me dio la fuerza, y le tiré un balazo. Mi esposo le hizo una cortada grandota en la cabeza a uno de mis hijos y al otro le rajó la piernita. El primero se me murió, pero el segundo sobrevivió. Mi esposo salió corriendo, pero la policía lo encontró y lo echaron a la cárcel. ¡Sí, mi Virgencita es muy milagrosa, muy milagrosa! Yo le tengo mucha fe.*

4. Domestic violence is defined as "abuse committed against an adult or a fully emancipated minor who is a spouse, former spouse, cohabitant, former cohabitant, or person with whom the suspect has had a child or is having or has had a dating or engagement relationship." Penal Code Section 13700(b), http://www. leginfo.ca.gov/cgi-bin/displaycode?section.

5. Domínguez and Maya-Jariego 2018; O'Neal, Beckman, and Spohn 2016; White and Roosa 2012; Zadnick, Sabina, and Cuevas 2016.

6. Similarly, Orsi (2005, 60) in his study of the Virgin Mary maintains that "Mary is called on to mediate family disputes, to judge behavior, and to listen to the most intimate sorrows and fears."

7. James, Brody, and Hamilton 2013.

8. The English text is a loose translation of the original quote that reads as follows: *Porque, así como me crié, cuando me casé nomás [nada más] bajaba mi cabeza cuando mi esposo me insultaba. Yo pensaba que si le respondía lo estaba desobedeciendo. Él me platicaba de las otras mujeres con las que andaba y me daba detalles, y yo nomás [nada más] lloraba.*

9. The English text is a loose translation of the original quote that reads as follows: *Le recé a La Virgen de Guadalupe para que me diera fuerzas [jadeando por el
aire y alzando su voz] para poder gritarle de nuevo. Le rezaba para que yo pudiera
ser yo. Esto era algo imposible de hacer, pero me agarré de La Virgen de Guadalupe.
Me dije: "Ella me dará fuerzas y le diré exactamente cómo me siento." Fui donde
estaban mis hijas y les dije: "Rezamos a La Virgen antes de que se duerman." Una
señora que era una pariente lejana y vivía con nosotros en México me dijo una vez que
rezara el Salmo 140 cada vez que tuviera problemas con mi esposo. El salmo habla del
hombre malvado . . . Que puede causar daño y cómo puede ser apaciguado. Me se la
oración de memoria. Dice: "Líbrame, Señor, del hombre perverso, defiéndeme del hombre violento, de los que en su corazón planean maldades y provocan discordias todo el
día: afilan su lengua como la de una serpiente, en sus labios tienen veneno de víbora.
Protégeme, Señor, de la mano del malvado, defiéndeme del hombre violento, de los que
planean derribarme. Los soberbios me ponen trampas, tienden una red bajo mis pies,
y en mi sendero colocan lazos" (Salmo 140: 1–4).*

10. The English text is a loose translation of the original quote that reads as follows: *"El momento es ahora." Le dije: (levantando su voz y cambiando su tono), "No
sé qué está pasando. Yo no soy la misma. Soy una persona diferente. Ahora estoy aquí
en los Estados Unidos y conozco mis derechos. Quiero que me respetes y que si tienes
algo que decir, que lo digas con modales."*

11. The English text is a loose translation of the original quote that reads as follows: *Yo siempre le pido a Dios con todo mi corazón y él siempre me escucha. "Te
pido en nombre de Dios y de La Virgen que cambies." Me dijo: "Si no te callas, te voy
a romper la boca." Entonces, sentí mi estómago temblar y mi abdomen me empezó a
doler mucho. Le dije: "Por tu culpa voy a perder a mi hijo." No me siento bien. Mis
manos temblaban, mi boca, [y] todo mi cuerpo. Sentí como si el mundo se derrum-
bara sobre mí. Entonces mi hija mayor le dijo: "¡Cállate!" Fue entonces cuando él le
dijo: "Llama a la policía si quieres y verás lo que soy capaz de hacer."*

12. The English text is a loose translation of the original quote that reads as follows: *Mi hija me dice: "Mami, era La Virgen." Mis hijos tienen fe en Dios y La Virgen.
Le digo a mis hijos, La Virgen me ha ayudado mucho. Si no hubiera sido por ella, no
habría tenido la fuerza ese día y las cosas serían las mismas.*

13. The English text is a loose translation of the original quote that reads as follows: *Como mencioné en mi entrevista, mi papá era alcohólico. Uno de sus amigos
con el que se emborrachaba era el hombre que ahora es mi esposo. Recuerdo haberlo
visto caminando por la calle arrastrando y golpeando a mujeres, era un mujeriego. Yo
miraba por la ventana y me decía a mí misma, no a mí. Yo tenía un novio en aquel
entonces [y] él era un muy amoroso y los dos estábamos profundamente enamorados.
Un día en la cantina, mi papá se emborrachó y dio mi mano en matrimonio a ese
hombre, todo por un par de tragos.*

14. The English text is a loose translation of the original quote that reads as follows: *Él siempre se aseguraba de que yo comiera cuando llegaba a la casa del trabajo.*

Tuvimos una buena vida. Mi esposo me ayudaba con las tareas de la casa mientras yo trabajaba. Hacía arroz y tortillas para toda la familia. [Llorando añadió] ¿Cómo no voy a extrañarlo?

15. The English text is a loose translation of the original quote that reads as follows: *No soy la misma de antes. El tomar clases en el centro me ha ayudado mucho. Especialmente a ser mucho más fuerte. Me ayudado a estar más segura de mi misma con mi esposo, con mis hijos, [y] con mis responsabilidades. Antes, yo era muy sumisa y lloraba por todo [y]ara todo. Antes, tenía muchos problemas con mi esposo, y mi familia. Mi matrimonio estaba prácticamente destruido.*

16. The English text is a loose translation of the original quote that reads as follows: *Soy una feminista cuando defiendo mis derechos como mujer. Cuando tenemos que tomar una decisión por el bien de nuestros hijos. Como por ejemplo, cuando no quiere hacer algo y logró hacerle ver las cosas, como cuando mi hija quería ir a acampar con los otros niños de su escuela.*

17. The English text is a loose translation of the original quote that reads as follows: *Si ella ve que las mujeres están siendo humilladas, no estaría de acuerdo. Por eso se apareció, para que hubiera igualdad en la tierra. Creo que de esta manera La Virgen es una feminista. Los hombres no deben ser más poderosos que las mujeres. Así es como [yo] la veo.*

18. Quote originally in English.

19. The English text is a loose translation of the original quote that reads as follows: *Me gustan esos [métodos anticonceptivos]. Los usé y no ofendí a nadie. Si no los hubiéramos usado, habríamos tenido siete, [u] ocho niños. Creo que los métodos anticonceptivos no matan a nadie ni son dañinos. ¿A quien ofendes? El sexo es una cosa y los niños son otra. Es mucho más hermoso si son planiados [planeados].*

20. Zavella 1997.

21. Marín and Gómez 1997, quoted in González-López 2005, 245.

22. González-López 2005.

23. Hurtado 2003.

24. The English text is a loose translation of the original quote that reads as follows: *A pesar de que la Iglesia Católica lo desaprueba, creo que ella entendería que es necesario para tener familias más pequeñas [y] para poder criar a los hijos. Antes las mujeres tenían diez hijos o más, y era difícil criarlos. Pues yo pienso que si estaría de acuerdo.*

CHAPTER 8

1. For example, people borrow from various religious traditions to create something completely new (Roof 1993, 2001). Roof (2001) found that unlike their parents, the baby boomer generation integrates various spiritual beliefs to their own, resulting in what he calls a "reflexive spirituality." For an in-depth analysis of Chicana spirituality see Pérez 2007; Delgadillo 2011.

2. For further reading on Chicana feminist representations of Our Lady of Guadalupe see Pérez 2007; Serna 2011; Herrera-Sobek 2001; Mesa-Bains 2003.

3. There were a couple of *Las Damas* who had heard about the Chicana/o movement, but did not know much about it.

4. For further reading on the controversy, see Gutiérrez 2010.

5. Quote originally in Spanish: *Puedo ver lo que los artistas están tratando de comunicar, pero La Virgen no necesita ser pintada de una manera diferente. Ella se mueve a través de la fe que tenemos en ella.*

6. See Davalos 2008.

7. The English text is a loose translation of the original quote that reads as follows: *Para mí . . . bueno . . . ahora conociendo la historia . . . uno piensa un poco . . . sobre la persona . . . no de la pintura . . . porque [La Virgen] le concedió un milagro y fue capaz de mostrar su cuerpo de nuevo. Pero, sobre la persona que hizo la pintura y lo que tiene que decir . . . el mensaje que da es diferente. Porque si mi marido . . . fuera a ver esta foto donde está así . . . no . . . es porque quienquiera que vea esta foto, no lo sé . . . un joven, se excitaría . . . Por eso digo que no es bueno . . . es algo del diablo. Las Virgen se supone que es algo de Dios . . . algo sagrado.*

8. The English text is a loose translation of the original quote that reads as follows: *Seguir los principios de tu religión es algo diferente. Si eres un buen católico, sigues las reglas. Pero, nunca vas a ver a La Virgen de Guadalupe como un ejemplo para seguir o tratar de ser como ella. Ella es original, ella es especial.*

9. The English text is a loose translation of the original quote that reads as follows: *Si veo la pintura desde un punto de vista religioso, la veo como una falta de respeto. Si la veo desde la perspectiva del arte, entonces la veo más como lo que hizo en esta representación es parte de su profesión.*

10. The English text is a loose translation of the original quote that reads as follows: *Quería decir lo que realmente sentía acerca de la representación, pero por respeto a las otras mujeres del grupo decidí quedarme callada. Yo era una prostituta, y escuchar a las otras mujeres criticar a "Nuestra Señora" porque ella parecía una prostituta me lastimó.*

11. For reading on pregnancy and depression among Latina teenagers, I recommend Corcoran 2016.

12. The English text is a loose translation of the original quote that reads as follows: *Las mujeres que han tenido una bonita infancia no pueden ver a La Virgen como yo la veo. No pueden relacionarse con la pintura porque no han sufrido. Yo sí puedo ver lo que Alma López está tratando de decir, y estoy totalmente de acuerdo.*

13. The English text is a loose translation of the original quote that reads as follows: *La pintaría completamente desnuda, con los brazos abiertos. No se avergonzaría de su sexualidad. Yo también dibujaría alrededor de ella, un condón, píldoras anticonceptivas, una lata de cerveza, una jeringa y dos jóvenes luchando. El mensaje de mi Virgen sería el de prevención de embarazo, pandillas y drogas.*

14. Hurtado 2003.

CONCLUSION

1. See also León 2004 and Goizueta 1996.
2. For a further analysis of the "chain of memory," see Hervieu-Léger 2000.
3. Lifton cautions against concluding that a person can become protean on the spur of the moment. The protean self, he contends, emerges "from a certain social and historical context" (Lifton 1993, 2).
4. Cook 1989; Sandoval 1991; and Zepeda 2016.

Bibliography

Adams, Heidi L., and Lela Rankin Williams. 2011. "What They Wish They Would Have Known: Support for Comprehensive Sexual Education from Mexican American and White Adolescents' Dating and Sexual Desires." *Children and Youth Services Review* 33 (10): 1875–1885.

Ahrold, Tierney K., and Cindy M. Meston. 2010. "Ethnic Differences in Sexual Attitudes of U.S. College Students: Gender, Acculturation, and Religiosity Factors." *Archives of Sexual Behavior* 39 (1): 190–202.

Alba, Francisco. 2016. "Changing Fortunes: Mexico and Mexican–US Migration." In *Migration in an Era of Restriction and Recession*, edited by David L. Leal and Nestor P. Rodriguez, 39–55. Switzerland: Springer International Publishing.

Alfaro, Sammy. 2010. *Divino Compañero: Toward a Hispanic Pentecostal Christology.* Vol. 147. Eugene, OR: Wipf and Stock.

Alfaro Alvarez, Jessica. 2005. "La Retórica del Poder. Miradas Respecto del Feminismo, las Mujeres y lo Social. Análisis del Discurso de la Iglesia Católica." *Athenea Digital: Revista de Pensamiento e Investigación Social* (7): 105–113.

Ammerman, Nancy Tatom. 2007. *Studying Everyday Religion: Challenges for the Future.* Oxford, New York: Oxford University Press.

———. 2013. *Sacred Stories, Spiritual Tribes: Finding Religion in Everyday Life.* New York: Oxford University Press.

Ammerman, Nancy T., and R. R. Williams. 2012. "Speaking of Methods: Eliciting Religious Narratives through Interviews, Photos, and Oral Diaries." *Annual Review of the Sociology of Religion*: 117–134.

Amnesty International. 2005. *Mexico: Justice Fails in Ciudad Juárez and the City of Chihuahua.* https://www.amnestyusa.org/reports/mexico-justice-fails-in-ciudad-juarez-and-the-city-of-chihuahua/.

Anderson, Charles W. 1963. "Bankers as Revolutionaries: Politics and Development Banking in Mexico." In *The Political Economy of Mexico: Two Studies*, edited by William P. Glade Jr., 103–185. Madison: University of Wisconsin Press.

Andión, Eduardo, Diego Lizarazo, and Margarita Zires. 2007. *Interpretaciones icóni-cas: estética de las imágenes*. México, D.F., San Ángel: Siglo XXI.

Anzaldúa, Gloria. 1987. *Borderlands/La Frontera: The New Mestiza*. San Francisco, CA: Spinsters/Aunt Lute.

———. 1996. "Coatlalopeuh, She Who has Dominion over Serpents." In *Goddess of the Americas/La Diosa de las Americas*, edited by Ana Castillo, 52–55. New York: Riverhead.

Aquino, Maria Pilar. 1992. "Perspectives on a Latina's Feminist Liberation Theology." In *Frontiers of Hispanic Theology in the United States*, edited by Allan Figueroa Deck, 23–40. Maryknoll, NY: Orbis Books.

———. 1996. "Feminist Theology, Latin American." In *Dictionary of Feminist Theologies*, edited by Letty M. Russell and J. Shannon Clarkson, 116. Louisville, KY: Westminster John Knox.

———. 2008. "Living on the Border." *Journal of Feminist Studies in Religion* 24: 121–125.

Arrizón, Alicia. 2014. "'Invisible Wars': Gendered Terrorism in the US Military and the Juárez Feminicidio." In *Gender, Globalization, and Violence: Postcolonial Conflict Zones*, edited by Sandra Ponzanesi, 177–194. New York: Routledge.

Asencio, Marysol, ed. 2010. *Latina/o Sexualities: Probing Powers, Passions, Practices, and Policies*. New Brunswick, NJ: Rutgers University Press.

Avishai, Orit. 2010. "What to Do with the Problem of the Flesh? Negotiating Orthodox Jewish Sexual Anxieties." *Fieldwork in Religion* 7 (2): 148–162.

Bacallao, Martica L., and Paul R. Smokowski. 2007. "The Costs of Getting Ahead: Mexican Family System Changes After Immigration." *Family Relations* 56 (1): 52–66.

Beauvoir, Simone de. 1949. *The Second Sex*. Translated and edited by H. M. Parshley. Harmondsworth, UK: Penguin.

Becker, Marjorie. 1987. "Black and White and Color: Cardenismo and the Search for a Campesino Ideology." *Comparative Studies in Society and History* 29 (3): 453–465.

Berru Davis, Rebecca. 2009. "Guadalupita: La Virgen Peregrina—An Ethnographic Study." *Perspectivas: Hispanic Theological Initiative Occasional Papers* (Fall): 22–49.

Bermudez, J. Maria, and Jay A. Mancini. 2013. "Familias fuertes: Family Resilience among Latinos." In *Handbook of Family Resilience*, 215–227. New York: Springer.

Bhopal, Kalwant. 1998. "South Asian Women in East London: Motherhood and Social Support." *Women's Studies International Forum* 21 (5): 485–492.

Brown, Anne S., and David D. Hall. 1997. "Family Strategies and Religious Practice: Baptism and the Lord's Supper in Early New England." In *Lived Religion in America: Toward a History of Practice*, edited by David D. Hall, 41–68. Princeton, NJ: Princeton University Press.

Burkhart, Louise M. 1993. "The Cult of the Virgin of Guadalupe in Mexico." In *South and Meso-American Native Spirituality: From the Cult of the Feathered Serpent to the Theology of Liberation*, edited by Gary H. Gossen and Miguel Leon-Portilla, 198–227. New York: Crossroad.

Cadena, Gilbert. 1995. "Religious Ethnic Identity: A Socio-Religious Portrait of Latinos and Latinas in the Catholic Church." In *Old Masks, New Faces: Religion and Latino Identities*, Vol. 2, edited by Anthony M. Stevens Arroyo, 33–58. New York: Bildner Center for Western Hemisphere Studies, CUNY.

Cadena, Gilbert R., and Lara Medina. 1996. "Liberation Theology and Social Change: Chicanas and Chicanos in the Catholic Church." In *Chicanas and Chicanos in Contemporary Society*, edited by Roberto M. De Anda, 99–111. Boston: Allyn and Bacon.

Calavita, Kitty. 2007. "Immigration, Social Control, and Punishment in the Industrial Era." In *Race, Gender, and Punishment: From Colonialism to the War on Terror*, edited by Mary Bosworth and Jeanne Flavin, 117–133. New Brunswick, NJ: Rutgers University Press.

Cantú, Norma E. 2000. *La Quinceañera: Towards an Ethnographic Analysis of a Life-Cycle Ritual*. Guadalupe Cultural Arts Center.

Carranza, Mirna E. 2013. "Value Transmission among Salvadorian Mothers and Daughters: Marianismo and Sexual Morality." *Child and Adolescent Social Work Journal* 30 (4): 311–327.

Castañeda-Liles, Socorro. 2008. "Our Lady of Guadalupe and the Politics of Cultural Interpretation." In *Mexican American Religions: Spirituality, Activism, and Culture*, edited by Gastón Espinosa and Mario García, 153–179. Durham, NC: Duke University Press.

Castillo, Ana, ed. 1996. *Goddess of the Americas: Writings on the Virgin of Guadalupe*. New York: Riverhead.

Castillo, Fernando Muñoz. 2001. "Teatro Maya Peninsular (Precolombino y Evangelizador)." *Assaig de Teatre: Revista de l'Associació d'Investigació i Experimentació Teatral* (29): 149–154.

Castro Dopacio, María Jesús. 2010. *Emperatriz de las Américas: La Virgen de Guadalupe en la Literatura Chicana*. Biblioteca Javier Coy d'Estudis Nord-Americans 67. Valencia, Spain: Universidad de Valencia.

CBSNews. 2009. "'Basic Instinct' Screenwriter Finds God." http://www.cbsnews.com/news/basic-instinct-screenwriter-finds-god/.

Charlesworth, Dacia. 2001. "Paradoxical Constructions of Self: Educating Young Women about Menstruation." *Women and Language* 24 (2): 13–20.

Chávez, Eduardo. 2006. *Our Lady of Guadalupe and Saint Juan Diego: The Historical Evidence*. Lanham, MD: Rowman & Littlefield.

Cianelli, Rosina, et al. 2013. "Unique Factors that Place Older Hispanic Women At Risk for HIV: Intimate Partner Violence, Machismo, and Marianismo." *Journal of the Association of Nurses in AIDS Care* 24 (4): 341–354.

Cisneros, Sandra. 1996. "Guadalupe the Sex Goddess." In *Goddess of the Americas: Writings on the Virgin of Guadalupe*, edited by Ana Castillo, 46–51. New York: Riverhead.

Cook, Elizabeth Adell. 1989. "Measuring Feminist Consciousness." *Women and Politics* 9 (3): 71–88.

Corcoran, Jacqueline. 2016. "Teenage Pregnancy and Mental Health." *Societies* 6 (3): 21.

Correll, Timothy Corrigan, and Patrick Arthur Polk. 2014. "Productos Latinos: Latino Business Murals, Symbolism, and the Social Enactment of Identity in Greater Los Angeles." *Journal of American Folklore* 127 (505): 285–320.

Cotera, Marta. 1997. "Our Feminist Heritage." In *Chicana Feminist Thought: The Basic Historical Writings*, edited by Alma M. García, 41–44. New York: Routledge Press.

Cravey, Altha J. 1998. *Women and Work in Mexico's Maquiladoras*. Lanham, MD: Rowman & Littlefield.

Crenshaw, Kimberle Williams. 1989. "Demarginalizing the Intersection of Race and Sex: A Black Feminist Critique of Antidiscrimination Doctrine, Feminist Theory and Antiracist Politics." *University Of Chicago Legal Forum*: 139–167.

Davalos, Karen Mary. 2003. "La Quinceañera." In *Velvet Barrios*, edited by Alicia Gaspar de Alba, 141–162. New York: Palgrave Macmillan.

———. 2008. "La Quinceariera: Making Gender." In *Perspectives on Las Américas: A Reader in Culture, History, & Representation*, edited by Matthew Gutmann, Feliz V. Matos-Rodríguez, Lynn Stephen, and Patricia Zavella, 299–316. Malden, MA: Blackwell Publishing.

Davie, Grace. 2007. "Vicarious Religion: A Methodological Challenge." In *Everyday Religion: Observing Modern Religious Lives*, edited by Nancy Ammerman, 21–36. New York: Oxford University Press.

DeAnda, Neomi Dolores. 2011. "Images of God, Imago Dei and God's Relationship with Humanity through the Image of Mary's Breast Milk: A Focus upon Sor María Anna Águeda De San Ignacio (1695–1756)." PhD dissertation, Loyola University, Chicago.

Deardorff, Julianna, Jeanne M. Tschann, and Elena Flores. 2008. "Sexual Values among Latino Youth: Measurement Development Using a Culturally Based Approach." *Cultural Diversity and Ethnic Minority Psychology* 14 (2): 138.

de la Rosa, Rolando V. 2005. "History of the Rosary." *Landas: Journal of Loyola School of Theology* 19 (1): 92–100.

De La Torre, Miguel A. 2007. *A Lily Among the Thorns: Imagining a New Christian Sexuality*. San Francisco: Jossey-Bass/John Wiley & Sons.

Delgadillo, Theresa. 2011. *Spiritual Mestizaje: Religion, Gender, Race, and Nation in Contemporary Chicana Narrative*. Durham NC: Duke University Press.

De Troyer, Kristin, ed. 2003. *Wholly Woman, Holy Blood: A Feminist Critique of Purity and Impurity*. Harrisburg, PA: Trinity Press International.

Diaz-Stevens, Ana Maria. 1993. "The Saving Grace: The Matriarchal Core of Latino Catholicism." *Latino Studies Journal* 4 (3): 60–78.

———. 1994. "Latinas and the Church." In *Hispanic Catholic Culture in the U.S.: Issues and Concerns*, edited by Jay P. Dolan and Allan Figueroa Deck, 240–277. Notre Dame, IN: University of Notre Dame Press.

Dolan, Jay P. 1985. *The American Catholic Experience: A History from Colonial Times to the Present.* New York: Doubleday.

Domínguez, Silvia, and Isidro Maya-Jariego. 2008. "Acculturation of Host Individuals: Immigrants and Personal Networks." *American Journal of Community Psychology* 42 (3–4): 309–327.

Donato, Katharine M. 1993. "Current Trends and Patterns of Female Migration: Evidence from Mexico." *International Migration Review* 27: 748–771.

Durand, Jorge, Douglas S. Massey, and Fernando Charvet. 2000. "The Changing Geography of Mexican Immigration to the United States: 1910–1996." *Social Science Quarterly* 81 (1): 1–15.

Durand, Jorge, Douglas S. Massey, and Rene M. Zenteno. 2001. "Mexican Immigration to the United States: Continuities and Changes." *Latin American Research Review:* 107–127.

Ebaugh, Helen Rose Fuchs, and Janet Saltzman Chafetz. 2002. *Religion Across Borders: Transnational Immigrant Networks.* Walnut Creek, CA: AltaMira Press.

Edelblute, Heather B., Sandra Clark, Lilli Mann, Kathryn M. McKenney, Jason J. Bischof, and Christine Kistler. 2014. "Promotoras across the Border: A Pilot Study Addressing Depression in Mexican Women Impacted by Migration." *Journal of Immigrant and Minority Health* 16 (3): 492–500.

Elizondo, Virgilio P. 1977. *Our Lady of Guadalupe as a Cultural Symbol: The Power of the Powerless.* Publisher not identified.

———. 1980. *La Morenita: Evangelizer of the Americas.* San Antonio, TX: Mexican American Cultural Center.

———. 1993. "Hispanic Theology and Popular Piety: From Interreligious Encounter to a New Ecumenism." *Proceedings of the Catholic Theological Society of America* 48: 1–14.

———. 1997. *Guadalupe, Mother of the New Creation.* Maryknoll, NY: Orbis Books.

———. 1998. *San Fernando Cathedral: Soul of the City.* Maryknoll, NY: Orbis Books.

———. 2000. *Galilean Journey: The Mexican-American Promise.* New York: Orbis Books.

———. 2007. "Culture, the Option for the Poor, and Liberation." In *Option for the Poor in Christian Theology,* edited by Daniel G. Groody, 157–168. Notre Dame, IN: University of Notre Dame Press.

Elizondo, Virgilio P., and Timothy M. Matovina. 1998. *Mestizo Worship: A Pastoral Approach to Liturgical Ministry.* Collegeville, MN: Liturgical Press.

———. 1998. *San Fernando Cathedral: Soul of the City.* Maryknoll, NY: Orbis Books.

Ellison, Christopher G., Brian K. Finch, Daniell Nicole Ryan, and Jennifer J. Salinas. 1992. "Trinitarian Monotheism and the Birth of Popular Catholicism: The Case of Sixteenth-Century Mexico." *Missiology: An International Review* 20 (2): 177–204.

Elsasser, Nan, Kyle MacKenzie, and Yvonne Tixier y Vigil. 1980. *Las Mujeres: Conversations from a Hispanic Community.* New York: Feminist Press at CUNY.

Espín, Orlando O. 1992. "Trinitarian Monotheism and the Birth of Popular Catholicism: The Case of Sixteenth-Century Mexico." *Missiology* 20 (2): 177–204.

———. 1994. "Popular Catholicism among Latinos." In *Hispanic Catholic Culture in the U.S.: Issues and Concerns,* edited by Jay P. Dolan and Allan Figueroa Deck, 308–359. Notre Dame, IN: University of Notre Dame Press.

———. 1997. *The Faith of the People: Theological Reflections on Popular Catholicism.* Maryknoll, NY: Orbis Books.

———. 2006. "Traditioning: Culture, Daily Life and Popular Religion, and Their Impact on Christian Tradition." In *Futuring our Past: Explorations in the Theology of Tradition,* edited by Orlando Espín and Gary Macy, 1–22. Maryknoll, NY: Orbis Books.

———. 2013. "Mary in Latino/a Catholicism: Four Types of Devotion." *New Theology Review* 23 (3): 16–25.

Espinosa, Gastón. 2014a. *Latino Pentecostals in America.* Boston, MA: Harvard University Press.

———. 2014b. *William J. Seymour and the Origins of Global Pentecostalism: A Biography and Documentary History.* Durham, NC: Duke University Press.

Facio, Elisa, and Irene Lara, eds. 2014. *Fleshing the Spirit: Spirituality and Activism in Chicana, Latina, and Indigenous Women's Lives.* Tucson: University of Arizona Press.

Falicov, Celia J. 2007. "Working with Transnational Immigrants: Expanding Meanings of Family, Community, and Culture." *Family Process* 46 (2): 157–171.

Feline Freier, Luisa. 2009. "How Our Lady of Guadalupe Became Lutheran: Latin American Migration and Religious Change." *Migraciones Internacionales* 5 (2): 152–190.

Fernandez, Raul E., and Gilbert G. Gonzalez. 2012. *A Century of Chicano History: Empire, Nations and Migration.* New York: Routledge.

Fernandez-Kelly, Patricia. 2007. "Borders for Whom? The Role of NAFTA in Mexico-U.S. Migration." *Annals of the American Academy of Political and Social Science* 610 (1): 98–118.

Fitzgerald, David. 2008. *A Nation of Emigrants: How Mexico Manages Its Migration.* Oakland: University of California Press.

Flores, Richard R. 1995. *Los Pastores: History and Performance in the Mexican Shepherds' Play of South Texas.* Washington, DC: Smithsonian Institution Press.

Flores, Yvette G. 2013. "Latina Sexuality: De (re) Constructing Gender and Cultural Expectations in Midlife." *Women, Gender, and Families of Color* 1 (1): 85–101.

Franco, Jean. 1989. *Plotting Women: Gender and Representation in Mexico.* New York: Columbia University Press.

Freppon, Jackie. 2002. "The Veil." *Catholic Planet,* accessed March 21, 2016, http://www.catholicplanet.com/articles/article51.htm.

Gabaccia, Donna. 1991. "Immigrant Women: Nowhere at Home?" *Journal of American Ethnic History* 10 (4): 61–87.

Gamboni, Darío. 2009. "The Underground and the Virgin of Guadalupe: Contexts for la Virgen del Metro, Mexico City 1997–2007." *Anales del Instituto de Investigaciones Estéticas* 95 (Fall): 119–153.

Garcia, Lorena. 2012. *Respect Yourself, Protect Yourself: Latina Girls and Sexual Identity.* New York: New York University Press.

———. 2015. "Sexual Respectability and Peers." In *Gender Through the Prism of Difference*, 5th ed., edited by Maxine Baca Zinn, Pierrette Hondagneu-Sotelo, Michael A. Messner, and Amy M. Denissen, 184–195. New York: Oxford University Press.

Garcia, Lorena, and Lourdes Torres. 2009. "New Directions in Latina Sexualities Studies." *NWSA Journal* 21 (3): vii–xvi.

Gaspar de Alba, Alicia, and Alma López, eds. 2011. *Our Lady of Controversy: Alma López's "Irreverent Apparition."* Austin: University of Texas Press.

Geertz, Clifford. 1973. *The Interpretation of Cultures.* London: Fontana.

Gendzel, Glen. 2009. "It Didn't Start with Proposition 187: One Hundred and Fifty Years of Nativist Legislation in California." *Journal of the West* 48: 76.

Gereffi, Gary, David Spener, and Jennifer Bair, eds. 2009. *Free Trade and Uneven Development: The North American Apparel Industry after NAFTA.* Philadelphia: Temple University Press.

Goffman, Erving. 1959. *The Presentation of Self in Everyday Life.* Garden City, NY: Doubleday.

Goizueta, Roberto S. 1995. *Caminemos con Jesús: Toward a Hispanic/Latino Theology of Accompaniment.* Maryknoll, NY: Orbis Books.

———. 1996. "US Hispanic Popular Catholicism as Theopoetics." In *Hispanic/ Latino Theology: Challenge and Promise*, edited by Ada María Isasi-Díaz and Fernando F. Segovia, 261–288. Minneapolis, MN: Fortress Press.

———. 2003. "Our Lady of Guadalupe: The Heart of Mexican Identity." In *Religion and the Creation of Race and Ethnicity: An Introduction*, edited by Craig R. Prentiss, 140–151. New York: New York University Press.

Gonzales, Patrisia, and Roberto Rodriguez. 1997. *Gonzales/Rodrigues Uncut and Uncensored.* Berkeley, CA: Ethnic Studies Library Publications.

González, Fidel, Eduardo Chávez Sánchez, and José Luis Guerrero. 1999. *El Encuentro de la Virgen de Guadalupe y Juan Diego.* Mexico City: Editorial Porrúa.

Gonzalez, Gilbert G. 2015. *Guest Workers or Colonized Labor?: Mexican Labor Migration to the United States.* New York: Routledge.

González-López, Gloria. 2004. "Fathering Latina Sexualities: Mexican Men and the Virginity of their Daughters." *Journal of Marriage and Family* 66 (5): 1118–1130.

———. 2005. *Erotic Journeys: Mexican Immigrants and Their Sex Lives.* Berkeley: University of California Press.

———. 2007. "Confesiones de mujer: The Catholic Church and Sacred Morality in the Sex Lives of Mexican Immigrant Women." In *Sexual Inequalities and Social Justice*, edited by Niels Teunis and Gilbert H. Herdt, 148–173. Berkeley: University of California Press.

———. 2009. *Travesías Eróticas: La Vida Sexual de Mujeres y Hombres Migrantes de México*. Mexico City: Grupo Editorial Miguel Angel Porrúa.

———. 2015. *Family Secrets: Stories of Incest and Sexual Violence in Mexico*. New York: New York University Press.

González Navarro, Moisés. 2001. *Cristeros y agraristas en Jalisco*, vol. 2. Mexico City: El Colegio de México.

Granziera, Patrizia. 2004. "From Coatlicue to Guadalupe: The Image of the Great Mother in Mexico." *Studies in World Christianity* 10 (2): 250–273.

Greeley, Andrew. 2000. *The Catholic Imagination*. Berkeley: University of California Press.

Green, Ali. 2009. "Priest, Blood, Sacrifice: Re-Membering the Maternal Divine." *Feminist Theology* 18 (1): 11–28.

Griffith, R. Marie. 1997. "Submissive Wives, Wounded Daughters and Female Soldiers: Prayer and Christian Womanhood in Women's Aglow Fellowship." In *Lived Religion in America: Toward a History of Practice*, edited by David D. Hall, 160–195. Princeton, NJ: Princeton University Press.

Guerrero, Andres G. 2008 (reprint). *A Chicano Theology*. Eugene, OR: Wipf and Stock.

Gutiérrez, David G. 2010. "A History of Latina/o Sexualities." In *Latina/o Sexualities: Probing Powers, Passions, Practices, and Policies*, edited by Marysol Asencio, 13–37. New Brunswick, NJ: Rutgers University Press.

———. 2012. "The New Turn in Chicano/Mexicano History: Integrating Religious Belief and Practice." In *Catholics in the American Century: Recasting Narratives of US History*, edited by Appleby, R. Scott, and Kathleen Sprows Cummings, 109–134. Ithaca, NY: Cornell University Press.

Gutiérrez, Gerardo. 2015. "Identity Erasure and Demographic Impacts of the Spanish Caste System on the Indigenous Populations of Mexico." In *Beyond Germs: Native Depopulation in North America*, edited by Catherine M. Cameron, Paul Kelton, and Alan C. Swedlund, 119. Tucson: University of Arizona Press.

Gutiérrez, Gustavo, and Caridad Inda. 1988. *A Theology of Liberation: History, Politics, and Salvation*. Edited by Caridad Inda and John Eagleson. Maryknoll, NY: Orbis Books. First published, 1971.

Gutiérrez, Laura G. 2010. *Performing Mexicanidad: Vendidas y Cabareteras on the Transnational Stage*. Austin: University of Texas Press.

Guzman, B., and Claudia Kouyoumdjian. 2013 "Latina Adolescent Sexual Desire." In *The Essential Handbook of Women's Sexuality*, Vol. 1, edited by Donna Castañeda, 71–92. Santa Barbara, CA: ABC-CLIO.

Hall, David D., ed. 1997. *Lived Religion in America: Toward a History of Practice*. Princeton, NJ: Princeton University Press.

Hardin, Michael. 2002. "Altering Masculinities: The Spanish Conquest and the Evolution of the Latin American Machismo." *International Journal of Sexuality and Gender Studies* 7 (1): 1–22.

Henderson, Timothy J. 2011. *Beyond Borders: A History of Mexican Migration to the United States.* Vol. 13. New York: John Wiley & Sons.

Heredia, Luisa. 2009. "'Welcoming the Stranger': The Catholic Church and the Struggle for Immigrant Rights in Los Angeles." *Woodrow Wilson International Center for Scholars* (4): 20.

Herrera-Sobek, María, ed. 2001. *Santa Barraza, Artist of the Borderlands: Rio Grande/ Rio Bravo (5).* Texas: A & M University Press.

Hervieu-Léger, Daniéle. 1997. "'What Scripture Tells Me': Spontaneity and Regulation within the Catholic Charismatic Renewal." In *Lived Religion in America: Toward a History of Practice,* edited by David D. Hall, 22–40. Princeton, NJ: Princeton University Press.

———. 2000. *Religion as a Chain of Memory.* New Brunswick: Rutgers University Press.

Howe, Cymene, Suzanna Zaraysky, and Lois Ann Lorentzen. 2009. "Devotional Crossings. Transgender Sex Workers, Santisima Muerte, and Spiritual Solidarity in Guadalajara and San Francisco." In *Religion at the Corner of Bliss and Nirvana,* edited by Lois Ann Lorentzen, Joaquin Jay GonzalezIII, Kevin M. Chun, and Hien Doc Du. Durham and London: Duke University Press.

Hughes, Jennifer Scheper. 2010. *Biography of a Mexican Crucifix: Lived Religion and Local Faith from the Conquest to the Present.* New York: Oxford University Press.

———. 2014. "Intimate Devotions and Local Histories: Archival Approaches to the Study of Colonial Mexican Religion." *History of Religions* 54 (1): 94–97.

Hurtado, Aída. 2003a. *Voicing Chicana Feminisms: Young Women Speak Out on Sexuality and Identity.* New York: New York University Press.

———. 2003b. "Underground Feminisms: Inocencia's Story." In *Chicana Feminisms: A Critical Reader,* edited by Gabriela F. Arredondo, Aida Hurtado, Norma Klahn, Olga Najera-Ramirez, and Patricia Zavella, 260–290. Durham, NC: Duke University Press.

Hurtado, Aída, and Mrinal Sinha. 2016. *Beyond Machismo: Intersectional Latino Masculinities.* Austin: University of Texas Press.

Hussain, Kiran M., et al. 2015. "Unveiling Sexual Identity in the Face of Marianismo." *Journal of Feminist Family Therapy* 27 (2): 72–92.

Isasi-Díaz, Ada María. 1996. *Mujerista Theology: A Theology for the Twenty-First Century.* Louisville, KY: Westminster John Knox Press.

———. 2004. *La Lucha Continues: Mujerista Theology.* Maryknoll, NY: Orbis Books.

Isasi-Díaz, Ada María, and Yolanda Tarango. 1992. *Hispanic Women: Prophetic Voice in the Church.* Philadelphia, PA: Fortress Press.

James, Lois, David Brody, and Zachary Hamilton. 2013. "Risk Factors for Domestic Violence During Pregnancy: A Meta-Analytic Review." *Violence and Victims* 28 (3): 359–380.

Johnson, Maxwell E. 2002. *The Virgin of Guadalupe: Theological Reflections of an Anglo-Lutheran Liturgist.* Lanham, MD: Rowman & Littlefield.

Juárez, Ana M., Stella Beatríz Kerl-McClain, and Susana L. Gallardo. 2016. "Theoretical Shifts in the Analysis of Latina Sexuality." In *Are All the Women Still White?: Rethinking Race, Expanding Feminisms*, edited by Janel Hobson, 107–132. Albany: State University of New York Press.

Koniak-Griffin, et al. 2006. "Contemporary Mothering in a Diverse Society." *Journal of Obstetric, Gynecologic, & Neonatal Nursing* 35 (5): 671–678.

Lafaye, Jacques. 1976. *Quetzalcoatl and Guadalupe: The Formation of Mexican National Consciousness, 1531–1813*. Chicago: University of Chicago Press.

Lagarde, Marcela. 1990. "Los cautiverios de las mujeres: madresposas, monjas, putas, presas y locas." *Universidad Nacional Autónoma de México*.

Lara, Irene. 2008a. "Goddess of the Americas in the Decolonial Imaginary: Beyond the Virtuous Virgen/Pagan Puta Dichotomy." *Feminist Studies* 34 (1/2): 99–127.

———. 2008b. "Tonanlupanisma: Re-Membering Tonantzin-Guadalupe in Chicana Visual Art." *Aztlán: A Journal of Chicano Studies* 33 (2): 61–90.

León, Luis D. 2004. *La Llorona's Children: Religion, Life, and Death in the U.S.–Mexican Borderlands*. Berkeley: University of California Press.

León Portilla, Miguel . 1969. *Pre-Columbian Literatures of Mexico*. Norman: University of Oklahoma Press.

León Portilla, Miguel, and Lysander Kemp. 1962. *The Broken Spears*. Boston: Beacon Press.

———. 2000. *Tonantzin Guadalupe: Pensamiento Náhuatl y Mensaje Cristiano en el Nican Mopohua*. Mexico City: Fondo de Cultura Económica.

———. 2012. *Aztec Thought and Culture: A Study of the Ancient Nahuatl Mind*. Vol. 67. Oklahoma: University of Oklahoma Press.

Lifton, Robert Jay. 1993. *The Protean Self: Human Resilience in an Age of Fragmentation*. Chicago: University of Chicago Press.

Lobo, Titiana. 2015. *Entre Dios y e l Diablo*. Editorial Costa Rica. PDF e-book.

Lopez, Sonia A. 1997. "The Role of the Chicana Within the Student Movement." In *Chicana Feminist Thought: The Basic Historical Writings*, edited by Alma M. García, 100. New York: Routledge Press.

Lozano-Díaz, Nora O. 2002. "Ignored Virgin or Unaware Women: A Mexican-American Protestant Reflection on the Virgin of Guadalupe." *A Reader in Latina Feminist Theology: Religion and Justice*, edited by María Pilar Aquino, Daisy L. Machado, and Jeanette Rodriguez, 204–216. Austin: University of Texas Press.

Loya, Gloria Inés. 2002. "Pathways to a Mestiza Feminist Theology." In *A Reader in Latina Feminist Theology*, edited by María Pilar Aquino, Daisy L. Machado, and Jeanette Rodríguez, 216–240. Austin: University of Texas Press.

Levitt, Peggy. 2006. "Redefining the Boundaries of Belonging: The Transnationalization of Religious Life." In *Everyday Religion: Observing Modern Religious Lives*, edited by Nancy T. Ammerman, 103–120. New York: Oxford University Press.

———. 2007. *God Needs No Passport: Immigrants and the Changing American Religious Landscape*. New York: New Press.

Luckmann, Thomas. 1967. *The Invisible Religion: The Transformation of Symbols in Industrial Society.* New York: Macmillan.

MacMillen, Sarah. 2011. "The Virtual Pilgrimage: The Disappearing Body from Place to Space." *Journal of Religion & Society* 13 (2011): 1–19. https://dspace.creighton. edu/xmlui/bitstream/handle/10504/64281/2011-3.pdf?sequence=1.

Maramaldi, Peter, Tamara J. Cadet, and Usha Menon. 2012. "Cancer Screening Barriers for Community-Based Older Hispanics and Caucasians." *Journal of Gerontological Social Work* 55 (6): 537–559.

Margolis, Jeffrey R. 1995. "Closing the Doors to the Land of Opportunity: The Constitutional Controversy Surrounding Proposition 187." *University of Miami Inter-American Law Review* 26: 363–401. http://repository.law.miami.edu/umialr/vol26/iss2/5.

Marín, Barbara VanOss, and Cynthia A. Gomez. 1997. "Latino Culture and Sex: Implications for HIV Prevention." In *Psychological Interventions and Research with Latino Populations*, edited by Jorge G. Garcia and Maria Cecilia Zea, 73–93. Needham Heights, MA: Allyn & Bacon.

Martin, Patricia P., ed. 1992. *Songs My Mother Sang to Me: An Oral History of Mexican American Women.* Tucson: University of Arizona Press.

Massey, Douglas S. 2013. "America's Immigration Policy Fiasco: Learning from Past Mistakes." *Daedalus* 142 (3): 5–15.

Massey, Douglas S., Jorge Durand, and Nolan J. Malone. 2002. *Beyond Smoke and Mirrors: Mexican Immigration in an Era of Economic Integration.* New York: Russell Sage Foundation.

Massey, Douglas S., and Kristin E. Espinosa. 1997. "What's Driving Mexico-US Migration? A Theoretical, Empirical, and Policy Analysis." *American Journal of Sociology* 102 (4): 939–999.

Matas, Amanda, and James L. Rodríguez. 2014. "The Education of English Learners in California Following the Passage of Proposition 227: A Case Study of an Urban School District." *Penn GSE Perspectives on Urban Education* 11 (2): 44–56.

Matovina, Timothy. 2002. "Companion in Exile: Guadalupan Devotion at San Fernando Cathedral, San Antonio, Texas, 1900–1940." In *Horizons of the Sacred: Mexican Traditions in U.S. Catholicism*, edited by Timothy Matovina and Gary Riebe-Estrella, 17–40. Ithaca, NY: Cornell University Press.

———. 2005. *Guadalupe and Her Faithful: Latino Catholics in San Antonio, from Colonial Origins to the Present.* Baltimore, MD: Johns Hopkins University Press.

———. 2009 "Theologies of Guadalupe: From the Spanish Colonial Era to Pope John Paul II." *Theological Studies* 70 (1): 61–91.

Matovina, Timothy, and Gerald E. Poyo, eds. 2015. *¡Presente!: US Latino Catholics from Colonial Origins to the Present.* Eugene, OR: Wipf and Stock.

Matovina, Timothy, and Gary Riebe-Estrella. 2002. *Horizons of the Sacred: Mexican Traditions in U.S. Catholicism.* Ithaca, NY: Cornell University Press.

McGuire, Meredith B. 1990. "Religion and the Body: Rematerializing the Human Body in the Social Sciences of Religion." *Journal for the Scientific Study of Religion* 29: 283–296.

———. 2003. "Why Bodies Matter: A Sociological Reflection on Spirituality and Materiality." *Spiritus: A Journal of Christian Spirituality* 3 (1): 1–18.

———. 2007. "Embodied Practices: Negotiation and Resistance." In *Everyday Religion: Observing Modern Religious Lives*, edited by Nancy T. Ammerman, 187–200. New York: Oxford University Press.

———. 2008. *Lived Religion: Faith and Practice in Everyday Life.* New York: Oxford University Press.

Medina, Lara. 1998. "Los espíritus siguen hablando: Chicana Spiritualities." In *Living Chicana Theory*, edited by C. Trujillo, 189–213. Berkeley, CA: Third Woman Press.

———. 2005. *Las Hermanas.* Philadelphia, PA: Temple University Press.

Medina, Néstor. 2014. *Mestizaje: Remapping Race, Culture, and Faith in Latino/a Catholicism.* Maryknoll, NY: Orbis Books.

Menchaca, Martha. 2001. *Recovering History, Constructing Race: The Indian, Black, and White Roots of Mexican Americans.* Austin: University of Texas Press.

Mercer, Danielle, et al. 2015. "Intersectionality at the Intersection." *The Oxford Handbook of Diversity in Organizations*, edited by Regine Bendl, Inge Bleijenbergh, Elina Henttonen, and Albert J. Mills, 435–453. New York: Oxford University Press.

Merino, Joel. 2002. *Tepeyac en Nueva York.* Puebla, Mexico: Benemérita Universidad Autónoma de Puebla.

Mesa-Bains, Amalia. 2003. "Domesticana: The Sensibility of Chicana Rasquachismo." In *Chicana Feminisms: A Critical Reader*, edited by Gabriela F. Arredondo, Aída Hurtado, Norma Klahn, Olga Nájera-Ramírez, and Patricia Zavella, 298–315. Durham, NC: Duke University Press.

Meyer, Jean A. 2008. *The Cristero Rebellion: The Mexican People between Church and State 1926–1929.* Cambridge: Cambridge University Press.

Mills, C. Wright. 1959. *The Sociological Imagination.* New York: Oxford University Press.

Mora, Pat. 1994. "Coatlicue's Rules: Advice from an Aztec Goddess." *Prairie Schooner* 68 (4): 76–78.

Moraga, Cherríe. 1983. "Entering the Lives of Others: Theory in the Flesh." In *This Bridge Called My Back: Writings by Radical Women of Color*, edited by Cherríe Moraga and Gloria Anzaldúa, 21–22. New York: Kitchen Table, Women of Color Press.

———. 1996. "El mito Azteca." In *Goddess of the Americas: Writings on the Virgin of Guadalupe*, edited by Ana Castillo, 68–71. New York: Riverhead.

Nabhan-Warren, Kristy. 2005. *The Virgin of El Barrio: Marian Apparitions, Catholic Evangelizing, and Mexican American Activism.* New York: New York University Press.

Nakhid, Camille, et al. 2015. "Intersectionality Revisited: Moving Beyond the Contours of Race, Class, Gender." Notes on an Intersectionality Symposium. *New Zealand Sociology* 30 (4): 190.

Nanko-Fernández, Carmen M. 2015. "Lo Cotidiano as Locus Theologicus." In *The Wiley Blackwell Companion to Latino/a Theology*, edited by Orlando Espín, 15–34. Malden, MA: Wiley.

Napolitano, Valentina. 2009. "The Virgin of Guadalupe: A Nexus of Affect." *Journal of the Royal Anthropological Institute* 15: 96–112.

Newcomer, Daniel. 2004. *Reconciling Modernity: Urban State Formation in 1940s León, Mexico*. Lincoln: University of Nebraska Press.

Nieto-Gomez, Anna. 1997. "La Chicana: Legacy of Suffering and Self-Denial." In *Chicana Feminist Thought: The Basic Historical Writings*, edited by Alma M. García, 48–50. New York: Routledge.

Nuñez, Alicia, Patricia González, Gregory A. Talavera, Lisa Sanchez-Johnson, Scott C. Roesch, Sonia M. Davis, and Linda C. Gallo, et al. 2016. "Machismo, Marianismo, and Negative Cognitive-Emotional Factors: Findings from the Hispanic Community Health Study/Study of Latinos Sociocultural Ancillary Study." *Journal of Latina/o Psychology* 4 (4): 202–217.

Odem, Mary E. 2004. "Our Lady of Guadalupe in the New South: Latino Immigrants and the Politics of Integration in the Catholic Church." *Journal of American Ethnic History* 24 (1): 26–57.

Olivarez, Elizabeth. 1997. "Women's Rights and the Mexican American Woman." In *Chicana Feminist Thought: The Basic Historical Writings*, edited by Alma M. García, 131–136. New York: Routledge Press.

O'Neal, Eryn Nicole, Laura O. Beckman, and Cassia Spohn. 2016. "The Sexual Stratification Hypothesis: Is the Decision to Arrest Influenced by the Victim/Suspect Racial/Ethnic Dyad?" *Journal of Interpersonal Violence*: http://journals. sagepub.com/doi/10.1177/0886260516651093.

Orsi, Robert A. 1996. *Thank You, St. Jude: Women's Devotion to the Patron Saint of Hopeless Causes*. New Haven, CT: Yale University Press.

———. 2005. "The Cult of the Saints and the Reimagination of the Space and Time of Sickness in Twentieth-Century American Catholicism." In *Religion and Healing in America*, edited by Linda L. Barnes and Susan S. Sered, 29–47.

———. 2010. *The Madonna of 115th Street: Faith and Community in Italian Harlem, 1880–1950*. New Haven, CT: Yale University Press.

———. 2011. "Belief." *Material Religion: The Journal of Objects, Art and Belief* 7 (1): 10–17.

Overmyer-Velazquez, Rebecca. 2005. "Christian Morality in New Spain: The Nahua Woman in the Franciscan Imaginary." In *Bodies in Contact: Rethinking Colonial Encounters in World History*, edited by Tony Ballantyne and Antoinette Burton, 67–83. Durham, NC: Duke University Press.

Pastor, Marialba. 2010. "El Marianismo en México: Una Mirada a su Larga Duración." *Cuicuilco* 17 (48): 257–277.

Peña, Devon G. 2014. *The Terror of the Machine: Technology, Work, Gender, and Ecology on the US-Mexico Border.* Austin: University of Texas Press.

Peña, Elaine A. 2008. "Beyond Mexico: Guadalupan Sacred Space Production and Mobilization in a Chicago Suburb." *American Quarterly* 60 (3): 721–747.

———. 2011. *Performing Piety: Making Space Sacred with the Virgin of Guadalupe.* Berkeley: University of California Press.

Peña, Milagros, and Lisa M. Frehill. 1998. "Latina Religious Practice: Analyzing Cultural Dimensions in Measures of Religiosity." *Journal for the Scientific Study of Religion* 37 (4): 620–635.

Pérez, Laura E. 1998. "Spirit Glyphs: Reimagining Art and Artist in the Work of Chicana Tlamatinime." *MFS Modern Fiction Studies* 44 (1): 36–76.

———. 2007. *Chicana Art.* Durham, NC: Duke University Press.

———. 2008. "Hybrid Spiritualities and Chicana Altar-Based Art: The Work of Amalia Mesa-Bains." In *Mexican American Religions: Spirituality, Activism, and Culture,* edited by Gastón Espinosa and Maria T. García, 339–358. Durham, NC: Duke University Press.

Pesquera, Beatriz, and Denise Segura. 1997. "There is No Going Back: Chicanas and Feminism." In *Chicana Feminist Thought: The Basic Historical Writings,* edited by Alma M. García, 294–309. New York: Routledge Press.

Phipps, William E. 1980. "The Menstrual Taboo in the Judeo-Christian Tradition." *Journal of Religion & Health* (19): 298–303.

Pineda, Ana Maria. 2004. "Imagenes de Dios en el Camino: Retablos, Ex-Votos, Milagritos, and Murals." *Theological Studies* 65 (2): 364–379.

Pineda-Madrid, Nancy. 2006. "Traditioning: The Formation of Community, the Transmission of Faith." In *Futuring Our Past: Explorations in the Theology of Tradition,* edited by Orlando Espín and Gary Macy, 204–226. New York: Orbis Press.

———. 2011. *Suffering and Salvation in Ciudad Juárez.* Minneapolis, MN: Fortress Press.

Plaza, Rosío Córdova. 2003. *Los Peligros del Cuerpo: Género y Sexualidad en el Centro de Veracruz.* Madrid: Plaza y Valdés.

Poncela, Anna M. Fernández. 2000. *Mujeres, Revolución y Cambio Cultural: Transformaciones Sociales versus Modelos Culturales Persistentes.* Vol. 37. Anthropos Editorial. Mexico: UAM-Xochimilco.

Poole, Stafford. 1995. *Our Lady of Guadalupe: The Origins and Sources of a Mexican National Symbol, 1531–1797.* Tucson: University of Arizona Press.

Powers Vieira, Karen. 2005. *Women in the Crucible of Conquest: The Gendered Genesis of Spanish American Society, 1500–1600.* Albuquerque: University of New Mexico Press.

Purnell, Jennie. 1999. *Popular Movements and State Formation in Revolutionary Mexico: The Agraristas and Cristeros of Michoacán.* Durham, NC: Duke University Press.

Raffaelli, Marcela, and Stephanie Green. 2003. "Parent-Adolescent Communication About Sex: Retrospective Reports by Latino College Students." *Journal of Marriage and Family* 65 (2): 474–481.

Raming, Ida, Gary Macy, and Bernard J. Cooke. 2004. *A History of Women and Ordination: The Priestly Office of Women: God's Gift to a Renewed Church.* Vol. 2. Lanham, MD: Scarecrow Press.

Ranke-Heinemann, Uta. 1990. *Eunuchs for the Kingdom of Heaven: Women, Sexuality and the Catholic Church.* New York: Doubleday.

Reese, Leslie. 2012. "Storytelling in Mexican Homes: Connections Between Oral and Literacy Practices." *Bilingual Research Journal* 35 (3): 277–293.

Rivera, Mayra Rivera. 2010. "Unsettling Bodies." *Journal of Feminist Studies in Religion* 26 (2): 119–123.

Rodriguez, Jeanette. 1994. *Our Lady of Guadalupe: Faith and Empowerment Among Mexican-American Women.* Austin: University of Texas Press.

———. 1996. "Guadalupe: The Feminine Face of God." In *Goddess of the Americas/La Diosa de las Américas: Writings on the Virgin of Guadalupe,* edited by Ana Castillo, 25–31. New York: Riverhead Books.

Rodríguez, Pepe. 1997. *Mentiras fundamentales de la Iglesia Católica.* Barcelona, Spain: Ediciones B.

Romo, Laura F., Magali Bravo, and Jeanne M. Tschann. 2014. "The Effectiveness of a Joint Mother–Daughter Sexual Health Program for Latina Early Adolescents." *Journal of Applied Developmental Psychology* 35 (1): 1–9.

Romo, Laura F., Rebeca Mireles-Rios, and Aida Hurtado. 2016. "Cultural, Media, and Peer Influences on Body Beauty Perceptions of Mexican American Adolescent Girls." *Journal of Adolescent Research* 31 (4): 474–501.

Romo, Laura F., Erum Nadeem, and Claudia Kouyoumdjian. 2010. "Latino Parent–Adolescent Communication about Sexuality: An Interdisciplinary Literature Review." In *Latina/o Sexualities: Probing Powers, Passions, Practices, and Policies,* edited by Marysol Asencio, 62–74. New Brunswick, NJ: Rutgers Press.

Roof, Wade Clark. 1993. *A Generation Of Seekers: The Spiritual Journeys of the Baby Boom Generation.* New York: HarperCollins.

———. 2001. *Spiritual Marketplace: Baby Boomers and the Remaking of American Religion.* Princeton, NJ: Princeton University Press.

Rull Fernández, Enrique. 1986. *Autos Sacramentales del Siglo de Oro.* Barcelona, Spain: Plaza y Jants.

Rusch, Dana, and Karina Reyes. 2013. "Examining the Effects of Mexican Serial Migration and Family Separations on Acculturative Stress, Depression, and Family Functioning." *Hispanic Journal of Behavioral Sciences* 35 (2): 139–158.

Sagarena, Roberto Lint. 2009. "Making a There There: Marian Muralism and Devotional Streetscapes." *Visual Resources* 25 (1–2): 93–107.

Sánchez, David. 2009. "Guadalupe and the Resistance: Ancient and Contemporary Counterimperial/Colonial Discourses." *Perspectivas: Hispanic Theological Initiative Occasional Papers* (Fall 2009): 8–21. Available at http://www2.ptsem. edu/uploadedFiles/HTI.

Sánchez, Miguel, Francisco de Siles, Luis Lasso de la Vega, and Francisco de Barcenas. 1982. "Imagen de la Virgen Maria madre de Dios de Guadalupe: milagrosamente aparecida en la ciudad de Mexico: celebrada en su historia, con la profecia del capitulo doze del Apocalipsis." In *Testimonios históricos Guadalupanos*, edited by Ernesto de la Torre Villa and Ramiro Navarro de Anda, 152–267. Mexico City: Fondo de Cultura Económica.

Sandoval, Chela. 1991. "US Third World Feminism: The Theory and Method of Oppositional Consciousness in the Postmodern World." *Genders* 10: 1–24.

Schüssler Fiorenza, Elisabeth. 2001. *Wisdom Ways: Introducing Feminist Biblical Interpretation*. Maryknoll, NY: Orbis Books.

Segura, Denise A., and Jennifer L. Pierce. 1993. "Chicana/o Family Structure and Gender Personality: Chodorow, Familism, and Psychoanalytic Sociology Revisited." *Signs* 19 (1): 62–91.

Segura, Denise A., and Patricia Zavella. 2007. *Women and Migration in the US–Mexico Borderlands: A Reader*. Durham, NC: Duke University Press.

Serna, Cristina. 2011. "It's Not About the Virgins in My Life, It's About the Life in My Virgins." In *Our Lady of Controversy: Alma López's Irreverent Apparition*, edited by Alicia Gaspar de Alba and Alma López, 165–194. Chicana Matters Series. Austin: University of Texas Press.

Sewell, Marilyn. 2002. *Resurrecting Grace: Remembering Catholic Childhoods*. Boston, MA: Beacon Press.

Sharma, Sonya. 2008. "Young Women, Sexuality and Protestant Church Community Oppression or Empowerment?." *European Journal of Women's Studies* 15 (4): 345–359.

Stein, Gabriela L., Alexandra M. Cupito, Julia L. Mendez, Juan Prandoni, Nadia Huq, and Diana Westerberg. 2014. "Familism through a Developmental Lens." *Journal of Latina/o Psychology* 2 (4): 224–250.

Stevens, Evelyn P., and Ann Pescatello. 1973. *Marianismo: The Other Face of Machismo in Latin America*. Pittsburgh, PA: University of Pittsburgh Press.

Taylor, Diana. 2004. "Scenes of Cognition: Performance and Conquest." *Theatre Journal* 56: 353–572.

Tilly, Charles. 1973. "Does Modernization Breed Revolution?" *Comparative Politics* 5: 425–447.

Torres, Valerie. 2010 "*La Familia* as *Locus Theologicus* and Religious Education in *Lo Cotidiano* [Daily Life]." *Religious Education* 105 (4): 444–461.

Trujillo, Carla Mari, ed. 1991. *Chicana Lesbians: The Girls Our Mothers Warned Us About*. San Antonio, TX: Third Woman Press.

———. 1998. "La Virgen de Guadalupe and Her Reconstruction in Chicana Lesbian Desire." In *Living Chicana Theory*, edited by Carla M. Trujillo, 214–231. Berkeley, CA: Third Woman.

Tuck, Jim. 1982. *The Holy War in Los Altos: A Regional Analysis of Mexico's Cristero Rebellion.* Tucson: University of Arizona Press.

Turner, Kay. 2008. "*Voces de Fe*: Mexican American *Altaristas* in Texas." In *Mexican American Religions: Spirituality, Activism, and Culture,* edited by Gastón Espinosa and Maria T. García, 180–205. Durham, NC: Duke University Press.

Tweed, Thomas A. 1997. *Our Lady of the Exile: Diasporic Religion at a Cuban Catholic Shrine in Miami.* Oxford: Oxford University Press.

———. 2010. "Mary's Rain and God's Umbrella: Religion, Identity, and Modernity in the Visionary Art of a Chicana Painter." *Material Religion* 6 (3): 274–303.

Ugarte, Sandra. 1997. "Chicana Regional Conference." In *Chicana Feminist Thought: The Basic Historical Writings,* edited by Alma M. García, 153–154. New York: Routledge Press.

USCCB (US Conference of Catholic Bishops). 2005. "Seven Themes of Catholic Social Teaching." http://www.usccb.org/beliefs-and-teachings/what-we-believe/catholic-social-teaching/seven-themes-of-catholic-social-teaching.cfm.

Vanderwood, Paul. 2000. "Review: Religion: Official, Popular, and Otherwise." *Mexican Studies/Estudios Mexicanos* 16 (2): 411–441.

Vásquez, Manuel A., and Marie F. Marquardt. 2003. *Globalizing the Sacred: Religion across the Americas.* New Brunswick, NJ: Rutgers University Press.

Villar, Maria Elena, and Maritza Concha. 2012. "Sex Education and Cultural Values: Experiences and Attitudes of Latina Immigrant Women." *Sex Education* 12 (5): 545–554.

Villegas, Jorge, Jennifer Lemanski, and Carlos Valdéz. 2010. "Marianismo and Machismo: The Portrayal of Females in Mexican TV Commercials." *Journal of International Consumer Marketing* 22 (4): 327–346.

Weisbrot, Mark, Stephan Lefebvre, and Joseph Sammut. 2014. *Did NAFTA Help Mexico? An Assessment after 20 years.* No. 2014-03. Center for Economic and Policy Research (CEPR).

White, Michael J., Frank D. Bean, and Thomas J. Espenshade. 1990. "The US 1986 Immigration Reform and Control Act and Undocumented Migration to the United States." *Population Research and Policy Review* 9 (2): 93–116.

White, Rebecca, and Mark W. Roosa. 2012. "Neighborhood Contexts, Fathers, and Mexican American Young Adolescents' Internalizing Symptoms." *Journal of Marriage and Family* 74 (1): 152–166.

Wilkin, Holley A., S. Vikki, and J. Sandra. 2009. "The Role of Family Interaction in New Immigrant Latinos' Civic Engagement." *Journal of Communication* 59 (2): 387–406.

Young, Julia G. 2013. "The Calles Government and Catholic Dissidents: Mexico's Transnational Projects of Repression, 1926–1929." *The Americas* 70 (1): 63–91.

———. 2015. *Mexican Exodus: Emigrants, Exiles, and Refugees of the Cristero War.* New York: Oxford University Press.

Zadnik, Elizabeth, Chiara Sabina, and Carlos A. Cuevas. 2016. "Violence against Latinas: The Effects of Undocumented Status on Rates of Victimization and Help-Seeking." *Journal of Interpersonal Violence* 31 (6): 1141–1153.

Zavella, Patricia. 1993. "Feminist Insider Dilemmas: Constructing Ethnic Identity with 'Chicana' Informants." *Frontiers: A Journal of Women Studies* 13 (3): 53–76.

———.1997. "Feminist Insider Dilemmas: Constructing Ethnic Identity with 'Chicana' Informants." In *Situated Lives: Gender and Culture in Everyday Life*, edited by Louise Lamphere, Helena Ragoné, and Patricia Zavella, 42–61. New York: Routledge Press.

———. 2003. "Talkin' Sex: Chicanas and Mexicanas Theorize about Silences and Sexual Pleasures." In *Chicana Feminisms: A Critical Reader*, edited by Gabriela F. Arredondo, Aida Hurtado, Norma Klahn, Olga Najera-Ramirez, and Patricia Zavella, 228–253. Durham, NC: Duke University Press.

———. 2008. "Playing with Fire: The Gendered Construction of Chicana/Mexicana Sexuality." In *Perspectives on Las Américas: A Reader in Culture, History, & Representation*, edited by Matthew Gutmann, Feliz V. Matos-Rodríguez, Lynn Stephen, and Patricia Zavella, 229–244. Malden, MA: Blackwell.

———. 2015. "Fleshing the Spirit: Spirituality and Activism in Chicana, Latina, and Indigenous Women's Lives." *Aztlán: A Journal of Chicano Studies* 40 (1): 231–235.

Zepeda, Candace. 2016. "Chicana Feminism." In *Decolonizing Rhetoric and Composition Studies*, edited by Iris D. Ruiz and Raúl Sánchez, 137–151. New York: Palgrave Macmillan.

Zinn, Maxine Baca. 1979. "Field Research in Minority Communities: Ethical, Methodological and Political Observations by an Insider." *Social Problems* 27 (2): 209–219.

———. 1982. "Familism among Chicanos: A Theoretical Review." *Humboldt Journal of Social Relations* 10 (1): 224–238.

Zires, Margarita. 1994. "Los Mitos de la Virgen de Guadalupe. Su Proceso de Construcción y Reinterpretación en el México Pasado y Contemporáneo." *Mexican Studies/Estudios Mexicanos* 10 (2): 281–313.

———. 2014. *Las Transformaciones de los Exvotos Pictográficos Guadalupanos (1848–1999)*. Frankfurt am Main, Germany: Vervuert.

Zuniga, Jennie. 2015. "Mothers and Daughters: Conversations about Sexuality." PhD dissertation, California State University, Northridge.

Index

Figures are indicated by an italic *f* following the page number.